the cinema of NEIL JORDAN

DIRECTORS' CUTS

Other titles in the Directors' Cuts series:

the cinema of
NEIL JORDAN

dark carnival

carole zucker

WALLFLOWER PRESS LONDON & NEW YORK

First published in Great Britain in 2008 by
Wallflower Press
6 Market Place, London W1W 8AF
www.wallflowerpress.co.uk

A catalogue record for this book is available from the British Library

ISBN 978-1-905674-41-1 (paperback)
       978-1-905674-42-8 (hardback)

Book design by Rob Bowden Design

Printed and bound in Poland; produced by Polskabook

CONTENTS

ACKNOWLEDGEMENTS

I must first thank those who have supported my project with grants and aid: the Social Sciences and Humanities Research Council from whom I received two grants, and the Concordia Aid to Scholarly Activities fund which has been most forthcoming in their sponsorship of my research. I have many, many people to thank for the work they did in helping me research Irish cinema and then the films of Neil Jordan. I must express my gratitude to Emer and Kevin Rockett, Luke Gibbons and John Hill for their pioneering work on Irish cinema. I also thank Heather McDougall, Paul Monticone and Antoinette Prout for their very special input into this volume. I am most grateful to Anna McLeish and Laurel Wypkema. This book truly could not have been completed without the massive amounts of research and very generous, unending support of two people: Andrea Ariano and Chris Meir. They were my research assistants as the book was developing, and were munificent in carrying out the many tasks asked of them. My gratitude to Yoram Allon, Editorial Director at Wallflower Press, for keeping me on the straight and narrow, and to Editorial Manager Jacqueline Downs (a.k.a. Warrior Princess) for her kindness, exceptional editorial skills and keen sense of humour. I want to thank Bart Testa of the University of Toronto who has helped me more than he will ever know by being a patient and generous reader of my writing; his criticism has been invaluable to me. I must also acknowledge the angel at my table who is always there for intellectual and emotional support, Kristian Moen of the University of East Anglia. I am also very grateful to Neil Jordan for his generosity in permitting me access to his personal archives, and his personal assistant Sarah Smith for her support. Thanks too to Stephen Rea for agreeing immediately to write the foreword for this book; his emotional intelligence is a great model for anyone who wants to be an actor. Finally, and as always, I have no words to express the truly inexpressible – the time, the patience, the advice, the commitment, the encouragement of my husband Mario Falsetto, whose selflessness, constancy and profound love is intertwined in all of my undertakings. This book is dedicated to him.

The first I knew of Neil Jordan, in fact the first anyone knew, was of Jordan the writer. His collection of short stories, *Night in Tunisia*, came out in 1976 (and was awarded the Guardian Fiction Prize) and his novel *The Past* was published in 1980. Back then, people who had read his work, including myself, would not have been surprised to see Neil joining a certain cadre of respected Irish prose authors such as John McGahern and Edna O'Brien. What happened next, his screenplay of *Angel*, came as quite a surprise, then, and not least for me, because it became clear that I was lucky enough to be in his line of vision as a candidate for the role of Danny. I remember he handed me the script and Danny's saxophone and asked, 'Why don't you see if you want to do this?'

I had never done a film before, and it was Neil's first film too. *Angel* was the first project that the Irish Film Board invested in, and it was a miraculous thing at that time to be involved in an indigenous Irish film, when hardly anything was being made. But of course the other miraculous thing was how the script shared many of the qualities of his fiction. I often hear *Angel* being spoken of as a genre, almost a noir-ish, piece, but actually there is a lot more going on in that film. Just like in his writing, it doesn't take place in the world that we all know and share, but in Neil's own world, maybe what you would call Jordanland.

What makes that fictional space special is that it is connected to the common experience in oblique ways. Sure, *Angel* is ostensibly about the conflict in the north, and it *is* engaged with history in a concrete way, but the action takes place on an intangible, highly ambiguous level of experience that was to become increasingly recognisable as Neil's as his directing career progressed. His stories have their roots in specific times and places but he has always been more interested in much less localised themes. This refusal to be formulaic is what made *Angel* and everything since then so intriguing. The vision that suffuses that first film came to the screen already complete and fully intact; he was in immediate possession of it from the start.

When I consider *The Crying Game*, for example, the thought that strikes me is: who else but Jordan would have based it on such a preposterous premise as the romantic entanglement of an IRA man and the transvestite lover of the soldier that he has abducted? At first sight, it seems to be such a lurid situation, but because it is in Neil's hands, it becomes something tender and real. Neil has an incredible instinct which manifests itself as immense confidence in what he is able to achieve, and this is what explains the degree of control he has over his films, something that was fully formed even with *Angel*. During that shoot, his spontaneity and readiness to take an alternative approach caused a lot of criticism from practically every department – the art department, make-up, you name it. What was going on was that some people did not know what he was talking about because he saw everything differently, he challenged everybody. He was impatient, intolerant of interference; he wouldn't wait for the lighting rigs to be set up properly, or for the camera to be put in some notionally correct position, he just wanted to set things up in an unexpected, sometimes under-lit, way, press ahead and shoot.

All of these tendencies were initially put down to the inexperience of a debutant, but really I think his vision replenished the craft of many of us who were fortunate enough to work with him. Instead of directing actors by telling us what to do, he would remind us of what the narrative was. And if things changed as we went along, which they often did, he would rewrite rather than re-direct. He had no compunction at all about throwing out his own great scenes and writing them afresh – he was almost cavalier with his own creations. For example, while we were sitting around waiting for everybody to set up the penultimate scene of *Angel*, the scene with the faith-healer boy in the caravan, Neil re-wrote the entire thing in around ten minutes. He worked quickly then and he still does. At one point during the shooting of *Interview with the Vampire*, I remember I needed to get a robe fixed at the last minute, but Neil was talking to me about the scene we were about to do, so he just put the robe right himself and carried on talking throughout, without missing a beat.

I have acted in nine films directed by Neil Jordan, yet most of this foreword is concerned with *Angel*. The reason for this is that that film set the tone for so much of what was to come for me as an actor, in particular his reluctance to indulge in too much characterisation. By this I mean that the characters of Neil's films are not defined so much by the dialogue they engage in with one another, rather they are always in dialogue with themselves in some important sense. That was definitely the case in *Angel*, but also in so many of the films that followed: *The Crying Game*, *The Butcher Boy*, *The End of the Affair* and *Breakfast on Pluto*, to name just some. The sense of an inner life, of a private emotional existence, that we can see in so many of his films comes from Neil's intense feeling of ownership of his own stories. Every time he tells me a new story and describes his next project, it is as though a precious secret has been revealed to him. And of course it has.

If any contemporary filmmaker may be called an auteur, it is Jordan. The phrase 'A Neil Jordan Film' that we see at the start of his work actually means something; it means that you are in a very particular territory. It is as meaningful as 'A Robert Altman Film' or 'A Jean-Luc Godard Film' – it is a guarantee that what you are about to see is not like a film by anybody else. He has a particular way of creating electric tension by holding back, by refusing to tell the viewer what to think; a good example is that penultimate scene in *Angel*, where the audience is left asking itself 'What does it mean?' and so also '*How* does it mean?' When Samuel Beckett observed of James Joyce's writing that it 'is not about something; it is that something itself' he might also have been describing a key characteristic of Neil Jordan's tendency to treat the process of filmmaking as a journey with a mysterious destination, a destination which can really only be described as the film itself.

My comments here are an actor's appreciation of a director, and for that reason I hope they fit well with Carole Zucker's compelling series of analyses in this volume. Unusually for an academic publication, this book is written by someone who has both experience in and an understanding of what performance is. Carole's critical instincts allow her to appreciate how writing becomes incarnate, if that is the right word, in the actions of an actor. This instinctive approach is something that she shares with the object of her study, and which in my opinion qualifies her to speak with insight, originality and authority on Neil Jordan and his films.

Stephen Rea
Dublin, 2007

'I love those who yearn for the impossible.'
– Goethe

INTRODUCTION

'Surely all art is the result of having been in danger, of having gone through an experience all the way to the end, to where no one can go any further.'
                                                    – Rainer Maria Rilke

With each successive outing, Neil Jordan – without doubt the most interesting film-maker to emerge thus far from Ireland – astonishes the viewer with the eclectic, catholic range of his interests. From *Angel* (1982) to *The Brave One* (2007), Jordan's peregrinations through genre often loosen or immolate the boundaries between categories. Jordan is truly idiosyncratic, always experimenting with form, unafraid to change styles from film to film. He is a master at creating moods and situations which can be sensed, but which are too complex to be grasped immediately. Jordan is a filmmaker who loves both the image and the use of language that expresses and transforms meaning. He has no trepidations about making bold, *outré* gestures in his work, and is easily one of the most poetic, intelligent and gifted of contemporary filmmakers.

As much as Jordan experiments with form and generic convention, his work tends to circulate around repeated themes. Among them are: a fascination with storytelling, and how the stories are told by various modes of performance; the quest for identity and wholeness; meditations on innocence; permutations of the family unit; violence and its attendant psychic and physical damage; impossible love and erotic tension; the dark and irrational aspects of the human soul; and characters who are, in some way, haunted by loss. His films continually embrace the deepest question one can ask: what does it mean to be human? A signal aspect of Jordan's work is his approach to character. He does not have a strong investment in probing the characters' psychology in the traditional sense; he is most interested in their immediate feelings, those moments of revelation and sensation so beloved by the Romantics. One knows very little about Jordan's characters, their backstories are minimal, at best; we enter their lives *in medias res*. And yet, one cannot call these films apsychological (in the way one might consider the work of Antonioni), because there is access to the characters' emotional sensibilities and temperature. Characters have definition and amplitude; feelings are experienced and enacted; emotional journeys occur that result in major alterations of a character's life. Jordan's main concern is with something I would call 'sensual meaning', that which is provisional and fleeting, and made up of the melding of image, sound, performance, narrative and dialogue; one intuits not only from character traits, but from sensory materials. Although Jordan's films may be read through the filter of theoretical, historical and cultural perspectives, it is really the experiential component that most interests the filmmaker. He has repeatedly said that abstract thought holds no interest for him. I think of Jordan as a postmodern romantic; postmodern in that he destabilises boundaries, appropriates a variety of artistic referents and transfuses genres, romantic in his embrace of perception, intuition and sensation. Perhaps most importantly, Jordan's work is embedded within a mythopoeic sensibility; it is the crucial overarching feature of his work.

The director does not want to diminish the irreducible mystery that subtends human behaviour and being-in-the-world; Jordan wishes to set forth the kaleidoscopic array of feelings that make the human condition so enigmatic. My approach in this book is to explore the films within the specific context of aesthetic, psychological and intellectual ideas that illuminate Jordan's work. It is not my objective to theorise about the films, but to view them within a history of ideas. I will not offer a complete reading of each, but rather focus on one or several particular patterns or areas of significance that colour the director's individual films.

It is important to underscore that a work on Neil Jordan would be impossible without contextualising him as a filmmaker who came into adulthood just as 'the Troubles' resurfaced in Ireland in the late 1960s. I begin by examining two films, *Michael Collins* (1996) and *Angel* that situate the filmmaker's response to the political climate. I look at the reception of *Michael Collins* as this illuminates the prevalent attitudes towards Ireland's dark history. Some knowledge of the Anglo-Irish War, the Irish Civil War, and the participants in the tragic drama of Collins' brief life is absolutely necessary to address the film. Yet the conclusion I draw from my exploration of the film is that Jordan is much more interested in the mythopoeic dimensions of the Easter Uprising and the ensuing conflicts. While Jordan's film is grounded in the painful human struggles endured by Collins and his comrades, ultimately the director paints on a larger canvas. I discuss the mythic cycle of ritual sacrifice and bloodletting – assayed in the work of social anthropologist Mircea Eliade (amongst others) – as it is inscribed in the conflicts of Irish history.

While *Angel* is a way of comprehending the violence of the Troubles, the specifics of sectarian hostilities are left ambiguous. The director utilises the political turmoil to interrogate the journey of a lone individual who gradually loses his connection not only with the external world, but also with his selfhood, as he becomes a self-appointed executioner, avenging the death of a girl he barely knew. The central question is: what happens to a human being once he becomes enmeshed in violence?

Angel is the first time Jordan uses the considerable skills of Stephen Rea, who will go on to become a fixture in the director's films. Jordan manifests a strong personal vision in his debut film, but also his great indebtedness to European art cinema, particularly the New German Cinema and Italian films. There is a good deal of experimentation with off-screen sound, colour and genre, and the latter is something Jordan will play with throughout his career, most often juggling several genres within the same film.

I would submit that Jordan's films function on a deeper and more universal level than has been appreciated heretofore and thus my analysis is interdisciplinary in nature, using art history; cultural anthropology; psychology; philosophy; literary criticism; history; narratology; the uses of myth and fairy tales; spirituality; storytelling and performance studies, and so forth. It presents a challenge to the ways in which one comprehends Jordan's films. It is my contention that the director's stories interface with precepts and configurations informed by Celtic myth and folklore; the fairy tale; Romanticism and the Gothic. Here, I take an observation by Richard Kearney as a point of departure. Kearney writes about the Irish Revivalist mindset as one that wishes to recapture a lost homeland, while the modernist mind is propelled towards the notion that prefers discontinuity to continuity, diversity to unity, conflict to harmony, novelty to heritage. The tension and fusion of these positions as exemplified by Jordan's work are labelled postmodern by Kearney (1988: 12–14). I would posit Jordan as an artistic hybrid, inventively recasting his literary and national heritage in a postmodern light. The issue of hybridity in Jordan's work is an important one. The question becomes: how does a contemporary artist remain in dialogue with ancient and centuries-old literary-historical schemata, while creating his unique, highly individuated imaginative world? How are the social, artistic, historical, spiritual and philosophical concerns of these anterior movements etched into the filmmaker's worldview and creative impulses?

The preoccupations that dominate Jordan's work take much from Irish folklore, at base dealing with the polarities and contradictions within human nature that engender complexity of character. Jordan sees himself as first and foremost 'an Irish filmmaker and as an Irish writer' (McIlroy 1986: 118), and his psychic connection with Ireland is woven through his storytelling and the director's bond, often ironic, to subjects derived from Irish folklore. Jordan's link with Yeats, with whom he shares a childhood in mystical, iconic Sligo, in the equally fabled west of Ireland, can be found in his concern for the marriage of the real world and the imaginary, the everyday and the mystical, the familiar and unfamiliar. As Richard Kearney writes: 'It is striking how many modern Irish authors have spoken of being in transit between two worlds, divided between opposing allegiances' (1988: 14). L. P. Curtis discusses the oscillating nature of Irishness as manifested in the country's film and literary characters as 'a kind of Celtic Jekyll and Hyde, shifting between two extremes of behaviour and mood ...

liable to rush from mirth to despair, tenderness to violence, and loyalty to treachery' (1969: 51). One does not have to labour to find such characters in *Angel*, *The Crying Game* (1992), *Interview with the Vampire* (1994), *Michael Collins*, *The Butcher Boy* (1997), *The End of the Affair* (1999) and *The Brave One*.

The divided, mystical mind finds its most potent manifestation in the film *In Dreams* (1999) where the two main characters are able to enter the permeable boundaries of each other's psychic and literal worlds. The filmmaker taps into the distinctly Irish *anima mundi*, Yeats' term for 'a cosmic storehouse of symbols' (Kearney 1988: 19), much like Jung's collective unconscious, where the lone, confused self can find a cathartic, if bloody knowledge. The mythic reciprocity of beauty and terror, the 'terrible beauty' (Kearney 1988: 217) of which Yeats writes, where the fearsome and the sublime fuse, is a subject common to Jordan's films.

A link is made between the act of storytelling, an integral mode within Jordan's work, with regard to Walter Benjamin's famous essay, 'The Storyteller' (1934) and performance, the primary route through which stories are told. The work actors engage in to create the performances we witness on-screen is virtually ignored by film scholars. For this reason, I approach *The Crying Game* from the perspective of performance and its connection with storytelling. Nearly every article written about the film focuses on identity politics at the expense of the very human drama that is enacted. While *The Crying Game* is a good example of naturalistic performance, I compare it with *Interview with the Vampire* in which, for the most part, the acting is quite stylised. Acting is a way of conveying story, but more than that it is a creative act in itself, rarely brought to one's attention in anything more than a history of taste (that is, 'I liked it', 'I didn't'). Actors are to us as shamans were to the ancients: they share stories and experience, something Benjamin finds sadly lacking in modern society.

Unlike the sacred and national origins treated in myth and legend, fairy tales – another form of storytelling – are a narrative form that engages with personal and social origins, providing a rich body of cultural imagery and history for a filmmaker concerned with the peregrinations of identity. Moreover, the instability of fairy tales, historically contingent, forever reworked by the new teller, allows for the kind of artistic manipulation which serves the director's examinations of the power of narrative and myth. Rather than following the paths of archetypal and structural absolutes or overlaying moral and social codes in his use of fairy tales, Jordan builds upon the disruptive elements of this durable narrative form.

Marina Warner writes of how 'all the wonders that create the atmosphere of fairy tales disrupt the apprehensible world in order to open spaces for dreaming alternatives … The dimension of wonder creates a huge theatre of possibility in the stories: anything can happen' (Warner 1994a: xvi). While the sense of enchantment that often accompanies ruptures in identity and narrative allows for rearrangements of the real, for Jordan it frequently entails a fundamental loss, the impossibility of healing what really hurts.

Jordan captures the threat of change and the uncertainty of desire implicit in fairy tales, as well as the often catastrophic effects of growing up. His use of the fairy tale is not a correction or parody of their supposedly outdated values; rather, he investigates what it means to listen to fairy tales, what it means to trust narrative and what it means to follow their paths. His films often show the messy results of fairy tales, the awkward ways in which we interact with our shared store of narratives and the complex inter-relation of past and future that make fairy tales such vivid material for impassioned pastiche.

Because Jordan began his career as a fiction writer, and for the most part writes his own scripts, an examination of the literary modes that operate in his fiction and writing for the screen is indispensable. The discussion of Jordan as a writer looks at the similarities between his award-winning fiction and the film *The Miracle* (1991). We see how film can do what the written word cannot, and vice versa. Many of Jordan's preoc-cupations with father/son relationships and adolescent sexual confusion are explored; the theme of mother/son incest, a topic rarely explored in film or literature, is para-mount in *The Miracle*, and the film provides an outstanding example of the way in which Jordan prefers to work close to the edge. The second section of the chapter inter-rogates the narrative structures of *The Butcher Boy*, adapted from Patrick McCabe's contemporary classic of Irish fiction. The film's unusual and bold narrational devices are inscribed in its use of voice-over, which complicates the notion of point of view in the film.

Another literary model to which Jordan's work is bound is English Romanticism, where of great concern is the transcendence of the material world to a greater spiritual reality. The triad of subject, mind and spirit speaks to the emphasis on the world as experienced through the senses and perceptions of the individual (much like the 'sensual meaning' of Jordan's films invoked earlier). Relating to the *anima mundi* is the correlation of the individual mind with the mind of the absolute. This was the very essence of imagination to the Romantics, and is a quintessential belief of the origin and value of art for Jordan; it is the filmmaker's quest to interact imaginatively with the external world. A crucial subject for the Romantics, as for Jordan, is the idyllic time of childhood, but an idyll that is short-lived and tinged with the sense of what is lost over the course of a human life. The paradisal child often assumes a perverse and ironic dimension for Jordan, a rendition of childhood that bespeaks the Romantic agony and despair at the fallen world. A bond is made between childhood and imagination on the one hand and reason on the other. Jordan's obsession with father/son relationships and questions of origin and identity surface in his first publication, in the title story of *Night in Tunisia* (1980b), and are pervasively interwoven throughout the filmmaker's oeuvre.

The unholy trinity of sin, pleasure and death attains a powerful presence in Jordan's work. In the fallen world, anxiety is provoked over the existence of God, particularly as expressed by Satan and the fallen angels, and such figures haunt Jordan's films. Romantic tropes such as diasporic figures and exile, mourning and melancholy, dreams and the exotic find their way into *The Crying Game* and *Interview with the Vampire*, amongst other films.

Jordan taps into the darker side of Romanticism, which shades off into the Gothic. The Gothic is a movement of excess; it revolves around transgression and anxiety about the limits and boundaries of society and culture. Passion and excitement are the overriding effects of the Gothic, reason is untamed, 'social propriety and moral laws' are subject to ambivalence and uncertainty (Botting 1996: 3). The Gothic proffers a threat through a confusion of supernatural and natural forces; imaginative excesses and delusions; religious and human evil; mental disintegration and spiritual corruption (see Botting 1996: 2). In the nineteenth century what was externalised previously as terror and literal menace now became – as we approached the founding of the human science of psychology – horror, an internalised, disturbed psychic state. Sexual conflicts abound, and madness is a reflection of the despair, guilt and angst that destabilises all boundaries. The sublime mystery of the Romantics becomes the uncanny for the Gothic. Once we reach the twentieth century the site of horror is located in the institutions such as psychiatric hospitals and the criminal underworld.

This description could very well act as a précis for Jordan's filmography. Jordan is the interrogator *par excellence* of the boundaries of a desacralised world. The limits of rationality, individual freedom and sexual identity, are, among other concepts, subject to Jordan's scrutiny. The abrogation of convention is tied to the disintegration of social adhesion that characterises the millennial era.

Jordan's films often contain the iconic Gothic image of the labyrinth, 'a place of all forms of excessive, irrational, and passionate behaviour … also the site in which the absence or loss of reason, sobriety, decency and morality is displayed in full horror' (Botting 1996: 83). The dread woods of *The Company of Wolves* (1984); the underbelly of London in *Mona Lisa* (1986); the subterranean vampire sarcophygi in *Interview with the Vampire*; the drowned city and the tangled hospital corridors of *In Dreams* – all are maze-like constructions that position Jordan's creations firmly within the Gothic arena.

The chapter on *The End of the Affair*, an adaptation of Graham Greene's novel, looks at the process of adaptation from book to film, and includes an examination of three different drafts of the screenplay that Jordan wrote. It is a way of grappling with, and developing a better understanding of, the writer's craft. In dealing with *The End of the Affair* one cannot help but be engaged by the film's spiritual elements, an aspect that often hovers over each of Jordan's films but is here articulated in a profound and provocative way. Finally, the performances in *The End of the Affair* are explored; the actors convey a subtle minimalism, certainly light years away from the performance style in *Interview with the Vampire*, making manifest Jordan's need to continually experiment with style and content.

The chapter on the filmmaker's recent works begins with an examination of *The Good Thief* (2002), a film largely about Nick Nolte, surely amongst the finest actors of his generation, and a quintessential American rebel. Without Nolte's presence the film would be an exercise in style, as Jordan takes some risks with the film's formal coordinates. *The Good Thief* is concerned with a junkie gambler with six prison sentences behind him, who still hopes for redemption. Although there are allusions to Christian symbology, this is essentially a film about masculinity and vulnerability, kindness and malefic manipulation, isolation and belonging. The film's stylistic expressiveness is most apparent in the flamboyant use of the hyperkinetic camerawork of Chris Menges which throws us headlong into a wild underworld of sex, drugs, Leonard Cohen and world music. One of the film's central conceits is that the characters communicate largely through the mode of (mostly) phantasmatic storytelling, the more exotic and unbelievable, the better.

Jordan collaborates once more with McCabe on *Breakfast on Pluto* (2005), and like *The Butcher Boy* it is once again about the perplexing structure of the family. The episodic film deals with transvestism in Ireland from the late 1960s to the first few years of the 1970s, just as inhibitions were being tossed out the window. Kitten, the protagonist, is unabashedly transgendered, and must suffer for what was then considered (in Ireland certainly) a sin against God. The resilient Kitten has an overriding ambition in life – to become a middle-class hausfrau, pushing a pram around town. Jordan has never shied away from material about the homoerotic – transvestites, transsexuals, bisexuals and even straight people appear with regularity in his films and fiction. *Breakfast on Pluto* ends on an upbeat note, however fanciful this may appear, making it vitally different to Jordan's other films that end with breakdown (*Angel*), ambiguity (*Mona Lisa*, *The Crying Game*, *Interview with the Vampire*) or death (*Michael Collins*, *In Dreams*, *The End of the Affair*). At a deeper level, *Breakfast on Pluto* concerns Kitten's search for wholeness and healing, and it is in many ways one of Jordan's most hopeful films. This is followed immediately by *The Brave One*, which is played in the key of hopelessness. The main character, a woman whose ferocious quest for vengeance turns her into a serial murderer, is never recuperated into 'normal' society. The viewer has no reason to believe that her rampage has run its course or that her enactment of violence has in any way served to heal her profound wounds. It is surely Jordan's bleakest film to date.

Jordan is deeply invested in what Mikhail Bakhtin calls the dark carnival. The filmmaker's work is transgressive and takes pleasure in overturning the stability of the viewers' attachment to normality. He is particularly interested in the ambiguous and the liminal spaces where the cheerful and sinister combine in 'esoterics of celebration' (Bakhtin in Morgan 2002: 137). Bakhtin's notion of the carnivalesque in its melancholy phase turns comedy into pathology. In the construct of the dark carnival, the carnival atmosphere of food, laughter, death, drink and sex, originally part of the robust assertion of life … is lost. Life and death are perceived solely within the sealed-off individual life (see Bakhtin 1981: 199–200). The Russian author writes of 'the disappearance of laughter's regenerating power', and he sees laughter 'cut down to cold humour, irony, and sarcasm … there is no hint of its power of regeneration' (1968: 38).

Taken together, the various discussions in this book are enmeshed in a highly suggestive structure in which each subject area resonates off of the other. It is a conceptualisation of often complicated, poetic and dense work. I believe that I am conveying notions about the work that will broaden, deepen and enliven the films' significance.

CHAPTER ONE

Irish Film/History and Mythopoesis

Michael Collins: 'A Terrible Beauty is Born'

> [It was] a story waiting to burst. Maybe because it has remained unmade for
> so long. Or maybe because this particular part of Irish history was an embar-
> rassed secret for so long. The main opposition to the film will be from within
> this country. There's a series of resentments, sectarian and class differentiation
> that disguise themselves here as politics. And maybe the main objection is
> that the story is being told at all, in any form.
>
> – Neil Jordan

Neil Jordan's remarks on the reception of *Michael Collins* proved to be prescient, if
somewhat understated. As a filmmaker and screenwriter he undertook the task of
chronicling one of the most iconic figures in Irish history: a man who still arouses
fervent responses of reverence or antipathy eighty years after his assassination at the
age of 31. Jordan's film covers six of the most turbulent and complicated years in
Irish history, recounting events that continue to call forth passionate, dissonant and
conflicting perspectives.

Here, a brief synopsis of the historical and political background to Jordan's film
project is warranted. After a brief prologue, the film begins with the Easter Sunday
Uprising of 1916, in which a group of Irish nationalists, agitating for an independent

Republic free from the centuries-long colonisation of the British Empire, occupied the General Post Office in Dublin. They were quickly routed by the superior English military forces; the leaders of the uprising were executed with undue haste for treason, while the remaining participants, including Michael Collins, were jailed. Upon Collins' release from prison in 1917, he was one of the main organisers of the Irish Volunteers (soon to be known as the Irish Republican Army (IRA)), and the political arm of the movement, Sinn Féin. The goal of the secret society was to use physical force, tantamount to guerrilla warfare, to gain independence from the British, and to establish Home Rule for Ireland. Looking for a ceasefire in the Anglo-Irish War (1919–21), which showed no signs of abating, the British invited the Irish to Westminster for negotiations.

Collins was sent to London as Ireland's representative. A treaty was signed which left Ireland in its modern-day configuration: a self-governing parliamentary republic in the South, and the partition of the six northern counties, which remain under British rule. Collins' failure to bring home a treaty that united Ireland and freed it of the English presence created a rift among supporters of the IRA. Although the Treaty was ratified by popular vote, Eamon De Valera (also known as 'The Chief'), the president of Sinn Féin, and later Taoiseach (Prime Minister) and President of Ireland intermittently from 1932–73, stormed out of the Irish Parliament with his supporters in tow, effectively dividing the nascent republic into two factions, those for and against the Treaty. As the Chairman of the new Provisional Government, Collins tried to organise the transfer of power to the Irish Free State from colonial rule. He was faced with growing threats and armed rebellion from De Valera's anti-Treaty units of the IRA, known as the Irregulars. A civil war was fought in 1922 between the two factions, which effectively ended with the assassination of Collins by members of the IRA whose identity has never been established.

Jordan first completed a script for *Michael Collins* in 1983; it languished unmade while other competing Collins projects made the rounds of Hollywood studios. A version to be directed by Michael Cimino, with a script by playwright and RTE (Radio Telefís Éirann) producer Eoghan Harris, came close to achieving fruition, but subsequently funding fell apart. In light of Jordan's unexpected breakthrough with *The Crying Game* and *Interview with the Vampire*, his Collins project was green-lit by Warner Bros. in 1994. At that time, a cease-fire in the hostilities between the British and Republican paramilitaries had been declared. Had this not been the case, it is doubtful that a major studio would have touched such a controversial subject. The project was budgeted at over $30 million, a phenomenal amount of money for an Irish film at the time, albeit one supported by a major Hollywood studio. Still, Warner Bros. was squeamish about the release of the film, and was particularly wary of screening it for the Irish press (see Sheehey & Traynor 1996).

Even before the film was released, a great uproar ensued, with much being written about *Michael Collins* and the surrounding controversies. The conservative English newspapers declared it to be 'an anti-British travesty', 'two hours of sheer lies' and 'a deceitful piece of propaganda' (see Crowdus 1997: 15–16). *Michael Collins* was even called nothing more or less than a recruitment film for the IRA (Dwyer 1996: 12).

Perhaps the most extreme response came from London-based critic Phillip Johnson, who demanded that the film be withdrawn from circulation (see Dwyer 1996: 12). It is crucial to understand why the film provoked such an explosive response within the critical community. The heart of the matter is really: who owns Irish history? As Ronan Fanning, Professor of Modern History at University College, Dublin, writes, 'The perverting impact of the Northern Irish war upon Irish history and historiography since 1969 is but an example of the axiom that truth is the first casualty of war' (1997: 18).

Fanning is referring to the revisionists, a vocal group in Ireland whose basic contention is that the violence that marked Ireland's past – the Anglo-Irish War and the Civil War particularly – was wholly unnecessary. They believe, without any apparent basis in fact, that a treaty was available, and would have been signed without a war. They largely blame Michael Collins for what they call the 'violence and mayhem' (Lee 1996: 16). They refuse to admit that the Republic was founded by Sinn Féin supporters, in spite of the fact that the party bearing that name was overwhelmingly voted into power in a legitimate popular election in 1918. In essence, the revisionists (amongst others) refuse the legacy of violence that Michael Collins represents. As Professor Joe Lee writes, 'Because in Anglo-Irish relations, it is only Anglo violence that is legitimate. Irish violence is, by definition, terrorist' (1996: 17).[1]

Apart from the revisionist view of Collins, there was a very lengthy and very public argument between Eoghan Harris and Neil Jordan. For months, one could not open an Irish newspaper without reading letters to the editor or op-ed pieces siding with or vilifying either position. Harris's main contention (and we must naturally view this quarrel in light of his position as the author of an aborted film about Collins) is that Jordan's script dehumanises Collins, largely by repudiating his sexuality, and his image as a sort of Irish Don Juan. It is largely taken to be true that Collins, while in London before the Treaty talks, had a serious affair with Hazel Lavery, an 'earthy and experienced' woman, who was a close friend of both Prime Minister Lloyd George and his minister, Winston Churchill (see Harris 1996). As Harris writes: 'since she was sexually involved with Collins, it beggars belief that she could have had no part in his change of heart' (1996: 9). In other words, it is Harris's claim that Collins' decision to sign the Treaty negotiating away Northern Ireland was largely the result of his affair with Lavery. Harris further accuses Jordan of wishing away Collins' eleven years spent working in London, 'the centre of swinging Edwardian England' (ibid.) thus making Collins into a more acceptable naïf from County Cork. Harris mainly blames all of this on the Catholicism of Collins' biographers, and writes that 'Collins without a sex life is nothing but a murderous seminarian' (1996: 10). Elsewhere, Harris calls Jordan a 'Neo-Fascist' (see Maconghail 1996/97: 2). The latter remark is based on Walter Benjamin's idea that the romanticisation of violence provides a conduit for the success of fascist aesthetics, and that Jordan's main objective is to choreograph history in order to sweep away critical distance, comparing Jordan's work (quite shamelessly) to Leni Riefensthal's *Triumph of the Will* (1935). Harris is supported in his contentions by Queens University of Ulster Political Science professor, Paul Bew, who also condemns the film's Anglophobia, and sanctimoniously adds to the list of complaints Jordan's

Michael Collins (Liam Neeson) and Eamon De Valera (Alan Rickman) wait for sentencing after the failure of the Easter Uprising of 1916

gratuitous use of obscenities, and the filmmaker's historical inaccuracies (for example, incorrect armaments), and most importantly takes issue with Jordan's statement that Collins wanted to take the gun out of Irish politics (see Bew 1996: 8).

By contrast, there are a group of historians who defend Jordan's right to depart from documentary-style accuracy (see Donovan 1995: 11). The Irish press were, for the most part, passionate advocates of the film. Michael Dwyer in *The Irish Times* called *Michael Collins* 'the most important film made about Ireland in the first century of cinema' (1996: 12); Hugh Linehan also in *The Irish Times* sagely comments that 'it's enough that it has stimulated so much debate' (1996: 19) after what Neil Jordan has called a period of 'collective amnesia' (*The South Bank Show*, 1996), about a series of events that have calcified in people's minds and deserve examination. The main reservation about the film expressed on both sides of the Atlantic was the perception that the love story, with Julia Roberts as Collins' fiancée, Kitty Kiernan, represented an insipid and unnecessary distraction from the quintessential story of men, guns and politics.

One passage of the film has elicited the greatest opprobrium from the anti-Collins historians and critics. It begins with the Twelve Apostles, Collins' crack team of gunmen, assassinating a member of a group of elite British intelligence officers brought in to put an end to Republican aspirations. After a brief scene of Collins (Liam Neeson) crying over the broken, dead body of Ned Broy (Stephen Rea), we move to the famous Croke Park massacre, organised as an immediate retaliatory move following the assassinations by the IRA. The British send in an armoured car to a Sunday football match in Dublin; critics used the Croke Park sequence to discredit Jordan's accuracy, saying such artillery was not in use at the time. Jordan admits taking liberties with the scene in order to accommodate the lengthy events in a dramatically compact manner, although this temporal compression does not deal with the use of incorrect armaments (Neil Jordan, *Michael Collins* DVD commentary). Jordan was also criticised for showing the IRA assassins facing their victim and giving him an opportunity to pray before shooting him, while the British send in a faceless, inhuman killing machine to slaughter innocent civilians. But as pointed out by Tim Pat Coogan, the Croke Park massacre was worse than depicted in the film:

> [The] Auxiliaries and Tans made arrangements to surround Croke Park while the match was in progress, ostensibly to search the crowd for known Sinn Féiners. Later it was claimed in their defence that IRA men in the crowd fired first. But it is not denied that the security forces opened up on both crowd and playing field with rifles and machine-guns causing bloodshed and panic. Fourteen people died and hundreds were injured, none of them Tans or Auxiliaries … [The] Sam Maguire Cup … is named after one of the dead, Hogan, the Tipperary player who was shot on the playing field. (1991: 161)

The Auxiliaries and Tans were well-known for their brutality and blatant disregard for the civilian population. In one documented incident, 'Ellen Quinn of Kiltartan, County Galway, was killed sitting on her garden wall holding a child in her arms when a policeman took a pot shot from a passing lorry' (Coogan 1991: 145).

Perhaps the most significant and complex response to *Michael Collins* comes from cultural historian Luke Gibbons. Gibbons reminds us that three quarters of a century have elapsed since Collins was assassinated, and argues for the need to contextualise the film as a cultural object made in the mid-1990s. He begins his analysis by calling up various representations of Sinn Féin since the Troubles reignited in the late 1960s. It was an uneasy coincidence that Francis Ford Coppola's *Godfather* films of the 1970s intersected with the renewed sectarian violence in Ireland; it became valuable rhetorical propaganda for the British authorities to conflate political violence with organised crime, to embody the IRA as gangsters. Coincidentally, as if to reinforce this image of 'mindless thugs of the republican mafia produced by the nationalist ghettoes' (Gibbons 1997a: 51), the criminalisation policy towards Republican prisoners in the North was implemented in the mid-1970s. Gibbons sees Jordan's film as a rethinking of 'simplistic readings of political violence' (ibid.). *Michael Collins* refutes the sinister associations with *The Godfather* (1972) and the Mafia, and acts to humanise the IRA, thus repudiating the demonic portrayal of the political group by the revisionists. (Nonetheless, it also must be mentioned that *The Godfather* trilogy (1972–1990) has been criticised for its romanticisation of the Mafia.) Jordan's reconsideration of political violence, or probing of the consensus, dislocates the complacent view of the Northern conflict. It provokes questions about the war as glorious and romantic, and the Troubles as squalid and reprehensible, as well as questioning 'the relationship between realism and idealism, moderation and extremism, the state and violence – the connections between past and present, or indeed film and society' (Gibbons 1997b: 16). In this sense, *Michael Collins* can be seen as a 'shadow text' of the Troubles, regarding the inability of post-colonial societies to produce coherent narratives.

For Jordan, the movie – in its depiction of Collins and De Valera – is about 'an argument between a revolutionary and a politician, a passionate heart and a strategic, dispassionate mentality' (*The South Bank Show*, 1996). It is Jordan's disposition as a filmmaker to look for skewed versions of the family romance, and so it is that he casts Michael Collins and Eamon De Valera (Alan Rickman) in a choreography of son and father, or brother against brother; it is the director's claim that they can be viewed on a mythic level as Cain and Abel. He identifies himself at all times as a storyteller, not a historian, and is concerned with the larger canvas, that which lends itself to a more ecumenical reading. The mythopoeic aspect, and the distance between Jordan's work and historical actuality, becomes clear when we interrogate the meanings of the events that took place between 1916 and 1921 through the *optique* of myth and ritual.

In the Proclamation of 1916, the document addressed to the assembled crowd at the site of the General Post Office uprising, the legendary heroes of Irish myth Erin (Oisín) Cúchulainn, Mannanán, Caitlin Ni Houlihán, Fionn mac Cumhaill and his warrior band the Fianna are fiercely invoked, the long dead generations and Fenian forbears. The concept of sacrificial bloodletting is strongly identified as one of the foundational myths of the Irish Republic; it is no accident that Easter was the day chosen for the uprising (see Kearney 1988: 211). Martyrdom and the ancestor cult are part of the mythic ideology that informs the beginnings of the Irish nation, and are equally critical to Jordan's conception of Collins as a hero. As Mircea Eliade has written on the subject of myth and history, 'The historical personage is assimilated to his mythical model (hero etc.) while the event is identified with the category of mythical actions (fight with a monster, enemy brothers, etc.)' (1971: 44). In the same volume, Eliade writes: 'Struggles, conflicts, and wars, for the most part have a ritual cause and function. They are a stimulating opposition between two halves of a clan, or a struggle between the representatives of divinities ... but this always commemorates an episode of the divine and cosmic drama. War or the duel can in no case be explained through rationalistic motives' (1971: 29). The boyish grappling between Collins and Harry Boland (Aidan Quinn) becomes a fight to the death. Shortly before he is to be assassinated, and after Boland's death, Collins says to Kitty in a darkened hotel room: 'The papers said his last words were "Have they got Mick Collins yet?"' Kitty replies: 'It's not true Mick, you know it can't be...'. For the first time in the film, Collins appears thoroughly beaten, and weeps softly as he says to Kitty: 'I don't know anything any more...'

The mythographic and divine dimension of Collins is expressed not only by Liam Neeson's extraordinarily powerful presence, but by the film's *mise-en-scène*. At one point Collins is training the youthful IRA volunteers in the skills of warfare. Having only disused rifles at their disposal, the trainees despair of carrying out Collins' orders to steal guns from the Royal Irish Constabulary. Collins picks up a sod of turf and asks the assembled group: 'What's that?' One of the volunteers, laughing, says 'Sod of turf.' Collins replies, 'Wrong. That's a weapon. Fucking deadly. You don't believe me?' He attaches the turf to a metal hook and drenches it with petrol, lights it, and the sod goes up in flames. The gesture invokes the image of Prometheus bringing fire to mortals, and Neeson's divine appearance which turns him into what Northrop Frye would call 'the Hero of Myth'. For Frye, this type of hero 'must be superior in kind both to men and to environment; the hero is a divine being' (1957: 33). Normally this variety of myth is a story about a god found outside normal literary categories. In its tragic mode this figure may be a dying god, and the death of Christ provides a perfect example (see Frye 1957: 35–6). Collins' Promethean strain surely places him in this category, and the isolation in which the god finally finds himself is appropriate to the end of Collins' life. Before he sends the Twelve Apostles out to murder members of the elite British assassins, as Collins concludes his speech he says to the assembled group, 'I wouldn't force this on anyone.' There is a cut to a low-angle shot of a statue of the Christ figure surrounded by a bank of candles. Retroactively, we come to understand that a boy is saying his prayers before going out on his mission. The potent connection between Collins and Christ is forcefully made. Factually, Coogan writes about Collins:

> In the midst of the vortex he forced himself to study politics, literature, other countries' methods of economic development, anything which might benefit the country once he reached his objectives. Particularly in his last few years of life he continually worked to develop a philosophy for himself. And, throughout all this, he made a point of visiting friends or helpers who had been wounded or fallen ill. As the pressure intensified he tried to train himself to do without sleep and made a point of giving up smoking and drinking. 'I'll be a slave to nothing,' he boasted. (1991: 95)

There is no shortage of Judas figures in *Michael Collins*. One might say that both De Valera and Boland have betrayed their comrade. De Valera is found shaking and weeping the night before Collins' assassination. 'The Chief's' involvement in Collins' death has remained ambiguous, as it is in Jordan's film. What is interesting, however, is that a young boy (Jonathan Rhys-Meyers) acts as the go-between carrying messages from De Valera to Collins in County Cork, where the two men have arranged to meet. Collins gives the boy a message, and then asks, 'What's your name, kid?' The boy never responds, he merely leaves the room; and it is this boy who, in the ambush at Béal Na Bláth (The Valley of Flowers), aims his rifle and kills Collins. By giving him no identity and no real existence, the boy becomes a universal figure, one who plays his role in the death and martyrdom of Collins; it is seen as inevitable. As a biographer writes of Yeats:

> The tragic crises [infused] almost every event of public importance since the death of Parnell in 1891; but every tragic event became, in his eyes, an embodiment of his Great Wheel and its cycles of rebirth. And because he believed that historical cycles were crystallised mainly in the growth and development

of great nations, Yeats also referred to the patterns of death and rebirth in Irish culture as though they were mirrors of the whole world. (Seiden 1975: 138)

Eliade's work on myth and legend may well be applied to Collins and the mythic proportions of his story, which position the film as not merely a social fact, but as the repetition of a timeless ritual:

> Now, one fact that strikes us immediately: in such [primitive and archaic] societies the myth is thought to express the absolute truth, because it narrates a sacred history; that is, a transhuman revelation which took place at the dawn of the Great Time, in the holy time of the beginnings (in *illo tempore*). Being real and sacred, the myth becomes exemplary, and consequently repeatable, for it serves as a model, and by the same token as a justification, for all human actions. In other words, a myth is a true history, of what came to pass at the beginning of Time, and one which provides the pattern for human behaviour. In imitating the exemplary acts of a god or of a mythic hero, or simply by recounting their adventures, the man of an archaic society detaches himself from profane time and magically re-enters the Great Time, the sacred time. (1960: 23)[2]

It was the belief of Yeats and other members of the Literary Revival in Ireland, who, in various degrees, would have been supporters of nationalist aspirations in the world of poetry, theatre and literature, that beauty is the outcome of terror – a theme central to mythic logic. Consider De Valera's anti-Treaty speech: 'This Treaty bars the way to Independence with the blood of fellow Irishmen. And if it's only by civil war we can get our independence, so be it. The Volunteers may have to wade through Irish blood – in order to get Irish Freedom.' This sort of thinking is very much in the Romantic tradition that glorified the bloodletting of the French Revolution in the name of a sublime apocalypse. Yeats wrote in 'The Trembling Veil' (1922), 'And would not such a Unity of Culture and Image be impossible without some apocalyptic terror?' (in Kearney 1988: 217). The poet also writes in his poem 'Easter, 1916' (1921): 'Now and in time to come/wherever green is worn/they are changed, changed utterly/A terrible beauty is born' (2000a: 2104). Jordan rises very much out of the darker side of the Romantic legacy, and is culturally fused to Yeats' beliefs. The terrible beauty that Yeats speaks of is born and re-born out of periodic rites of terror, a ritual man must return to again and again, as it is only a temporary purchase of power that needs constant renewal. Cult practices and ritual mutilation and sacrifice of the victim go back to mythological cycles of renewal and rebirth (see Kearney 1988: 220–1); one need only listen to the speech that opens *Michael Collins* – or, for that matter, to watch Chris Menges' 'Twilight of the Gods' cinematography, shot largely at night, in dark spaces, and often in dream-like silhouette – to understand the religious and mythic underpinnings that subtend Jordan's vision of Collins. In the film's first dialogue scene, his friend Joe O'Reilly speaks to Kitty Kiernan in a darkened room:

Chris Menges' 'Twilight of the Gods' cinematography

You've got to think of him. The way he was. The way he fought the British without one ounce of hatred ... Some people have greatness flowing through them. They're what the times demanded. And life without them seems impossible. But he's dead. And life is possible. He made it possible. (Jordan 1996: 91)

The imputation of omnipotence and god-like powers to Collins reinforces access to an alternative world of consciousness; one that is removed from historical fact. Yeats and Lady Gregory wrote in their play *Cathleen ni Houlihan* (1902) about another Michael who forgoes marriage to a real woman and sacrifices his life at the altar of 'Mother Ireland' (see Gibbons 1995: 265). This element of sacrifice is why Julia Roberts' Kitty can never fully inhabit the role of a woman in Jordan's drama. Environments of a personal or domestic nature wherein women are positioned in less mythical narratives are barred to the character of Kitty.

Yeats evolved powerful theories about women and about what he called 'the goddess figure' (Meihuizen 1998: 34), who can be unintegrated or integrative. Unintegrated women were like Maud Gonne, and his platonic relationship with her was one of non-fulfilment; this sort of woman is associated with 'the sorrow of love, or unsatisfied love relationships' (ibid.). The integrative woman manifests herself as 'a soul image who is frequently redemptive in nature, and is also referred to by Yeats as daimon and spirit – she becomes an active aspect of Yeats' creative processes, both in terms of individual creativity and universal creativity ... central to Yeats' own creativity' (Meihuizen 1998: 35). Kitty Kiernan falls into the unintegrative category of women. As she visits shops in London to purchase her wedding gown for her marriage to Collins, there is a parallel montage showing the moments in County Cork leading to Collins' impending assassination. Kitty represents the 'sorrow of love', and its lack of fulfilment. Like Shakespeare's walled paradise images, the Yeatsian image of paradise also indicates a state of wholeness of existence. Indeed, rose and paradise are different expressions of the same wholeness. In the context of Yeats' note, the rose is a metonym for both paradise and Ireland, an identification of a similar order to Shakespeare's Eden (see Meihuizen 1998: 65). Kitty is a sort of rhetorical device who is used to engender the connections between two concepts of interest: the 'mythos of sacrifice' (Kearney 1988: 216), and Ireland as a rose.

The rose is an image that permeates both Irish folklore and Yeats. Central to the conceptualisation of Ireland as a rose is the idea of Ireland as a nation steeped in pride, sorrow, beauty, bloodshed, growth, death and renewal. As Yeats writes in 'To the Rose Upon the Rood of Time' (1893), a poem that celebrates myth, mysticism and sacrifice, 'Red Rose, proud Rose, sad Rose of all my days!' (1920: 155). In *The Company of Wolves*, the main character is named Rosaleen, after the 'dark Rosaleen' of Irish poetry, and the image of the rose engorged with blood can be seen as a symbol emerging from mythology (Meihuizen 1998: 64).

The scene in *Michael Collins* between Michael and Kitty Kiernan depicts them in the Gresham hotel during the pre-dawn assassinations of Bloody Sunday. The intercutting between the Collins/Kitty site and the assassinations evokes with tenderness and deathly chill the mythic reciprocity of beauty and terror in relation to both Ireland as a rose and the 'mythos of sacrifice'. As we see Collins' young volunteers carry out their orders, shooting dead each politician on their list before the city of Dublin awakes, there are cuts to scenes of Kitty and Michael in their hotel room, in which a bouquet of red roses is prominent.

Kitty likens the young volunteers to 'so many Valentines delivering bouquets'. She asks Collins if he sends a 'love note' with them, and if so what does it say? Collins sits on the edge of the bed and faces Kitty, who lies on her back and looks up at him; Collins holds one of the red roses between them, its outline silhouetted against an ashen sky outside their window. At length he replies with words inspired by his beloved rose, as he brushes Kitty's cheek with the flower: 'You know what it says, Kitty. It says give us the future; we've had enough of your past. Give us our country back; to live in, to grow in, to love.' As his (rather platitudinous) words are spoken, we return to the assassinations and back to Kitty, Collins, and their Red Rose. It is a remarkable moment of storytelling on Jordan's behalf, conveying with tragic clarity the meaning of Yeats' poem 'The Rose Tree' – 'terrible beauty' that emerges from the belief that 'There's nothing but our own red blood/ Can make a right Rose Tree' (2001: 88).

When Eoghan Harris complains about the de-sexualisation of Collins, one can see that his project was the very opposite of Jordan's. Harris wanted to incarnate a flesh-and-blood human being with all that implies, while Jordan's project embodies notions of 'martyrdom, apocalypse, and ritualistic commemoration'; his film presents a mythopoeic interpretation of Collins that is 'the interaction of imagination, politics and history', not the biography of a secular mortal (Jordan 1996: 80).

'Everything turns to everything else.'
                                        – Neil Jordan

Preceding his 1983 script on Collins, Jordan published his first novel, *The Past*. It is an imaginative response to the creation of the Irish Republic, both to the years leading to the traumatic moment in Irish history, the aftermath of these events and how they impact upon the novel's characters. The book contains conspicuous references to a figure named Michael O'Shaughnessy, patently modelled after Michael Collins, while Eamon De Valera is designated by his real name. The novel also uses time in a disjunctive manner, something that absorbs Jordan's attention in other films, especially in *The Company of Wolves* and *The End of the Affair*. The narration moves between first-person and third-person omniscient:

> He was from a Redmondite family, a lawyer with that blend of innocence and relentless idealism that was admirable then, really admirable, and that took the Free State to sully it. He was the best of them, by far the best of them, he was marked out for what would happen to him later, I've heard that said, having no way of knowing, my only memories of him are in the kindergarten school out near Mount Merrion, he'd come to visit us in his Free State uniform, the darling of the nuns with those glazed eyes that told you precisely how much he hated it, the heavy ridiculous belts and the shoulder pistols, he must have hated it even more than De Valera hated him, he would walk through the classroom in his wide boots, stammer while refusing the nuns' offer of tea and lift Rene on to his hip … I learned later it had always been like that, ever since she was old enough to know him, which is the trouble with public men I supposed, especially the kind of public men we had then. But those few brief meetings were enough to convince anyone of his innate goodness, the quiet enigma of him, which I suppose she inherited. (1980a: 13)

His humility (stammering before nuns) dispatches any thought that O'Shaughnessy (Collins) thinks of himself as someone deserving special obeisance, even as he is evidently revered by the nuns. He is too selfless, and still too much the boy from County Cork, to expect extraordinary treatment. O'Shaughnessy/Collins is further humanised when he takes his daughter, Rene, on his hip. His affection for her is evident throughout his appearance in the book. (The character is shot dead at a young age, as was Collins.) This passage presents the apotheosis of O'Shaughnessy/Collins, and portrays him as a colossal figure possessed of a remarkable and almost saintly character. His 'hatred' of the uniform and the arms he bears is reminiscent of Collins' conversation with Boland on board a ship:

> I hate them. Not for their race. Not for their brutality. I hate them because they've left us no way out. I hate whoever put a gun in young Ned Tannin's

hand. I know it's me, I have to do that. I hate them for making hate necessary. And I'll do what I have to, to end it. (Jordan 1996: 135)

One can sense the potency of Jordan's hero-worship of Collins; he imbues the figure with a quiet grandeur. Though O'Shaughnessy is assassinated relatively early in the book, he hovers over the narrative proceedings:

> He comes to realise as the car speeds towards Bray how much she has grown, between himself and the woman he rarely sees now, miraculously filling the absence between them, garnering her own life from the chaos between theirs. And the suspicion rears in his mind again with an elusive truth, with perhaps the last truth, the suspicion in Hyde Park, in the London railway hotels, in the figure of Casement being escorted from the club between a phalanx of policemen that the events which would take hold of him, whose pattern he thought he had divined at the time, were weaving quite a different pattern, that the great hatred and passion, the stuff of politics and the movements of men, were leading him merely to this child on his jaded knee, and that without this child on his knee those movements would have been nothing and would not, he almost suspects, have taken place. (Jordan 1980a: 60–1)

The 'great hatred and passion' O'Shaughnessy/Collins feels, the fatigue of battle ('his jaded knee') is balanced by the love he feels for the child. At the same time, the liberation of Ireland must be realised for the sake of ensuing generations, and his resolve is inflamed by this quest for freedom. Once again, Jordan softens the (potentially) rigid and soulless martyr, painting a portrait of a tired and agitated man whose selflessness in the face of the burden of his political mandate would be overwhelming, were it not for the child and those who would later inherit Ireland. On the other hand, we have Jordan's representation of De Valera, 'the gaunt schoolmaster', 'His pallid face, his gangling, unlikely bearing, his tenderness for mathematics and his strict academic air had been the butt of many private, rather caustic jokes' (Jordan 1980a: 45). The director has always shown disdain for De Valera and for the repressive parochialism of the Ireland in which Jordan grew up – De Valera's backward-looking view of Ireland as a place of little white cottages and its inconsequential relationship with the world outside its borders. Much of Jordan's contempt finds its way into his physical portrait of De Valera. In this passage, one of the novel's characters is pasting theatre posters on the town walls, where he finds a campaign poster of De Valera:

> There is a sharp aquiline nose, a rigorous mouth without a trace of humour, and a pair of wire-framed spectacles. The eyes on the poster reflect his own abstractions, and with it a quite terrifying certainty. They stare into the distance, embedded with the mathematics of vision. He watches as the damp spreads round the face. There is something foolish, horse-like in the features, which only adds to their allure. The corners of the mouth sweep downwards, in one clean line. (Jordan 1980a: 102)

The figure of De Valera represents the polar opposite on the spectrum of humanity to the loving, gentle, self-sacrificing O'Shaughnessy/Collins. The hawk-like face given to De Valera (and born out in photos) reflects the intransigent, mean-spirited and uninspired personality of De Valera. He is anything but the warm, lovable giant of a man who was so beloved by the Irish people that half a million mourners attended his funeral. Collins and De Valera come to personify the adversarial parameters of beauty and terror.

Angel: 'It's Like Nothing You Can Feel, and It Gets Worse'

> What I get the greatest pleasure out of is trying to make manifest how a perceiving eye can see and feel the world. I suppose really that fiction or any art is like sensual thinking. It's like thinking through one's senses [which] is deeper, more valuable than abstract thinking.
> — Neil Jordan (in Toíbín 1982: 17)

Angel, Neil Jordan's first directorial work, was filmed during a time of exceptional political violence in Ireland. The Troubles, the tensions and violent activity amongst the IRA, the Protestant Unionists and the occupying forces of the British Army in Northern Ireland exploded from the early 1970s onward. Retaliatory murders and bombings increased as the mediation between the British and Irish government was found unacceptable to both parties, particularly between representatives of Sinn Féin and the Ulster Unionists. The hunger strikes at the Maze Prison, first in 1980 and again in 1981, developed out of the British Parliament's decision to criminalise political prisoners. Those jailed for political crimes believed they were fighting a war, and as prisoners of war were entitled to a different status than the population of common criminals.

It was in this atmosphere, fraught with tension and sectarian turbulence, that Neil Jordan made *Angel*, his personal meditation on violence. The film had a difficult conception. John Boorman, the respected British director who has been a long-time resident of Ireland, was one of three members of the newly-created Irish Film Board (IFB) in 1980. In his capacity as a board member Boorman was generous in his financial support of *Angel*; this decision was vigorously decried by experienced Irish filmmakers. As Boorman says,

> I thought it was some kind of joke. I don't think this petty attitude is worth discussing. It was a relatively small investment [in *Angel*]. The Film Board will have its £100,000 back before the end of the year, plus their share of the profits. How could we have given money to Irish filmmakers when they boycotted the Board? I have to keep reminding myself that they are a group of malcontents and mad dogs. They are in love with martyrdom. (In Dwyer 1982: 27)

Jordan had previously worked with Boorman on *Excalibur* (1981) as a 'creative advisor', and had directed a 'making of' short of the film. Boorman's advocacy of

Jordan's film was perceived as an objectionable case of nepotism. The IFB provided £100,000 for the venture, while Britain's Channel 4 contributed the remainder of the £1 million budget. Boorman's subsequent resignation from the Board was provoked by the provincial narrow-mindedness of the protesting artists. Although the irritation of filmmakers who did not receive the boon of Boorman's financial beneficence is understandable, time has proven that Boorman's faith in Jordan was perspicacious and his instincts impeccable.

The pettiness did not stop with the funding of Jordan. There were also embittered complaints about the hiring of British cinematographer Chris Menges, who would go on to photograph several of Jordan's films. The squabbling disregarded the reality that Jordan's film provided employment for 45–50 Irish workers in varied capacities. Members of the crew campaigned against Jordan; arguments and non-compliance were their main tools for expressing their dissatisfaction. They simply did not think the fledgling director had the ability to direct a feature film (see Falsetto 2000: 224). Even at this early stage Jordan had a strong personal vision, if not the knowledge and experience to fully achieve it.

Angel was inspired by The Miami Show Band incident in which members of the band were shot while touring Northern Protestant towns on the way to Dublin. There was speculation that the attack was the work of ordinary criminals unmotivated by political concerns. When it became known that Jordan's film was based on this repellent episode in Irish history, he received death threats from both Protestant and IRA paramilitary groups. It is to Jordan's credit that he went ahead with the project in spite of the attempts at intimidation, and the unsettling lack of cooperation from the film's crew (see Falsetto 2000: 223–4).

The novice filmmaker was heavily influenced by European art cinema. At the time that Jordan made *Angel*, he cited Rainer Werner Fassbinder as an influence, but the impact of other directors, especially Wim Wenders, can also be detected. Many of Wenders' films are literally enacted on the border between East and West Germany, for example *Die Angst des Tormanns beim Elfmeter* (*The Goalkeeper's Fear of the Penalty Kick*, 1972), *Alice in den Städten* (*Alice in the Cities*, 1974), *Falsche Bewegung* (*Wrong Move*, 1975) and *Im Laufder Zeit* (*Kings of the Road*, 1976). Jordan skirts the areas that border Northern and Southern Ireland in *Angel*. More importantly, both Wenders and Jordan have a penchant for circuitous journeys across borders and boundaries of different kinds – both physical and emotional. There is also the cultural landscape of America that plays a role in much of their work, especially through musical traditions such as rock 'n' roll and jazz. Jordan has also expressed his admiration of Fellini. With that in mind, one can see similarities between the mute girl murdered in the opening incident of *Angel* and the silent blonde girl who beckons to Marcello Rubini (Marcello Mastroianni) at the end of Fellini's *La Dolce Vita* (*The Good Life*, 1960). *Angel* also alludes to Antonioni's *The Passenger* (1975) thematically, in its search for identity, limits, meaning and connectedness.

Angel begins with an onstage performance by Danny (Stephen Rea), playing the sax with his band. The film marks the first collaboration of the director and Rea, whom Jordan calls 'one of the most intelligent actors in the world' (Falsetto 2000:

225). Rea has come to be viewed as Jordan's *doppelgänger* because he has played the lead or a supporting role in nine of the director's films thus far. Before *Angel*, which marks Rea's debut in a major film, Rea had (and still has) a distinguished career in the theatre, both in Ireland, where he was a member of the Abbey Theatre, and in London venues, including the Royal National Theatre. Rea and playwright Brian Friel were the founding members of Field Day, a theatre troupe inaugurated in 1980, whose mandate was populist – to bring Irish plays, or translations by Irishmen of classical plays, to the Irish populace, many of whom had never been exposed to live theatre. The company has been criticised because none of their literary or theatrical ventures included women; it was not until 2002 that a volume of work by women has been published in the *Field Day Anthology of Irish Literature* (see Bourke 2002). Field Day toured the provinces in Ireland and Northern Ireland, and also brought their work to London. Rea speaks about his experience of working in England:

> I had the notion imposed upon me that you had to speak in a particular way if you were working in English theatre. Particularly if you were doing transla-tions of foreign classics. It seemed totally stupid to me that I should pretend to be English, to pretend I was Russian or German. I resented it very much and it robbed me of all the colour and emotion of my own accent. Because the standard English accent is part of a culture which is designed to conceal emotion; and Irish way of speech is more emotional, more poetic, more colourful: they express emotion in their language. (In Zucker 1999: 111)

The first section of *Angel* is a musical performance, an inaugural instanciation of the way in which performances of many kinds will resonate in the director's oeuvre. The seedy ballroom with gaudy disco lights and a huge pink neon sign at the front of the building create a sense of unreality. Yet backstage banter is handled naturalistically. This is a perfect example of the continuous tension between stylisation and realism that characterises many of the director's films. Rea's character Danny meets a deaf mute girl, Annie (Veronica Quilligan) and dances with her; his qualities of impulsiveness, kindness and compassion are communicated in the film's opening moments. Danny and the girl leave the club to the strain of angelic music written by Giovanni Fusco and they come across a tree strung with white lights, and a tinkling bell. Danny says: 'It's a wishing tree', thus connecting him to the animistic world of spirits. There is something child-like and untainted about Danny, qualities that will be undermined as the character makes his way through the film. Annie and Danny crawl into huge cement construction tubes; the scene is lit by the eerie glare of a red neon light. After an ellipsis, there is a cut back to the couple and Danny says, 'Bet they didn't teach you that at the convent school.' It is not clear precisely what has taken place, as they are both fully dressed. Conversation between the characters is impossible, but Danny's remark alerts the viewer to the fact that some kind of sexual act has been performed. (Jordan would not direct a scene of sexual intercourse until *The End of the Affair* in 1999.) They both watch the band's manager argue with a group of men outside the dance hall. The manager is shot, and before Danny can stop her, Annie wanders into the assassins' field of vision and she too is killed. The murderers then drive away just as the ballroom explodes in flames. Danny runs towards Annie's dead body and takes her in his arms. He shakes her as though she were alive, shouting, 'Why didn't you stay?' We next find Danny cradling the girl's limp form in the mouth of the cement tube. He, evidently in a state of shock, says, 'I'll teach you to sing'. There is a cut to men congregating around the burnt-out ballroom. Danny walks towards them carrying Annie's supine body. It is Bloom (Ray McAnally) and Bonner (Donal McCann). Bloom sees the body and say, 'Jesus Christ'. There is a cut to a close-up of a foot crunching on gravel; the shot is tinted blue. The next shot has Danny waking up in a sterile environment which we learn retroactively is a hospital. There is a return to the close-up of what we now perceive is an orthopaedic shoe, meant for a club foot. The frame is shared with a part of a body lying on the ground, blood pools around the heavy shoe. The elliptical style of editing and the use of synecdoche owe much to the conventions of European art cinema. This sequence offers a pre-eminent example of the way that Jordan utilises sound and image to create meaning, with little dialogue. An event of great significance has occurred, but no explanation is supplied for the bombing of the ballroom or the murder.

The opening sequence is important on a number of levels. It introduces the audience to Jordan's decidedly non-naturalistic use of colour: in a later scene at a club where Danny is playing, the room is enveloped in blue light, while the customers' tables are decorated with lamps lit by a red light; the bandstand, where Danny and his mates play, is awash in blue, then yellow; Danny exits the room and finds himself in orange neon light with palm trees of the same colour in the background. Jordan's use of colour is reminiscent of Wenders' films, where he uses a palette of vivid hues to bring a sense of unreality to his films as in *The Goalkeeper's Fear of the Penalty Kick*, *Wrong Move* and *The American Friend* (1977). Also, Wenders and Jordan share a fascination with neon lights.

Off-screen sound is used in intriguing ways in *Angel*. The film begins with music that we assume is non-diegetic, that is, not part of the depicted fictional world. When

Stephen Rea cradles the body of dead girl *á la pietà*

the film reveals Danny playing the saxophone, 'The Stan Getz of Armagh' as one of his bandmates suggests, the music can now be understood as being diegetic all along. The music that accompanies Danny is also used in unconventional ways. A solo saxophone is associated with the character and becomes a sonic representation of his presence in the film. The non-diegetic soprano voice heard when Danny and Annie meet outside is used on several occasions. We hear the angelic voice again when Danny finds the gun in the podiatrist's closet. It belongs to one of the men (Gerard McSorley) who was involved in the initial murders. The voice returns towards the end of the film when Danny revisits the ballroom, the site of the initial massacre. He is about to be shot by the crooked detective, Bonner (Donal McCann), when Bonner is killed by his fellow police officer, Bloom (Ray McAnally). We hear the soprano voice after Danny's saxophone riff has ended as it now merges with the off-screen sound of the helicopter. The soprano voice is clearly not part of the film's fictional world; it is like an angel hovering over and protecting Danny. This particular use of music also reminds one of the hauntingly beautiful non-diegetic voice that punctuates scenes in Antonioni's *Il Deserto rosso* (*Red Desert*, 1964). (The voice in *Angel* belongs to Cecilia Fusco whose husband Giovanni Fusco wrote the score for Antonioni's film.) The helicopter is never seen, but an unmistakable whirring sound is associated with the sight of papers being tossed about by the force of the chopper's rotating blades.

Additionally, there are two instances in the film where death is present, and where the aural quality of the dead is important. The policeman at the hospital where Danny has been taken first alludes to death when he says, 'It's so quiet now you'd think it was paradise.' A second comment is made in one of the morgue scenes, when the morgue attendant says, 'This is a dormitory. If you listen, you can hear them sleeping.' There is a sense that if one listens carefully, the dead have a voice – and this voice might very well be the soprano heard at various junctures throughout the film.

One of the scenes in which sound generates an interesting effect takes place when Danny and his group are playing at a psychiatric institution. As the band members exit, Danny stays behind to play his instrument and to test the reverberance of the room. Several people enter the room as he plays, and their footsteps are reproduced loudly on the soundtrack. We then cut to Danny playing, and return to a shot of the listeners. They have grown into a mass of people, but now we hear no footfalls at all. This set of shots is repeated twice, and each time more patients congregate. Again, there is a sensation that some otherworldly entity is active in Danny's life.

Angel, a film that might readily be called 'Avenging Angel', is so steeped in fury, rage and bloodshed that it invites the viewer to question the manner in which Jordan represents violence. The Troubles most certainly would have affected Jordan. In fact, it was on a boat to Ireland to attend the funeral of a relative who was the victim of a terrorist bombing that Jordan conceived the idea for *Angel*. There are (at least) two antagonistic views concerning the manner in which Jordan addresses the issue of violence during this bloody time in Ireland's history. The evil that we witness is both a characteristic of sectarian violence and also a sign of Danny's increasing loss of humanity. Richard Kearney writes that Jordan is looking at 'the psychic roots of violence and cutting through ideological conventions' (1988: 179). In exploring this

Neil Jordan shares an intimate moment with Honor Heffernan and Stephen Rea between takes on the set of *Angel*

mythic unconscious, the director shows how the refusal of ethical decision-making can lead to destructive fanaticism. Kearney sees Danny engaged in a personal quest for revenge which then becomes an 'impersonal madness'. Kearney's view is that *Angel* is a thriller only on the surface, while Jordan excavates the film's deeper psychological structure. And it is surely this deeper structure that most interests Jordan – 'the poetic, ethical and psychological dimensions of humanity' (Kearney 1988: 179). Kearney also claims that Jordan de-romanticises 'the cult of heroic violence which has fuelled sentimental nationalism' (1988: 183). I agree strongly with Kearney's views, especially when he notes that the exploration of violence and creativity has been one of the great subjects of art. Mention should be made as well of Jordan's treatment of genre, which will become an important factor in his personal style of storytelling. We shall see that the director often uses genre as a base from which to explore other issues: the neo-noir *Mona Lisa*; family drama in *The Miracle*; the heist in *The Good Thief* and the vigilante film in *The Brave One*; or as part of a mélange of genres that he imaginatively puts into play – for example, the political thriller and romance genres that underlie *The Crying Game* or the horror, comedy and melodrama that characterise *Interview with the Vampire*).

The alternative view of the violent subject matter of *Angel* comes from John Hill in *Cinema and Ireland*. Hill complains that 'by denying its political origins and motives, paramilitary violence is simply represented as criminal' (1988: 180). He goes on to say that 'the film's use of a decontextualising aesthetic strategy necessarily undermines the "legitimacy" or rationale of political violence, so it also adds to the legitimacy of the state by de-politicising its activities as well' (ibid.). Earlier in his interesting contribution to the book, Hill writes: 'Violence, in this respect, was not to be accounted for in terms of a response to political and economic conditions but simply as a manifestation of the Irish "national character"' (1998: 149). Hill compares the film to Carol Reed's *Odd Man Out* (1947), saying that Northern violence can only be seen as incomprehensible and destructive, which 'only helps to confirm a view of the "troubles" as unintelligible' (1998: 180). Hill, from his deep-seated Marxist perspective, seems oblivious to Jordan's interest in individuals as they move through the world. While he decries the universality of Jordan's views, he appears to be unconcerned by the fact that Jordan is first and always an artist and poet, not an ideologue. Jordan's 'decontextualising aesthetic strategies' can then conveniently be ignored; *Angel* ceases to be a film that fits easily within the context of European art cinema and, for Hill, becomes a missed opportunity for political analysis.

Another outstanding feature of *Angel* is Jordan's skill with dialogue, which is often quite extraordinary and accomplished for a young screenwriter (the director had written a script for Joe Comerford's *Traveller* (1981), and was so unhappy with the result that he decided he would direct his own films). While in the morgue, Bloom says to Danny: 'You want to watch nothing. It can take hold of you.' Again, when Bloom and Danny converse in a similar vein, Bloom says, 'It's deep. It's everywhere and nowhere.' Danny asks, 'What is?' Bloom responds, 'Evil.' It seems like a cross between pulp fiction and French existential novels.

A dialogue about 'nothing' occurs between the band's lead singer Dee (Honor Heffernan) and Danny:

> *Dee*:   You have to tell me something first.
> *Danny*:   It's nothing.
> *Dee*:   You're lying.
> *Danny*:   It's like nothing you can feel. And it gets worse.

As we shall see in chapter six, Jordan is heavily indebted to the English Romantic poets. The most troubling issue for the Romantics is the immanence of God versus the notion that God may not exist at all. In the context of *Angel*, the 'nothing' that Danny speaks of is not an absence, but a real presence which is the opposite of God. As the film draws to a close, Danny's wanderings take him to the home of Mary, played by Sorcha Cusack, a woman in great psychic pain. By now, thoroughly dazed and confused about his mission, Danny has come to kill another of the men he has adjudged guilty. Mary seems distracted and disturbed; she cuts Danny's hair at his request, but only finishes one side, making him look the holy fool. Mary asks about her husband:

> *Mary*:   Why do you want him?
> *Danny*:   I don't know anymore.
> *Mary*:   Hating is easy. That's what I found out. It just grows … that man whose clothes you're in … I hated him for years. I'd sit down next to him in mass and pray, 'Lord let me be free of him.' The priest told me, 'Love is kind.' But I never felt it.
> (She looks at a statue of Jesus)

> Wherever you stand his eyes stare right at you. Well, I'll
> show you what I felt.
> (She takes her husband's gun and shoots herself in the temple)

It is a completely unexpected moment in the film. While there has been a great deal of violence throughout, it is a shock when a woman takes a gun to her head on-screen, and the scene is difficult to watch. Understandably, the already discombobulated Danny's response is one of panic. He drives a pick-up truck back to the original scene of the ballroom. In a caravan, a child faith healer receives his 'parishioners' and conducts a laying on of hands. Danny enters the caravan in desperation; as soon as he meets the child, he collapses on the floor. The angelic music is heard on the soundtrack.

Danny is, in fact, very ill. He suffers from a sickness of the soul that began the night the mute Annie was killed, and with each murderous act of revenge, the state of his soul deteriorates. Within the narrative's trajectory, the scene with Mary is not so much about her – although she seems to be suffering from a malaise even deeper than Danny's – as it is about Danny's sickness. Antonioni has said that modern tragedy is different to the classical tragedy of a great man brought low by a flawed character. In the modern age, tragedy is about the loss of human feeling, a state Danny attains at the film's end. He has lost his moral and ethical compass in a world he no longer belongs to or comprehends. Danny has made the journey from a feckless, blasé musician, uncommitted to much in his life, to an obsessed murderer hell-bent on retribution. After a while, the cause of his bloody murders seems inconsequential, as he behaves more and more like the men he has killed.

CHAPTER TWO

Celtic Myth and Folklore: A Dimension Beyond Existence

'Folklore is at once *The Bible*, *The Thirty-Nine Articles*, and *The Book of Common Prayer*, and well-nigh all the great poets have lived by its light. Homer, Aeschylus, Sophocles, Shakespeare, and even Dante, Goethe, and Keats, were little more than folklorists with musical tongues.'

– W. B. Yeats, 'The Message of the Folklorist'

'[Ireland is] a world that teaches you the value of fables.'

– Neil Jordan

Myth and folklore

Walking down the thoroughfares of Dublin in the new millennium, one cannot help being mildly shocked at the changes wrought upon the city. In James Joyce's *Ulysses* (1934) (which takes place in 1904), the characters who inhabit Dublin collide with one another three or four times a day. Today, in the wake of the Celtic Tiger boom that began in the 1990s, one finds young professionals lined up outside the pubs of Dublin puffing away at now-forbidden cigarettes whilst talking on their mobile phones. A glut of BMWs, posh minimalist hotels, *haute couture* stores, and an ever-growing condo market have changed Dublin irrevocably.

Yet even in this secular, materialist climate, there remains a guttering belief in demons that inhabit the supernatural world. The immortals of legend are deeply implanted in the Irish consciousness and identity. They remain conjoined in eternal cycles, and are otherworldly beings that fund the Irish national identity. The belief in a metaphysical universe, according to Yeats, forms the foundation of an artist's creativity. Whether part of the oral or literary traditions, there lies an innate tension and a set of contradictions regarding the objectives of the gods at the core of these mythic stories: do they mislead or do they guide one's soul? The multitude of mythic, folkloric and symbolic elements that are mobilised in Ireland's history of supernatural folklore are vast indeed. The polarities and contradictions that exist within human nature are essential to Jordan's creative vision. The director has said that he likes to play with extreme contrasts, and the dualistic nature of Celtic myth and folklore reverberate in his work. A drama of body and soul, of history and myth, irradiates Jordan's film-making practice.

Some of the themes identifiable in Irish folklore that find resonance in Jordan's films include the *Sidhe* (Irish fairies) and their manifestation of 'the other'; 'the other' as a mind divided; spirituality and souls; folklore and mysticism in relation to the *anima mundi* and the mythic reciprocity of beauty and terror. As noted, Jordan is above all a teller of tales, with strong psychic bonds to folklore. The mythic or folkloric motifs that tend to repeat in his films and literature grow out of his awareness and connection with the traditions of Celtic legend.

Jordan's films provide a potpourri of contradictory impulses. He marries the real world with the imaginary, the everyday with the mystical, the familiar with the de-familiarised. It is an approach essential to, and largely influenced by, the 'Celtic Twilight' literary movement, associated with one of the most fascinating Celtic poet/activists to emerge from Ireland's formidable literary history: W. B. Yeats, an Anglo-Irish promoter of the late nineteenth-century Irish cultural revival, which was part of an attempt to encourage cultural nationalism in opposition to cultural provincialism. Yeats and his compatriots, notably George Russell and Lady Gregory, zealously fought for the restoration of a spiritual link and continuity with Irish tradition, as distinct from colonial dependency. In doing so, Yeats proselytised for the concept of 'Irishry': the apparent kinship of the Irish to psychic manifestations. In *Transitions: Narratives in Modern Irish Culture*, Richard Kearney discusses revivalism and modernism in relation to the Irish cultural revival. He identifies revivalism as an approach which presupposes an 'ideology of identity', and modernism as one which questions the very notion of 'origins', the latter challenging the correctness of the former. This important distinction is made to foreground the conflict that transpires between the two approaches, and enables us to attend to the 'essentially conflictual nature of contemporary Irish experience' (1988: 12).

Kearney continues: 'It is striking how many modern Irish authors have spoken of being in transit between two worlds, divided between opposing allegiances' (1988: 14). Jordan's complex and binary imaginative vision, to a certain degree, exemplifies Kearney's claim, although a reading of Jordan's work in which duality is a totalising quality would be contrived and reductive. These notions of a consciousness at war with itself are reinforced by the knowledge of Yeats' often contradictory and dynamic mind, driven by both revivalism and modernity, drawn to 'tradition, mythology and collective memory, and embracing individual creativity, autonomy, desire, play and will, the real and the imaginary' (Kearney 1988: 20).[1] As Yeats writes, 'No mind can engender till divided into two' (2000b: 244). Consider this comment made by Jordan in relation to the completion of his first three films, *Angel*, *The Company of Wolves* and *Mona Lisa*: 'They are all basically about the clash between the real world and the world of imagination and unreality, the conflict between dreams and reality. The constant concern is to do with realistic and surrealistic explanations of human behaviour and whether human beings answer to rational modes of thought or are inspired by things quite irrational and unknown to themselves' (in McIlroy 1986: 114).

> 'They don't believe in our gods. They remember older gods – they are nearer the magic of the animal world.'
>   – D. H. Lawrence

Before we examine Jordan's films more deeply it is necessary to investigate some of the essential components of Irish myth and legend. We are no longer in the realm of the quaint misty isle that espouses the spiritual perception of truths that resist intellectualisation. Ireland is rather a country which, like most places, has its own particular mythography. The *Sidhe*, Irish fairies descended from the Celtic gods, appear in their country's folklore as the Irish Celtic 'other'; Lawrence's remark above underscores the profound affinity of the mystical and the real – the visions of non-physical beings such as leprechauns, sylphs, water horses, salamanders, good angels and fallen angels and disincarnate human beings – heroic or common – which is one part of a mythology that can be traced back to centuries preceding the start of the Christian era.

The Irish Celtic gods known collectively as the *Tuatha Dé Danann* ('people of the goddess *Dana*'), amongst whom emerged Irish legends such as *Cúchulainn*, *Conchubar*, *Finn* and *Queen Maev* (said to be buried 'under the huge cairn of stones on Knocknarea' (Moore 1954: 43) in northwestern Ireland) and consequently seen around both Yeats' and Jordan's birthplace, Sligo, riding 'the lucent air' (ibid.). These gods were eventually forced to seek homes in the hills and seas of Ireland, in spite of their victory in a war against the evil *Fomors* (a group that challenged the gods who ruled the spirit world; see Moore 1954), following a prophecy that their centuries-long reign would soon come to an end. These hidden gods, with *Maev* as their Queen, became known as the *Aes Sidhe* ('people of the hills'), commonly abbreviated to *Sidhe*. The origin and nature of these entities support an Irish vision born of contradictions. An interest in the 'other' evolved out of a fascination with the unknown.

Irish folklorists or 'fairylorists', such as Crofton Croker, Douglas Hyde and Sir William and Lady Wilde, offer varying opinions on the relationship of these Irish fairies to their mortal counterparts. In his introduction to *The Trooping Fairies*, Yeats positions himself with William Wilde's *Irish Popular Superstitions* (1852) regarding the *Sidhes*' origins, debated and theorised by most 'fairylorists':

> Who are they? 'Fallen angels who were not good enough to be saved, nor bad enough to be lost,' say the peasantry. 'The gods of the earth,' says the Book of

Armagh. 'The gods of pagan Ireland,' say the Irish antiquarians, 'the *Tuatha De Danân*, who, when no longer worshipped and fed with meagre offerings, dwindled away in the popular imagination, and now are only a few spans high.' (2002: 10)

By offering this interpretation of the *Sidhe*, about whom 'everything is capricious', Yeats reveals their inherent complexity, and a disposition given to the contrary and contentious. Left in immortal limbo, bound to live between life and death, Heaven and Hell, these Irish fairies are simultaneously 'divine castoffs', yet 'no friends of man' (see Kinahan 1988: 47, 48). They are fated to exist within a soulless state and embittered of mortals who will find their place in Heaven: 'A man has a hope for heaven/But soulless a fairy dies/As a leaf that is old, withered and cold/When the wint'ry vapours rise' (Yeats 1966: 643).

Luke Gibbons refers to the oscillating nature of Irishness seen in many of the country's cinematic and literary characters as indicative of 'a kind of Celtic Jekyll and Hyde', one that shifts between 'two extremes of behaviour and mood' and 'liable to rush from mirth to despair, tenderness to violence, and loyalty to treachery' (1988: 218–19). As Jordan has said in many interviews, the Irish either talk ceaselessly or are taken by black, suicidal moods in which stony silence is the only attribute. This is certainly the case with several of Jordan's protagonists, notably the male ones: Danny, who transmutes from affable musician to merciless killer in *Angel*; Fergus (the name of a Celtic god),[2] who leaves the IRA to seek a life of peace and anonymity in *The Crying Game*; the mirror-opposite combination of Lestat (Tom Cruise) and Louis (Brad Pitt) in *Interview with the Vampire*; Francie (Eammon Owens), who shifts from childhood prankster to gruesome murderer in *The Butcher Boy*; and Michael in *Michael Collins*, surely the most infamous, mythic 'Celtic Jekyll and Hyde' in all of Jordan's films, a man who is considered the author of contemporary guerilla warfare and the 'big fella' who charmed nearly everyone who knew him. Claire of *In Dreams* (Annette Bening) and Erica (Jodie Foster) in *The Brave One* are the two female characters to exhibit this radical change of identity.

Linked to this notion of binaries is the ancient Celtic notion that there exists alongside every mortal 'a *Doppelgänger*, or dark shadow-self, or counter-part' – the Irish word is 'fetch' (see Moore 1954: 43–4). This theme is clearly conveyed in Jordan's films, as is the case with the IRA or Unionist assassins in *Angel*, who can be interpreted as multiple versions of Danny's fetch. The fetch can be racial, sexual or cultural. A spiritual fetch – a 'fallen angel' – resides in the dark recesses of his mind and is 'not good enough to be saved, nor bad enough to be lost' (Kearney 1988: 178). Somewhat less apparent, however, is Jordan's conception of Fergus and Jody (Forest Whitaker) in *The Crying Game*. More explicit readings can be ascribed to Jody as Fergus's fetch, and these include the racial (Fergus is white; Jody is black), the sexual (Fergus is heterosexual; Jody is homosexual) and the cultural (Fergus is Irish; Jody is English). Less obvious is the role that Jody plays as Fergus's spiritual fetch, once he has been killed.

As a British soldier taken hostage by Fergus and four other IRA members, Jody's death in *The Crying Game* is inevitable. When he runs from Fergus's gun and is hit by an oncoming Saracen tank arriving to foil the rebels' plans, Fergus cries out Jody's name as if one of his own comrades has been killed. Fergus's face is charged with despondency and loss as he grapples with the feelings that have built up over the previous 72 hours as a result of the unlikely bond formed with the English hostage. Following Jody's death Fergus goes into hiding and travels to England, fulfilling a last request that he look up Jody's 'wife' Dil (Jaye Davidson) and 'tell her I was thinking of her'. As Fergus develops complex feelings for Dil, he remains deeply troubled by the loss of Jody. Nearly all of Jordan's characters are in some way haunted by loss. In this way, Jody emerges as Fergus' spiritual fetch, a 'fallen angel' in the depths of his mind.

In addition to the shrine-like display of photos that decorate Dil's apartment and exacerbate Fergus's guilty conscience whenever he is there, Jody appears in Fergus's dreams three times. The first two show Jody in his cricket whites completing a fast bowl towards the camera (which can be taken as Fergus's dream point of view), as if challenging the Irishman to step up to the crease and bat, to make peace with his past and himself, to take care of Dil, and in doing so put all of their souls at peace. Significantly, the third time this dream-sequence occurs it follows Fergus's discovery of Dil's transvestism; he hits Dil, after which he throws up, and leaves in fear and disgust. This time, Jody walks casually towards the camera (Fergus's point of view), tossing the ball into the air continuously and smiling knowingly. He does not attempt a bowl, but instead turns and walks away with his back to Fergus's subconscious, still tossing the ball.

This marked change in Fergus's dream, I would argue, is indicative of his having failed the challenge assigned to him by Jody, as his spiritual fetch. Not long after this dream encounter, Fergus dresses Dil in Jody's cricket whites and shears her locks until she resembles an elfin version of Jody. Later, after Dil has been told the truth by Fergus, she stands dressed in cricket whites with gun in hand and her confessor tied to the bed, and demands a sign of contrition. Fergus submits and crushes his cheek against Dil's and says quietly but urgently, 'I'm sorry.'

Another important aspect of the *Sidhe*'s complex relationship with their Irish mortals is their finely-honed skill at 'glamouring': the ability to appear in several different guises, including human, in order to seduce and then steal or 'glamour' a mortal into their world of soulless perpetuity, to exist forever between life and death. In his poem 'Kidnappers' (1889) Yeats draws from Keats' poem 'Lamia' (1819) to suggest that the *Sidhe* have two faces and that 'one of the faces was false, and that the false face was the smiling one: the face of the lamia … The radiant welcome extended to man by the *Sidhe* masked a threat to man by its radiance' (Kinahan 1988: 52). One of several examples in Irish folklore of the *Sidhe*'s lamian skill at 'glamouring' occurs in Yeats' poem 'The Stolen Child' (1889) which also reveals the Irish mortal's continual struggle with tensions that arise between beauty and sorrow, life and what lies beyond: 'Come away, O human child!/To the waters and the wild/With a faery, hand in hand/ For the world's more full of weeping than you can understand' (1920: 39).

The immortal existence offered to the child by the deceiving *Sidhe*, in which they claim that the 'waters and the wild' will ensure eternal happiness, is something not on offer in the mortals' 'weeping' world. It is a temptation as alluring as the forbidden fruit was to Eve, and yet beautiful as it may be, it is the world's scourge. Irish Celtic folk-lorists and occultists, such as Yeats and George Russell, maintain that 'life prolonged, with pleasures infinite' is a life not truly lived because as Yeats observes in *The Celtic Twilight*, the 'soul cannot live without sorrow' (1902: 118). The temptation to succumb to the world of the unknown infiltrates Irish folklore while it reinforces its fascination with polarities, forever a reminder that 'there is this world and there is an alluring other world, but the two elements are forever at variance' (Kinahan 1988: 76).

An exemplary bit of glamouring occurs in *The Company of Wolves*. The central premise of the film is, of course, the warning Rosaleen (Sarah Patterson) continually receives from her Granny (Angela Lansbury): 'Don't stray from the path!' It is a warning to the young woman about the dangerous woods surrounding their homes, woods promising magical intrigue but beset with the danger of wolves. In many ways the likeness of these howling beasts in *The Company of Wolves* to the Celtic *Sidhe* is remarkable. They appear in human guise and Rosaleen meets a charming, handsome male with eyebrows that meet in the middle, a lycanthrope certainly, and one who clearly betokens a false 'lamia face'.

The wolves also exist between this world and the next, as indicated by the wolf/man's response to Rosaleen's question when they encounter one another in Granny's house: 'And where do you live? In our world or theirs?' 'Both. I come and go between them.' What makes this showdown different to the one Little Red Riding Hood experiences in the fairy tale, and intensifies the connection to Irish folklore, is that Rosaleen is more captivated than fearful from the moment she meets him in the woods; she is glamoured by the wolf/man (whether initially as food or as a companion remains ambiguous, given the multiple opportunities he has to eat her) and lured into joining his company of wolves.

In choosing to stray from the path of mortal life, Rosaleen, like Yeats' stolen child, takes the immortal path instead, 'to the waters and the wild/with a faery [wolf], hand in hand'. The final scene of the film reinforces the Celtic notion of glamouring further, when Rosaleen, upon waking from her fairy tale dream (a moment which in itself is an interesting example of Jordan's fascination with the real and the imaginary) screams in horror as the wolves burst into her bedroom and enter her reality, her mortal existence. It is at this point that Rosaleen experiences a moment of clarity, and as with the gullible 'stolen child', it is too late. Released from her dream-induced desire to join the beasts in their state of soulless perpetuity, Rosaleen has a split second to grasp her mortal life. Whether she does or not remains ambiguous. The film ends with a voice-over citing Perrault's *Le Petit Chaperon rouge* (1697), warning little girls to 'never trust a stranger' because 'sweetest tongue has sharpest tooth': the implication is that Rosaleen meets her fate with the wolves. This interpretation mirrors Irish folklorists' belief that once taken, 'glamoured souls were doomed to vanish on the day of judgement' (Kinahan 1988: 61).

Souls and spirituality, the metaphysical, leads us into an area of great interest to Yeats, George Russell and other Celtic occultists inspired by societies such as the Order of the Golden Dawn: the union of folklore and occultism. As we have already seen, Yeats' fascination with the journey of souls on both a real and mystical level filters through his work, stemming from his fascination with Druid lore and the philosophies of William Blake, as well as from the notion of the *anima mundi*.

In Dreams and the Anima Mundi

> 'I am happiest with stories that have the deepest resonance possible and if I can push it subtly in that direction I will. I work to create stories that illuminate the soul rather than the brain and try to make movies that are as universal as possible. To do that you have to tap into the collective unconscious.'
> – Neil Jordan (in Jackson 1991:19)

The *anima mundi* is a kind of 'cosmic storehouse of symbols, based on Plato's world of Eternal Forms and reformulated in Carl Jung's psychology of a collective unconscious' (Kearney 1988: 19). It surfaces emphatically in Jordan's films, rendering a Yeatsian environment caught between the waking and dreaming world. In Elizabeth Butler's words, this 'cosmic storehouse' contains treasures of the soul: 'The *anima mundi* is the sum of human wisdom, to which the individual gains access through the symbols of dreams and reverie, or through deliberate magical invocation' (1997: 17). 'We are thus organically linked to each other, to the dead, and to our former and future selves; the history of the world is a stream of souls, and not a catalogue of facts' (Kearney 1988: 19).

It is not difficult to relate Yeats' conception of the *anima mundi* to the philosophies of other visionaries, especially considering how Yeats was intrigued by the work of the poet William Blake.

> In Blake Yeats found too a confirmation of the innate spirituality of the Celt, for in the English poet's profound antipathy for materialism he had met a soulmate. He discovered in Blake's prophetic works, with their huge, epic canvases in which an essentially lyric, romantic artist communed with the spirits of ancient, Celtic Britain and with mythological figures conjured from the depths of mental life, an intimation of what an Irish literature could be like. It would not only take its sense of the other-world from the fairy lore of the countryside, its understanding of an essentially wild national character from the Irish peasantry, but its vision of racial mystique, and primal splendour from the kind of mythopoeic imagination which had informed Blake's monumental broodings on antiquity and on the current state of the spiritual world. (Brown 1999: 67)

Like Yeats, Jordan's creative vision taps into his own 'cosmic storehouse', and shares with us his distinctly Irish *anima mundi*, where 'small, endangered, confused symbolic selves hot on the trail of cathartic, magical knowledge' traverse the world as a 'stream of souls' (Kearney 1988: 19). In addition to Yeats, a great influence on Jordan's work is the theories of Jung which are strikingly close to the spiritual belief system of Yeats. In Jung's own words:

A more or less superficial layer of the unconscious is undoubtedly personal. I call it the *personal unconscious*. Yet this personal unconscious appears to rest upon a deeper layer that does not derive from personal experience and achievement but is inborn. This deeper layer I call the *collective unconscious*. I have chosen the term 'collective' because this part of the unconscious is not individual, but universal; in contrast to the personal psyche, it has contents and modes of behaviour that are more or less the same everywhere and in all individuals. (1963: 53)

The narrative patterns of *In Dreams* incontrovertibly reflect their mythic origin, and surely Claire is a mythological heroine. As Joseph Campbell writes: '[the hero of myth] carries the keys to the whole realm of the desired and the feared adventure of the discovery of the self' (1973: 8). In Jordan's postmodern Gothic fairy tale, Claire is a creative and all too sensitive woman. Her determination and her ability to endure the intolerable enables her to journey on her perilous quest for selfhood even at its most transgressive – in its unimaginable link with madness and the unconscious. Claire's voyage suspends the distinctions of the physical and the psychological; it leads her to a place of frightful foreboding. She grows from a beleaguered, frightened woman to an emblem of the fully realised self who is able to incorporate her shadow side, as Jung would say, and in the end, a level of ego-consciousness or wholeness as Claire comes to incorporate the beast within.

Claire follows, in many ways, the typical pattern of the hero's quest. She undergoes a symbolic rebirth as she drives her car off a cliff into the lake upon learning of her daughter, Rebecca's (Katie Sagona) murder. The nature of doubling that structures the film is in this case the raising of her daughter's murdered body from the water just as Claire drives her car off a precipice into the same watery grave. Otto Rank writes, 'Dreams of this sort are birth-dreams ... instead of hurling oneself into the water, it means emerging from the water, that is, to be born' (1914: 69). Water is a universal emblem of the womb, and this links Claire to Mother Earth, and nature itself, making her a potent force to be reckoned with. (Her status as a 'mommy' will have great importance in the film's dénouement.) Claire is re-born so that she can continue her heroic journey. After experiencing a death of sorts, Claire leaves the hospital a transformed person: her hair has been shorn (due to the ministrations of doctors attempting to find a physical site for her suicidal act) and she has thus become visually more androgynous.

In order to be reborn, she must lose herself (in a near-death experience) so that she may discover herself. As Campbell writes, 'the hero has died as a modern man; but as eternal man – perfected, unspecific, universal man – he has been reborn' (1973: 20). As the narrative progresses, Claire is stripped of her former identity as a wife and mother. If Claire is to truly accept her shadow side, she must accept her own madness and her powers, which make her an exile from the quotidian world. The concept of exile is prominent in Jordan's work, from *Angel* through to *The Brave One*. Only by embracing her insanity will she be able to reach the end of her quest. The notion of the shadow is comparable to the *animus* or *anima*; it is the sinister double of the heroine who resides within the depths of her unconscious. Jung describes this phenomena:

Claire (Annette Bening), after returning from a hospital stay, sports an androgynous look

They [*anima* and *animus*] seem to be functions or instincts which appear in a personal form when aroused from their dormant condition. But contrary to the functions attached to consciousness, they are always strangers in the conscious world. Because they permeate the atmosphere with a feeling of uncanny foreboding, or even with the fear of mental derangement, they are unwelcome intruders. In studying their psychic constituents – that is, the imaginative material manifested through them – we find any number of archaic and 'historical' connections, contents, archetypal images that we call mythological themes ... they obviously live or function in the deeper lays of the unconscious mind, in the phylogenetic substructures of the modern mind, the so-called *collective unconscious*. (1963: 20)

A characteristic pattern for the mythological hero is his or her setting forth from their normal environment to press forward to the threshold of adventure. The hero(ine) meets their shadow or darker self.; this shadow self, so well represented by Vivian (Robert Downey Jr) in *In Dreams*, guards the entrance to his private domain. One is reminded of the myth of Theseus, where the hero braves the danger of many tests to prove himself. Beyond this threshold lies

a shadow presence ... The hero may defeat or conciliate this power and go alive into the kingdom of the dark ... or be slain by the opponent and descent in death ... Beyond the threshold, then, the hero journeys through a world of unfamiliar yet strangely intimate forces ... When he arrives at the nadir of the mythological round, he undergoes a supreme ordeal and gains his reward. (Campbell 1973: 245–6)

The labyrinth imagery of the Theseus myth is replayed in different guises in *In Dreams*, such as the underwater town, Vivian's 'Good Apple' lair, the air ducts of the mental hospital Claire must crawl through to conquer the evil that is embodied by Vivian. Claire and Vivian fight to the death; his is a symbolic death and rebirth, and hers a literal death of the body. But she returns as a spiritual entity to haunt Vivian's consciousness and encourage his already highly developed sociopathy.

In the early scenes of *In Dreams* we witness Claire as she prepares her daughter for *Snow White*, a play put on by her school. They rehearse the lines together, and Claire fusses over Rebecca's costume. Rebecca plays the mirror which is asked, 'Who is the fairest of them all?' The aspect of doubling is important to Jung, and has also been a staple in Gothic literature since its inception. Jordan's postmodern conception of Snow White is that of an active heroine, decisively less passive than the fairy tale protagonist. Claire has no prince who is waiting to rescue her; she achieves fulfilment by accessing her paranormal powers. Claire is conscious, and thus unlike Snow White in her long sleep; Claire is able to forge a link between her conscious and unconscious self. Jordan's patterning of the film assumes the shape of the mythopoeic threat/hostility/escape pattern, which is the fairy tale mode of the mythic pattern of birth/quest/return. *In Dreams* presents us with an inverted version of *Snow White*. Whereas the fairy tale character traditionally moves from 'asexual to sexual individual, from an unattached and unmarried woman to a married one, and finally from a childless woman to a

Vivian (Robert Downey Jr) and Claire, 'doubles' sharing the frame

The battle between the 'self' and the 'other' reaches a violent and fatal climax

child-rearing mother' (Jones 1949: 179) Claire reverses this model; she goes from a child-rearing mother to a childless woman through the loss of her daughter, and from a sexual being to an asexual child playing 'mommies and daddies' with Vivian. Claire comes to understand herself as a powerful woman who needs no prince to make her life complete.

Just as Jordan returns again and again to mythic blueprints for his narratives,

> Yeats sought to make explicit relations between the mythic past and the modern moment ... past and present are juxtaposed to indicate that an order of things which found expression in a previous era is repeating itself in the modern world under another guise ... mythology is deemed to possess explanatory force for the modern mind. In such writing the incoherencies of the self, dispersed in time, memory and in self-division, the disorder of the social world and of history are momentarily made amenable to a transcendent pattern inscribed in the old tale. (Brown 1999: 211)

Equally ingrained in Jordan's Irish heritage is the filmmaker's preoccupation with the mythic reciprocity of beauty and terror discussed in the previous chapter on *Michael Collins*. As early as Jordan's film debut, *Angel*, the mythopoeic and romantic trope – this reciprocity of beauty and terror – emerges as one of the filmmaker's earliest preoccupations, re-conceptualised through the tensions that emerge between art and violence. In the film's opening sequence Danny finds his angel, a gentle and playful mute, only to witness her sudden and senseless murder by an unspecified paramilitary group. Danny begins his spiritual descent into a 'heart of darkness' (Kearney 1988:

176). It is a downward spiral which sees Danny, a gifted musician, convert to a soulless killing machine. When one looks at Danny, half his hair has been shorn and the other half has not, a most visible indicator of his position between two worlds. The tensions that emerge between art and violence are addressed by Jordan:

> The attraction of art, and perhaps the beauty of it, is that it can encapsulate all the beauty of sensual experience and at the same time allow you to meet this chaos and the darker side of your personality in, perhaps, the most meaningful way. Now violence to me – the attraction of violence – is the polar opposite to that. It does throw one into contact with chaos, with the darker side of human experience, with evil, and it does so, obviously, in the most brutal way imaginable. (In Comiskey 1982: 8)

Terror prevails, leaving the viewer to wonder if there is any possibility of redemption in the hell on earth that Danny inhabits.

CHAPTER THREE

Storytelling and Performance

'Provoke the unexpected. Expect it.'
— Robert Bresson

There are two distinct phases in Neil Jordan's independent filmmaking career thus far (that is, not including the Hollywood exercises). The first represents his work up to *The Crying Game*. This seminal phase consists of relatively small-budget projects that are, in the main, character-driven films that draw heavily on fairy tale allusions, the motif of storytelling, and which were generated mostly from original scripts developed by Jordan. The second half of his career is initiated by *Interview with the Vampire* and continues to the present. The films of this period are marked by more ambitious projects (big budgets, use of special effects, and so forth), and are somewhat more action-based (though it might be said that all of his films, regardless of their integration of action, must be considered as character-driven). This set of films continues to draw on fairy tale templates and the uncanny; and further, all of them have their basis in literature, history or other films (for example, *The Good Thief*). Amongst the films of this period, Jordan manifests his attraction to novels which feature first-person narration. This rhetorical predilection has been employed in a number of Jordan's adaptations. While I would not claim that the use of a narrator is a stylistic signature of Jordan's, the way one might articulate the strategy as an essential element in the films of Orson Welles or Robert Bresson, nonetheless, the continual attraction to the device bears witness to Jordan's career-long concern with storytelling.

For insight into this particular manifestation of storytelling, Walter Benjamin's essay 'The Storyteller' offers some assistance, providing a cursory glance at the history of storytelling as a social phenomenon – a culturally specific conception of storytelling – which is sadly falling away. In this history he makes a rather provocative assertion that the act of storytelling is inextricably bound to the transmission of human experience (see sections I and II especially), and this basic formulation is of the utmost importance to Jordan's particular process of spinning yarns.

Benjamin's essay is ostensibly a study of the life and writings of the obscure Russian writer Nikolai Leskov. From this point of departure, Benjamin launches into a rhapsodic elegy for the figure of the storyteller and the lost art of storytelling, and a lamentation for the decline of storytelling in contemporary culture. The primary reason for this devaluation of the storyteller is the concomitant decline in the value of experience. Benjamin contends that knowledge has become more important than experience. To illustrate this he points out that few World War One veterans' stories were sought out, but that scholarly books about the war were in vogue. In Benjamin's view storytelling is the sharing of experience, an important point for the films Jordan has made during the first period of his career.

The second section of Benjamin's essay expands upon the relationship between experience and storytelling; he hypothesises that experience is indispensable to the construction of storytelling. At this point, Benjamin declares that there are two crucial figures in the history of storytelling: the traveller, who accrued his experience while venturing around the globe; and the local storyteller (for example, a farmer or town doctor) whose experience stems from his lifetime study of one domain. Folklore as we know it, according to Benjamin, has been generated by the interpenetration of these two discursive figures.

In section nine, Benjamin's essay goes on to communicate the virtues of personalised narratives; his main point is that storytelling must engender reciprocity: the experience enunciated through the telling of the story, and the vital experience of hearing someone else's story. This seems to be an instinctive choice in Jordan's adaptations – to permit us to hear the stories of these characters. Here, Benjamin compares the oral tale to the story that one finds in newspapers, expressing displeasure that information and communication are in effect bastardising the term 'story', which is anything but an amalgamation of facts and expert interpretation. Instead he argues that the power of the real story lies in its resistance to factual accuracy and easy interpretation.

Benjamin emphasises, rather, the personal dimensions of storytelling which differentiate it from other mediums, including the written short story. In Benjamin's view the storyteller is the most important part of the story and he makes the point that every story must be filtered through a teller. Hence the famous aphorism 'Thus traces of the storyteller cling to the story the way the handprints of the potter cling to the clay vessel' (1968: 92). The importance attached to personalisation accounts for one of the most interesting choices made in *Michael Collins* – the addition of the narrator as the film's opening gambit. It also helps us to understand the power of first-person narration, and why Jordan employs this rhetorical device with some frequency. We like to hear people tell their stories, and Jordan has consistently sought out source novels with first-person narratives to enable this. Benjamin concludes this section of his essay with the analogy of storyteller as craftsman, a stance that retains his antipathy to mass production. He conveys more despair about modern man who is simply too impatient to hear a good story. Benjamin uses the example of the fairy tale which he points out has played a very important pedagogical role in personal development, but also a very palpable role in the shaping of human consciousness. This view echoes that of section two, and is one that reverberates in the works of, amongst others, Cristina Bacchilega, Marina Warner and Jack Zipes.

The Company of Wolves features a grandmother and granddaughter who communicate almost exclusively through stories, and in fact storytelling ultimately becomes the film's organising principle as we are absorbed into a 'Chinese-box' narrative which builds upon story after story. How is the act itself represented? Two points in Benjamin's essay are worth examining in relation to the film. The first has to do with the basic doctrine about storytelling and experience. What we witness in the film is, as stated in a claim I make in the next chapter, a female *bildungsroman* of sorts in which Rosaleen is slowly taken from the world of childhood and innocence and is ushered into the world of adulthood and experience. Her journey between the two realms is precipitated by her grandmother's stories, which are ostensibly based on Granny's vast experience of the adult world, and seek to inculcate in Rosaleen the proper wisdom (which Benjamin differentiates from the knowledge contained in news and novels) to guide her in her adult life. Interestingly, the education that Rosaleen receives takes the form of folk and fairy tales. Benjamin, in section 16, comments on the pedagogical nature of fairy tale telling, though he shows little interest in the type of dark social pedagogy deconstructed by Angela Carter and Neil Jordan, and is instead, like Yeats, more interested in man and myth.

The second important point that conjoins the film and essay has to do with the figure of the storyteller himself. It is interesting that in discussing the many storyteller archetypes (in section two) Benjamin fixates on males such as sailors and farmers, and virtually absents the old wife figure – one of humankind's most prolific storytellers. Reading Benjamin one would find little about this type, but Carter and Jordan bring her to the fore as one of humanity's central consciousness-moulding figures.

In Jordan's early films, from *The Company of Wolves* to *Mona Lisa*, *The Miracle* and *The Crying Game*, the persistent motif of storytelling is witnessed mainly in the form of characters who are united by this act. While *The Company of Wolves* is Jordan's most extensive examination of the social practice of storytelling, the subsequent films also employ the device, though for different reasons. In the case of *Mona Lisa* storytelling is a way for the central characters to make sense of a world which is frightening and confusing to them. George (Bob Hoskins) and Thomas's (Robbie Coltrane) relationship revolves to a great degree upon the telling of stories. In *The Miracle*, Jimmy (Niall Byrne) and Rose (Lorraine Pilkington) make sense of their world through the outlet of the stories they create. In both cases we witness a storytelling dynamic in which the story is a filter through which the characters try to understand a world they have yet to fully experience and comprehend. In Jimmy's case, his problems are exacerbated by the lack of a more experienced storyteller figure. Consider the scene after he discovers

Renée is his mother, when he tearfully tells his father, 'I should've heard it from you!' In many ways, the alienation Jimmy feels from his father, and the world at large, is encapsulated in this line which points up an absence of what Benjamin sees as one of our basic needs – shared experience. In *Mona Lisa*, the case is not quite the same. Though George, like Jimmy, can only comprehend the world through stories, his case is different because the genre of those stories is most *apropos*. He listens to Thomas's dark mysteries and also lives in one; he is relentlessly manipulated in a film noir style by Mortwell (Michael Caine) and his collaborators who purposely withhold important information from him. He needs a guide through this seamy aggregation of pimps, prostitutes and gangsters in which he finds himself. The film does not fit quite as neatly as *The Miracle* into Benjamin's sociological paradigm; nevertheless, the dynamic of story and experience is there.

In *The Crying Game* the story is employed in a much more subtle mode than in the previous films. Storytelling does do the two most important things: the tale of the scorpion and the frog communicates vital wisdom about human nature, and the transmission of that wisdom acts as a bond between Fergus and Jody. Later the mantle is passed on. As the film closes, we find Fergus in prison recounting the parable to Dil with great animation. Here the tale is told – or the part to which we are permitted access – to amuse Dil, and serves to form a circle of knowledge shared amongst the three characters.[1] On a further, perhaps more obscure level, when Jody, in a desperate mood, asks Fergus to tell him a story, Fergus begins (after some thought) to recite from Corinthians I. He begins: 'When I was a child I thought as a child…'. Fergus breaks off his story, unable to play along bravely, and obviously devastated by the certainty of Jody's execution. The passage in the Bible continues:

> … I understood as a child; but when I became a man, I put away childish things. Though I speak with the tongues of men and of angels, and have not charity, I am become as sounding brass or a tinkling cymbal. And though I have the gift of prophecy, and understand all mysteries, and all knowledge; and though I have not faith, so that I could move mountains, and have not charity, I am nothing.[2]

One can view the omission of the remainder of the passage in several ways. On a basic level it is Fergus's expression of remorse for the lack of charity displayed by his peers. On another level the idea of 'becoming a man' lends itself to questioning the meaning of masculinity. If this is what it means to become a man then Fergus here begins his revolt against traditional notions of masculinity and embraces, instead, a more generous and multivalent attitude that will mark his behaviour when he 'crosses the water' and meets Dil. The employment of storytelling in *The Crying Game* is subtle, but it is nonetheless consistent with previous uses of the motif which stresses human bonds (or their lack in the case of Jimmy and his father) as well as the various ways in which wisdom and experience are shared between these foolish mortals.

I have suggested a number of confluences between Jordan's films and the idea of storytelling as laid out by Benjamin. But one must exert caution here. In espousing his theory of what the storyteller should and should not do or be, Benjamin is writing from a Marxist perspective in which things such as the novel, academic scholarship and mass media are sites of privilege, whereas the story belongs to the people, that is, the proletariat. I think Jordan's take on the subject is significantly different and is born out of his own humanistic view of the world. Stories are what bind his characters together and storytelling is meant to form a unique bond between his films and their audience.

Performance: the soul made visible

> 'There is no overacting; there is only untrue acting.'
> – Stellan Skarsgård

As someone who came to academia from training and performing as an actor, I have always been dispirited by the way in which acting is largely neglected in film and cultural studies programmes. When it is discussed it is primarily from an ideological perspective: the actor is seen as an industrial commodity for the spectator's consumption; the actor is merely a repository, a blank screen for our repressed desires and fantasies; and lastly, the actor is a collection of 'signs'. The exclusion of human emotion, which must of necessity be an important component of performance studies, is part of the tendency to take the human out of the humanities. The expression of that humanity is precisely the actor's job to be emotionally available each moment so that the spectator can be astonished and/or taken on an unexpected journey. Not surprisingly, everyone has opinions about acting, and they do not have the slightest trepidation about expressing them even if they have virtually no understanding whatsoever regarding the creative role of the actor. Actors are normally at the core of narrative film; they bear a primary responsibility for telling the film's story. Yet actors are barely recognised for their artistry, much less for their role as intelligent and creative beings.

The subject of acting as seen from a cultural studies perspective focuses on movie stars as cultural artifacts, as sociological phenomena, or as a sign to be deciphered from a semiological viewpoint (for some examples, see the work of Richard Dyer, Christine Gledhill and James Naremore), and rarely, if ever, from a technical viewpoint that analyses the art and craft of acting. Analysis that treats acting as a significant component of a film is also absent from mainstream publications, and even from journals devoted to the study of cinema and drama. My approach to performance differs from the discourses on acting that predominates in Film Studies. Briefly, I am interested in actors, not stars. The physical actor has been theorised out of film; in order to rectify this I will address the importance of the human presence in film. Film acting is about urgency and immediacy with which certain actors express their selfhood and push the limits of their expressivity, and most importantly, how actors create a living, breathing character from the words on the page of a script.

Jordan's attachment to the plurality and permeability of the boundaries of human behaviour leads him to investigate diverse styles of acting. How can one style possibly serve to depict the complex and heterogeneous worlds he explores? The performances in his films have no discernible signature; one cannot perceive a 'Neil Jordan' style of acting. As with form and genre, he is committed to experimentation and diversity in performance, always in response to the particular story he is telling. One constant in Jordan's films is that there is rarely an elemental meaning that can be taken from witnessing a performance (Falsetto 2000: 251). The films are replete with moments that work on multifarious levels. Jordan as writer/director is a virtuoso at portraying the mystery and complexity of human feeling; sub-textual meanings are in abundance. I will investigate two of Jordan's films which serve as examples of his formidable work with actors, and best represent the range of acting styles in his films. *The Crying Game* engages with several performance issues: the interplay between work with non-professional and professional actors, a mix of radically different performance modes within the same film, and the way in which film style relates to and is a determining factor in performance. *Interview with the Vampire* is a study in the uses of ritual, hyperbole and theatricality in performance.

The Crying Game

'Who knows the secrets of the human heart?'
– Col in *The Crying Game*

In the aftermath of the surprising commercial success of *The Crying Game* and its generally excellent critical reception – the film enjoyed large-scale public support and garnered mostly excellent reviews in the popular press – critics of a certain persuasion targeted the filmmaker's perceived lack of 'correctness' in the handling of gender, race and post-colonial politics. Because the film is occupied, at least on a certain level, with a veritable hornet's nest of loaded issues such as homosociality, homosexuality, transvestism, interracial romance and sectarian violence in Ireland, it would have been odd for critics to overlook the representation of these matters. As nearly all of the criticism of *The Crying Game* has ideological roots, I wish to offer an alternative way of accessing the film.

The lack of sympathy amongst some critics for Jordan's film stems from a basic misapprehension of the director's artistic project. Jordan, even while using identity politics as an arena in which the narrative is played out, is much more intrigued by the fundamental humanity of his characters. As Jack Boozer writes, 'Jordan can hardly be accused of unawareness of the crises and conditions that exist. His focus simply emphasises the microcosm of individual character development, of any possibility of finding a path through the circulating signifiers that pass for contemporary meaning and truth' (1995: 179). Jordan is much more in sympathy with the ideas expressed by the poet/writer Tom Paulin when he said in an interview, 'I just wanted to displace the concept of national identity, the concept of belonging to your tribe, the idea of tradition and so on. I wanted to wreck that and replace it with something that's plural and infinite, something that's moving all the time' (in Hughes 1998: 125). Jordan's concern with the multiplicity of meanings inherent in human interactions is very much at the core of his filmmaking practice, and a signal aspect of his responsive working relationship with actors.

The first segment of *The Crying Game* presents the hostage-taking of a black British soldier, Jody, by an IRA unit. The paramilitary cell is led by Peter (Adrian Dunbar) and includes Fergus and Jude (Miranda Richardson) who, as the only woman in the unit, is given the task of seducing Jody to facilitate his capture. Fergus, alone amongst his comrades, almost instantly bonds with Jody. Most of the scenes that take place in this section are between Jody and Fergus – a flirtatious interplay immediately surfaces between the two men. It begins when Fergus suggests that Jody eat something, and lifts Jody's hood to delicately place bits of food in his mouth. There is something touching, with intimations of the erotic, about this gesture, and as the hostage sequence evolves the two men share genuine feelings for each other.

In these scenes, Stephen Rea as Fergus is fairly relaxed, and not given to a great deal of movement; he does very little 'emoting'. As the segments of the first part of the film progress toward Jody's eventual death, the emotional range, particularly on Rea's part, remains subtle and completely lacking in ostentation. For example, when Jody asserts that, without doubt, Fergus will have to kill him, Fergus's response is to look up and away; his anxiety is betrayed primarily by little more than the noticeable shallowness of his breathing. One of the few times Rea displays more externalised emotion is when Jody remarks on the innate lack of compassion of Fergus's 'people'. Fergus's anger is straightforward; he says, 'What the fuck do you know about my people?' In one beat, through the use of vocal intonation, a collision transpires between Fergus's IRA sympathies and his illicit connection to the British soldier's humanity, thus compromising his allegiance to the terrorist agenda.

Further, Fergus resents Jody's dehumanising circumscription of his identity; he fights throughout the film to retain his individuality, to resist categorisation by others. In terms of characterisation, Jordan has said:

> This guy Fergus is a Catholic and a nationalist, and he identifies himself with certain parameters. He thinks this is what he is, a political animal. He's wedded to violence. He feels that he's a soldier, and is justified in killing people he doesn't know for this cause. I was interested in setting this person up with his polar opposite, someone who is so far away from his experience: a black soldier who is gay, although Fergus didn't know it. If you throw this character on this journey, will he survive and will he change. (In Falsetto 2000: 237)

Most of the hostage scenes are shot in a fairly conventional way; the cutting follows the semantic flow with shot/reverse-shot editing patterns dominating. A greater sense of urgency develops as Jody comes to the realisation that he is unlikely to survive. As this happens, Jordan begins to cut to closer shots of each actor. Jody asks Fergus to look up Dil, his 'wife', and 'tell her I was thinking of her'. Fergus, now attached to the hostage, is visibly moved by Jody's request; tears are barely suppressed as he contorts his face in his effort not to cry. Fergus is told that he must kill Jody, and finds the prisoner sobbing. The expression on Rea's face reveals many different emotions simultaneously – feelings of impotence, guilt, confusion, pain and empathy. He wants to help, but

Teasing sexual identity: Jude (Miranda Richardson) tantalises Jody (Forest Whitaker)

he cannot; one can sense this complex of feelings without a great deal of motion or effort on the actor's part. Jody is desperately frightened, and Rea's face is charged with despondency and loss; the latter privation will resonate in the film's second half. There are cuts to closer and closer shots of each actor's face, with the camera moving in on them as they speak. This penultimate scene between Fergus and Jody is brimming with constrained but deep emotion. It plays very much like a passionate love scene.

Each Fergus/Jody scene has a very clear dramatic arc; as each scene is played out chronologically, the intensity builds. A great deal of this has to do with Jordan's talent as a writer, and the fact that two excellent, professional actors perform the scenes. If I have focused less on Forest Whitaker in this section, it is not because he is any less skilled, committed and truthful in these scenes than Stephen Rea. But Rea is so heavily inscribed in Neil Jordan's work that he deserves to be central to any discussion of it. As the director himself has said of Rea, 'Stephen's a remarkable actor … He's one of the best, genuinely most intelligent actors in the world' (in Falsetto 2000: 251). What I believe Jordan means in this statement is Rea's capacity for emotional intelligence – the ability to assess and embody the needs of a part – rather than (but not excluding) the actor's intellectual faculties. The profundity of an actor's emotional intelligence marks the difference between an actor who is simplistic and banal, and one who is inspired.

Rea has very definite ideas about film acting – what belongs on film and what does not. He said:

> I've always had a great love of Robert Mitchum … What it is I admire about his acting is that he's one of the great narrative actors. Nowadays everybody wants to 'show emotion'; everyone since the post-Brando Italian actors wants

to scream the house down and show their innards, and Mitchum simply thinks. He must have been wonderful for a director, because all you do is cut to Mitchum and he thinks something, and then you can take the movie in any direction you want. So, that's the kind of acting that I really admire, Bogart, Tracy, and those kind of guys ... great screen actors like Mitchum were very economical; they knew that the movie had to have a movement. (In Zucker 1999: 110–11)

One can readily see that frugality in Rea's performance in *The Crying Game*. The ability to let oneself alone in front of the camera, to allow oneself, and have the ability, to listen and respond in character is one of the most demanding and difficult styles of acting to achieve. One must have the focus, the relaxation, the technique and the naturalness to allow the camera to record the unimpeded beauty, the simplicity and complexity of being, in order to, as Sanford Meisner (the founder of the Neighborhood Playhouse in New York) put it, 'live truthfully in imaginary circumstances' (1987: 15). One may call this 'naturalism', or simply good acting. Lindsay Crouse has said of acting for film: 'You're very translucent when you're on film. You are a figure of light; your soul comes through. You can tell, easily, when someone is really doing it or not' (in Zucker 1995: 28). It is this type of 'dangerous' acting, letting the camera reveal your visible soul, that Stephen Rea displays in *The Crying Game*. It serves Neil Jordan's desire to construct multiple layers of meaning through the complex medium of his characters (see Antony Sher in Zucker 1999: 171, 182).

In every way, the first section of the film is very much a chamber piece. The shooting style is integral to defining the spatial parameters of Jody's imprisonment. But perhaps more importantly, in terms of the emotional and psychological universe Jordan sets up in the film, the tightly constructed and constricted style reflects the affective oppression of the IRA. This is a milieu that allows for little expressivity, other than the muted affection shared by the prisoner and his 'keeper'. In fact, Peter, the group leader, says at one point later in the film (after stubbing a cigarette out on Fergus's hand and whacking him in the face), 'I'm getting fuckin' emotional, and I don't want to get fuckin' emotional.' Jordan might easily have moved the camera more, or had less conventional set-ups. It is my claim that the film's style changes utterly, as does the latitude for expression, once Fergus 'crosses the water' and is released, fleetingly, from the suffocating world of IRA politics.

Once Fergus arrives in London and meets Jody's 'wife', Dil, the shooting style changes markedly. Most of the time the actors are together in two-shots; the shot/reverse-shot pattern is used sparingly. The takes are longer and more expansive; there is greater depth of field. More of the environment is revealed, whether in the Metro (the gay bar where Dil and Fergus meet), or in Dil's flat, the camera follows the actors around and through space. There is a sense of liberation in Fergus's relocation to these surroundings; he has a new job as a construction worker, and a new name, Jimmy. This section of the film is altogether less formal and restrictive.

Fergus's range of expression is given more latitude; although still subdued, Rea's performance in the London locale has more colour and variation than in the Jody sequences. After the 'discovery scene', when Fergus realises that Dil is a cross-dressing male, they meet at her workplace, Millie's hairdressing salon. A long dialogue scene ensues as the camera continually tracks with both characters. Fergus expresses incredulity at his own naïveté, while Dil, at least on the surface, stages a show of nonchalance. (*Fergus*: 'Thing is, you're not a girl, Dil.' *Dil*: 'Details, baby, details'). When they arrive at Dil's flat, she attempts to touch Fergus's face. Fergus refuses this offer of intimacy, instinctively moving away from Dil's outstretched hand. She says, 'Don't be cruel', as Fergus, in a very delicate move, cocks his head, submits, and in a whisper that is an aural caress, says, 'Okay'. It is a particularly telling, highly nuanced and unexpected response on the actor's part, coming directly out of the 'given circumstances' of the situation rather than the result of a premeditated, manipulated reality. Rea is showing us, rather than telling us, how his character feels with the most subtle and understated gestures and barely articulated dialogue.

He then reaches out to pat Dil in a big-brotherly, patronising way, almost as if to try to reinstate their relationship on a 'normal' footing: 'Be a good girl, go inside.' Dil stands her ground and looks directly at Fergus: 'Only if you kiss me.' Fergus stops for a moment, taken aback by the bluntness of the request. His body literally rocks backwards, then forwards on his heels as he moves closer to kiss Dil lightly on the lips with his eyes shut. Fergus then moves slightly backwards. The expression on his face is at once amorous, aroused, surprised and perplexed – the confused range of emotions his character might experience kissing another man. He lets out a short snort; he cannot believe what he has done. It is also a self-protective pulling back, as if to deny that he kissed Dil for any reason other than to satisfy a petulant request. Or perhaps it is partly an apology for his physical aggression upon learning Dil's 'secret'. His eyes remain in contact with hers, as Fergus tries to deny the significance of the kiss: 'Are ya happy now?' Dil maintains her cool, but suppressed anger shades her deadpan reply: 'Delirious.' Fergus lets out a big breath. Again, there is a play of emotions which transfuses his expression, of pleasure, fear, disbelief and perturbation.

The long scene is notable for several reasons. Firstly, it is often through the feelings rather than the words that contact is made. The tension between Dil and Fergus and the attraction/repulsion of their erotic interplay is largely declared in their movements towards and away from one another; their hesitant touching or refusal to make contact; the awkward, defeated or defiant postures each of them adopt. Language is secondary to this interchange; they are in response to one another in a way that transcends language. Each is emotionally available to the other, and the audience, like the actors, does not know what is going to happen next. There is an exquisite feeling of aliveness, of living in the unknown, of 'the first time' in this scene. As Sanford Meisner said, 'The quality of your acting depends on how fully you are doing what you are doing' (in Silverberg 1994: 61). Each actor responds to the minute changes in his partner; they work off of one another, and give up control for the sake of the truth of each moment. Neither partner directs the scene towards a goal. There is never a moment in which you feel either actor withdraw from the scene to determine the next move or the next response; they remain in sensitive contact with the gradations of each other's behaviour. In terms of the script, the sequence moves from point A to B; but

Dil (Jaye Davidson) and Fergus (Stephen Rea) about to kiss before the big 'reveal'

the unique way it moves, working with the moment-to-moment emotional fullness of the actors' responses to one another, is always exciting and unexpected.

Jaye Davidson gives a remarkable debut performance, and while we must give him credit for allowing himself to engage so fully in the proceedings, other factors are at play. When working with non-professional actors, because they have little technique to fall back on, a director usually has to film quickly. This suits Jordan's shooting style; he rehearses very little, and then only for the purpose of rewriting dialogue that sounds awkward when spoken by the actors. The director rarely does more than one or two takes. So, we are getting the raw moments of film acting. A professionally-inexperienced actor like Davidson will not have the technique or the skill to know how to build a scene. A professional actor like Rea, while working partly on an instinctual level, will have the working experience to know when he has achieved the truth of a scene. He will know how to tap into his emotions with facility and not offer facile emotions; it is Rea's job, particularly as a film actor, to be able to express himself with immediacy. Rea comments on working with a non-professional actor:

> Working with a non-actor is tricky … It's not that they're not talented, it's not that they're not conscientious, but it'd be like a professional footballer working with a non-professional footballer: it doesn't matter how good they are, they're bound to slip out of position. They don't have professional stand-ards; they couldn't have. So what non-actors sometimes do is pick up your tone. Like that scene at the end of *The Crying Game* where I'm tied to the bed and my character says he's sorry. We started doing that, take one, and I started

to fill up with tears, right? So take two, Jaye (Davidson) starts to fill up with tears as well. Take three, he's crying more than me, so that's the un-discipline that happens, because you don't just start a scene and go wherever it goes, you go into a scene thinking. You go in with a conscious notion of where you want to go with the scene and you don't let it knock you about all over the place ... What happens with a non-actor is that a scene more quickly loses its shape. That doesn't mean they're not brilliant – and Jaye was absolutely brilliant in it – but when they're being brilliant, you have to get it right then. The professional actor will get it, be able to do it again, and develop it. If I was doing a scene with Miranda [Richardson], the scene would automatically develop, because she's a fine professional actor. (In Zucker 1999: 115)

It is interesting to contemplate a remark Rea made about Lauren Bacall's performance in *To Have and Have Not* (1944): 'They all said she was so cool, but she says she was terrified, and if you look at it knowing that, all you can see is her fear. She's a young girl of nineteen' (in Zucker 1999: 116). I think this is true to a certain extent of Davidson. While he seems at ease with his transgender 'performance', there are moments of fear and uncertainty, often masked by superficial cool. But whatever underlying panic there might have been it is integrated into the performance, and serves to make it more real; there is none of the flamboyance that one might associate with transgender role-playing.

Ultimately, *The Crying Game* is a film resolutely entwined with the notion of identity as a performance. If one fully engages with a role one becomes something other, and new amplitude and fluidity is given to one's notion of self. Jordan says, 'Could people's narrow identifications of themselves change? ... It was an exploration of self. That's what I wanted to do with it. If you strip away all these masks human beings wear, is anything left underneath? Is anything left of Fergus when all this stuff is stripped away from him? In fact, there is, and he turns out to be a human being' (in Falsetto 2000: 238). Fergus and Dil are the ones who are capable of acting on feeling and instinct, and in response to the possibilities offered to them. They are the survivors in the film. Whether these characters are or will become connected in a sexual relationship is irrelevant. What is important is that both have broken through boundaries that had previously constricted their notions of selfhood; each can embrace unsettled positions regarding their identity. Rea says:

The emotional journey is that Fergus realises that you can love anyone. He goes from being a man who's got a very rigid code about who you can offer love to, and it doesn't include British soldiers, it doesn't include the British, it doesn't include loving other men, and it probably doesn't include black men, or black people. So by the end of the movie, he knows, and we all know and feel it, you can love anyone – race, gender, nationality are all meaningless. That wasn't a challenge for me, because I believe that with all my heart. It's wonderful to be in a movie where it really happens. I think that's what everyone responded to. (In Zucker 1999: 115)

If *The Crying Game* can be seen to turn upon a patently outrageous premise, 'A tranny meets an IRA terrorist' as Rea put it (in Zucker 1999: 116), the initial transgressive plot is made both sympathetic and believable through the small moments of truth that lie at the heart of the film. It is a paean to Neil Jordan's eclecticism that several years later he would be drawn to a project so different in dimension, scope and generic origin as to signal a significant movement in the director's oeuvre – *Interview with the Vampire*.

Interview with the Vampire

'I was waiting for you. Watching you watching me.'
– Louis in *Interview with the Vampire*

The fact that the main characters are vampires does not change Jordan's essential priorities; as he asks in *Interview with the Vampire*: what is love? What place does feeling have in the world? What makes people (or vampires) behave as they do? The question is, at base: what does it mean to be human? The fact that the film is not populated with ordinary mortals merely complicates this eternal mystery. As Armand (Antonio Banderas), the oldest vampire on earth, says of Louis, 'A vampire with a human soul. An immortal with a mortal's passion. You are beautiful, my friend.' Louis' dilemma – caught between his humanity and his inhuman appetite for blood – becomes the film's core conflict. The differences between *The Crying Game* and *Interview with the Vampire* that are of interest in this context are the ways in which the two films present performance. While in the former film the multifarious meanings of the narrative reside almost wholly in the intimate realm of the actors' expressions, gestures, postures and so forth, in *Interview with the Vampire* we must negotiate our way through the varied tones of the scenes. The import is not so much in the release of little feelings that may be witnessed in a naturalistic film, but in the unstable thrust of the material presented to us. Often, it is difficult to determine whether to gape in horror or to respond with laughter to a particular scene in *Interview with the Vampire*, if not both at once. So the movement in terms of acting is from the representational to the presentational. The more naturalistic films might be called 'micro-responsive', while *Interview with the Vampire* works on a canvas that is painted in an altogether bolder and more flamboyant palette of colours.

The Crying Game tenders provocative and naturalistic performances within the framework of Jordan's imaginative universe. In *Interview with the Vampire* the acting, in general, defies the prototypical traits of naturalistic performance, such as the valorisation of truthfulness and consistency, recognisable conventions of behaviour, the representation of 'authenticated life' (Burns 1972: 144), and positions itself firmly within the compass of excess. I have written at length on this subject elsewhere, and will comment briefly on the most salient aspects of 'excess' as a style of performance. Firstly, there is an emphasis on irony, commentary and self-consciousness. While I will argue later that *Interview with the Vampire* utilises the spatial configuration of the theatre in its *mise-en-scène*, it wreaks utter havoc with the Stanislavskian notion of being 'private in public'. If anything, the performances are meant to invoke the presence of the spectator; we are meant to know the actors are performing. Further, to explicate the notion of 'excess' as it applies to *Interview with the Vampire*,

> Our absorption in the performance largely depends on the actor's abilities, and further, on his or her capacity to choose creatively and well. The criteria by which these choices are more or less apt hinges on the style and demands of the narrative, i.e. in a narrative that is closer on the spectrum to realism, the criteria of 'truthfulness' and 'naturalness' would obtain. But [in cases where] the diegetic world presents a very heightened or otherwise distorted version of reality … the style of acting – governed by this weakened resemblance to the world we know – is not bound by the laws of naturalistic behaviour. And where the stricture to play naturalistically is relaxed, the style of performance may be inclined, in more interesting cases, to 'excess', to a de-familiarised notion of human behaviour. (Zucker 1993: 56)

Interview with the Vampire, situated in a particular sub-genre of horror, lays prior claim to a 'weakened resemblance' to the world of normality. But not all vampire films engage in the degree of ritual, stylisation and exaggeration so abundantly displayed in Jordan's film. It is, in great measure, about performance as spectacle, funded, as it is for much of the film, by copious amounts of theatrical rhetoric. The other necessary component of spectacle is the audience, the watcher of the spectacle. Jordan repeatedly sets up a relay between that which is presented to us and the trope of the watching figure, through the use of camera placement or movement and/or an actual embodied onlooker, thus acknowledging the viewer's spectatorial position and the watcher/watched motif. Of importance is Jordan's interest in horror and the Gothic. He is deeply intrigued by the human hunger for destruction and violence, a fascination that dates back from traditions of oral storytelling in pre-literate cultures.

A scene from *Interview with the Vampire* that is heavily inscribed with the patterns of spectacle and spectatorship takes place in a New Orleans brothel. The set is arranged very like a stage, with deep red brocade wallpaper and vivid colour throughout. The characters – a young prostitute (Helen McCrory), Lestat and Louis – are all positioned frontally with respect to the camera; one has a strong sense of peering at the scene through the 'fourth wall'. Lestat playfully (at first) bites the breast of the woman. Only slightly later do we – and she – perceive that her ivory dress is drenched in blood. She begins to scream. Lestat slits the prostitute's wrist and fills a wine glass with her blood. In a long shot emphasising the proscenium arch-like nature of the set, Lestat offers the beverage to Louis; Lestat is rectitude and courtliness personified. Louis reacts with revulsion to the liquid. Both actors are positioned in the foreground on opposing sides of the frame, the moaning woman is seated dead centre in the background; it is a strong, highly stylised composition that provides a pertinent backdrop to the excesses of the subject and performances of the film.

Lestat moves to the frightened woman, and with a great flourish kicks open a coffin lid and drops her body in with a thud; he hops onto the lid of the closed coffin

Lestat (Tom Cruise) toys with the screaming prostitute (Helen McCrory), reminding us of our own complicity in watching the spectacle played out for our delectation

with the panache and elegance of Errol Flynn. Louis watches the proceedings, horrified by Lestat's cruelty. The latter continues to toy with the shuddering prostitute; he is humorous and light-hearted. She states the obvious: 'It's a coffin', to which Lestat responds, 'So it is. You must be dead.' He strikes a pose, hand on cheek, as if contemplating the situation. The scene ends with a high-angle shot of the carnage; another prostitute lies dead in the foreground; Lestat has finished off the pitiful victim in the coffin. The audience is watching from a height, as if from the circle of a theatre. Reflexively, the viewer of the film becomes complicit in the act of watching this gruesome spectacle.

One can see the way in which sexuality, cruelty and theatricality are imbricated in this scene. There is a tension created between the icy barbarity of Lestat's actions, and the highly mannered and decorous behaviour with which he performs. This theatricalised cruelty is again in opposition to the more humane and human demeanour of Louis as he witnesses Lestat's remorseless conduct. The scene is paradigmatic of the complex fusion of tones of *Interview with the Vampire*. We are amused by Tom Cruise's stylised dandy, but at the same time horrified by his cool infliction of suffering. Again, one sees Jordan's penchant for working close to the edge, and placing the viewer in a position of discomfort where they must traverse a network of conflicting moods and emotions.

The theatricality of the first part of the film is displaced in its second half by scenes that take place in a real theatre, Le Théâtre des Vampires. The stage set looks very much like many of the film's New Orleans sets, with rich, deep colours, lit by evocative candlelight ('veneral' colours, as Jordan describes them in his DVD commentary), which emphasises the nature of spectacle. The audience within the film is unaware that this is a company of genuine vampires, who actually kill people on stage. Before viewing the main spectacle of the vampires' show, we see bits of a Grand Guignol performance, which was popular in Paris at the time. A reference to a different style of theatre, Commedia dell'Arte, is found earlier in the film, intercut with another theatrical and painterly rendering of Louis and Lestat feasting on a prostitute, reminiscent of the chiaroscuro and character positioning of Caravaggio's work.

In the Théâtre des Vampires a young girl is brought on stage, obviously terrified, calling out for help. Her outer garments are stripped off, her breasts sensuously bared. Just as a vampire is about to sink his fangs into her neck a sound resonates like a cannon shot. We see Armand, the leader of these 'decadent' vampires played with great authority and elegance by Banderas, upstage, dressed entirely in crimson; he tosses his long mane of black hair as flames shoot out of either side of the foreground of the shot. He is extraordinarily regal, and moves with the assurance of privilege.

Armand holds his arms out to the victim. The girl runs to Armand's open arms and buries her face in his chest, as though he had come to rescue her. He, in turn, puts on a show of solicitude, caressing her and stroking her hair. Suddenly he pushes her downstage, and raises both her arms to shoulder height. He whispers in one of her ears and then the other, saying, 'No pain. No pain'; it is a rhythmic ritual. She seems either resigned, hypnotised or fully paralysed with fear; she does not move. Armand removes her petticoat so that she is completely nude. The girl faints or collapses in his arms,

Armand (Antonio Banderas) brandishes his next victim for the delight of the theatre (and film) audience

as he bites her neck. The moment he sinks his teeth into her flesh he looks directly at Louis, in the balcony, who whispers, 'Monstrous.' Armand then raises the supine body of the girl over his head as the others in the troupe carry her off. An overhead shot shows the black-cloaked figures converging like famished rats on the girl's body. The curtain closes. Once again we, in our role as spectators, passively watch the savage performance invoked by the placement of the camera.

Desire and death coalesce in ritualised spectacle. Eroticism is a threat, lethally entangled with mortality. Louis, watching and passive, is a surrogate for the film audience who view the gruesome spectacle with the audience in the theatre. What makes this highly reflexive scene so disquieting is that it is performed in public. At one point, just as Santiago (a buffoonish vampire played by Stephen Rea, who studied tapes of *La Comedie Française* to perform his role) is about to bite the young girl, a woman in the audience stands up and cries out, 'Take me, Monsieur Vampire.'

It is like watching a rock show in which the entrance of the star (Armand) is charged with electric anticipation and a frisson of eroticism. The public's fascination with this ritual of submission to a diabolical figure is all the more haunting because they cannot differentiate between dramatised death (Grand Guignol) and a real murder that is played out for their delectation; that is a truly appalling idea. Yet, surely, Jordan is reminding us of our own enchantment with the profane. The spectacle demands to be watched; it merges the monstrous and the beautiful. We cannot fail to look, and that enraptured passivity, that magnetism provoked by ritual and spectacle, however evil or macabre, has a universal, timeless dimension. It is not limited to the world of vampires; it is endemic to humanity.

Apart from the scenes of spectacular theatricality, Jordan varies the temperature of the performances with more naturalistic moments. A sequence striking for its poignancy is the one in which Claudia (Kirsten Dunst) comes to understand that while her emotions and mentality change as she continues her existence, she will retain the physiognomy of a doll-like little girl. She says, 'It means that I shall never, ever grow up … Tell me how I came to be this thing.' There are no histrionics – the scene is very quiet and low-key – just a sad admission of who she is, and what she can never become. During the moments when Claudia expresses her anguish Louis silently weeps, averting his eyes from the girl; he finally admits that it was he who made her. It is important to be reminded that even amongst the undead there are redemptive moments of genuine sorrow and pain. The more naturalistic of these, though limited, provide a conduit between the imagined cosmos of the grotesque and excessive, and a world without severity and violence, a place of identifiable feeling.

As these elements indicate, Jordan is intelligent and skilled enough to know that he cannot sustain a long film with a non-stop show of pyrotechnics. He weaves scenes of ritual power and energy with moments of mournful tenderness, distancing us with potent images of heightened intensity and then moving us towards a position of sympathy for the devil.

CHAPTER FOUR

Postmodern Fairy Tales and Hybrid Genres

The Company of Wolves: 'A huge theatre of possibilities'

> 'The aggressive impulses of little girls leave nothing to be desired in the way of abundance and violence.'
> – Sigmund Freud

The fairy tale provides a potent tool for the interpretation of Neil Jordan's storytelling. Fairy tales are situated within an animistic universe governed by the belief that spirits, good and bad, inhabit all things and that thoughts and wishes are all-powerful over physical reality. All cultures are inspired by these primitive incorporeal beings. Freud argues that none of us has passed through this animistic stage of development without unconsciously retaining certain residues of it that remain capable of manifesting themselves in those feelings of fear and terror that he refers to as versions of the uncanny: 'everything that now strikes us as uncanny fulfils the condition of touching those residues of animistic mental activity within us and bringing them to expression' (Freud 1955a: 240–1).

This archaic and universal template of human consciousness achieves its most clear delineation in myth and legend. The relationship between myth and fairy tale has been much discussed amongst folklorists and cultural anthropologists. Jack Zipes is in agreement with Mircea Eliade when he declares that myth has a sacred function, and that fairy tales are essentially secular narratives through which one can discern 'the initiatory core' of the myth; in other words, these primal structures serve as the basis for all future storytelling (see Zipes 1994: 1–2). Fairy tale becomes myth, and myth can be viewed as fairy tale. Eliade ruminates further on this issue:

> it is not always true that the tale shows 'desacrilisation' of the mythical world. It would be more correct to speak of a camouflage of mythical motifs and characters; instead of 'desacrilisation', it would be better to say 'rank-loss of the sacred' … its content proper refers to a terrifyingly serious reality: initiation, that is, passing by way of a symbolic death and resurrection, from ignorance and immaturity to the spiritual age of the adult. (1963: 200–1)

We have examined the myths and legends that are specific to Irish culture. In this chapter we will begin with the way in which fairy tale constructs pervade and illuminate Jordan's work.

Unlike the religious and national origins treated in myth and legend, fairy tales are a narrative form that engages with personal and social origins. Because Jordan is so concerned with the peregrinations of identity, the fairy tale provides a rich body of cultural imagery, form and history for the director. Moreover, the instability of fairy tales – historically contingent, forever reworked by the new teller – allows for the kind of artistic manipulation that serves Jordan's examinations of the power of narrative and myth. Rather than pursuing archetypal and structural absolutes, or the underlying moral and social codes in his use of fairy tales, Jordan builds upon the disruptive elements of this durable narrative form.

References to fairy tales appear at turning points in Jordan's films, at decisive moments: *Angel*, where fairy lights frame the encounter of the musician and the girl who strays from the path and ends up dead; *The Company of Wolves*, where a young woman fantasises of tales and metamorphoses until her fairy tale dream shatters the separation between her actuality and her desires; *In Dreams*, where a pantomime performance of *Snow White* ends in a young girl's kidnapping and murder. Marina Warner writes of how 'all the wonders that create the atmosphere of fairy tales disrupt the apprehensible world in order to open spaces for dreaming alternatives … The dimension of wonder creates a huge theatre of possibility in the stories: anything can happen'[1] (1994a: n.p.). A sense of enchantment often accompanies ruptures in identity and narrative for Jordan, and allows for rearrangements of the real, frequently entailing a fundamental loss. Jacqueline Rose describes (and critiques) the ways in which the social conception of fairy tales and children's literature turn on 'the opposition between the child and the adult … between oral and written culture, between innocence and decay' (1984: 50). Jordan's cinematic fairy tales engage with these assumptions, and his fairy tales of personal desire and so cial devastation often end with the futility of returning to states of passivity, simplicity and blindness – the impossibility of healing what really hurts. The director captures the threat of change and the uncertainty of desire implicit in fairy tales; like Gustave Doré's erotic illustrations of Little Red Riding Hood's encounter with the wolf, Jordan's characters face the changes in their lives 'beset by powerful ambivalent feelings ... attracted and repelled at the same time' (Bettelheim 1976: 176).[2] Given the often catastrophic effects of growing up in the director's films, his fairy tale sensibility is much closer to the 'melodramatic depictions of desire, loss and self-immolation' of Hans Christian Andersen than the earthy ribaldry, playful irrationality or the pedantic moralism of other canonical fairy tales (Bettelheim 1976: 176). Jordan resists slotting fairy tales into prescriptive, rewarding structures of growing up. We hear the fable of the scorpion and the frog twice in *The Crying Game*, and rather than provide a moral for the film (much less a solution for the complex issues of political violence and the instability of social roles with which the film engages), the tale indicates the impossibility of solutions for a situation of suffering and misrecognition.

As well as incorporating fairy tale tropes and thematics within his films, the director reflexively engages with the formal, social and historical implications of fairy tales. Storytelling and the narrator's voice – essential to the history and expression of fairy tales – is a central aspect of Jordan's interrogation of the ways in which we respond to narrative (see Tatar 1992: 216). A probing of the limits of morality and the possibilities of dialogue within the situations of storytelling that circulate throughout *The Company of Wolves*, as well as tensions between storytelling and writing in *The End of the Affair* or storytelling and lying in *The Butcher Boy*, suggest the recurring interest the director has in the implications of the storyteller. *In Dreams* broadens this exploration of articulation by representing a range of ways – such as pantomime and illustration – in which fairy tales are expressed. While the reflexive examination of forms that articulate meaning are one route for Jordan's use of fairy tales, a historical self-awareness also accompanies many of his fairy tale allusions. Jordan's treatment of the history of fairy tales is visually present in *The Company of Wolves*, particularly in the baroque amalgamation of archetypal images in the set design by Anton Furst. In many respects, the pop culture references in *The Butcher Boy* and the intertext of *Psycho* (1960) (and its generic progeny) running through *In Dreams* suggest that the storytelling that grows out of popular culture (the horror film and social anxieties it addresses) can be seen as a contemporary expression of the fairy tale – albeit one with a peculiarly modern uncertainty in expressing myths of gender, childhood and family.

> Angela Carter's quest for eros, her perseverance in the attempt to ensnare its nature in her imagery, her language, her stories, drew her to fairy tales as a form and [before her death in 1992] she wrote some of the most original reworkings in contemporary literature.
>
> – Marina Warner (1994b: 248)

Carter and Jordan first met when she was an adjudicator on the *Guardian* Book Award committee; Jordan won the top prize for his collection of short stories, *Night in Tunisia*. They would reconnect at the centenary fête of James Joyce's birthday in Dublin. Carter had written a radio play of her short story 'The Company of Wolves' (1979), and was then commissioned to write a 30-minute screenplay by Channel 4, although after she met with Jordan they decided to make it into a feature film.

The novelist and reticent filmmaker met, in the person of Carter, someone who was as outspoken as he was reserved. Jordan is skilled at creating moods and situations of great subtlety and complexity, using both image and language to transmit feelings and transform meaning. He shares with Carter a delight in exploring transgressive impulses that interrogate fundamental human behaviours: the project of probing the construction and meaning of identity (and identities), sexuality, violence and mortality that astonish their audience. As Marina Warner put it: 'many of Angela's heroines ... resemble the literary text of the kind Angela herself was writing: ornate, bejewelled, artificial, highly wrought prose playing hide-and-seek ... with the chatty, downmarket, vulgar, unadorned personae of the characters underneath the greasepaint and the costume' (1994b: 248). Jordan's films map out the darkness that lurks beneath their flamboyant exterior, and while Carter's work may deal with iniquity, it is always leavened with a *jeu d'esprit*. Both writers share a sensibility that embraces the sensual and the textural – Jordan in an exquisite, sensitive way, Carter in the name of the outrageous. If we think of the Carter/Jordan relationship in terms of Jungian archetypes, Carter is the externalised mask and Jordan the shadow side of the process of creation.

As an enthusiastic listener/reader of both folk and fairy tales, and as a writer who draws from many versions of each, oral and literary, Carter tells tales that reactivate lost traditions, trace violently contradictory genealogies and flesh out the complex and ritual workings of desire and narrative. As Cristina Bacchilega writes about *The Company of Wolves*, 'meta-narrative is most definitely the name of the game in this parodic, deliberately overly-symbolic movie' (1997: 67).

On his part, Jordan distinguishes between two traditions of fantasy: one is exemplified by Cocteau's *Beauty and the Beast* (1946), which Jordan considers surreal; the other by 'silly comic book-like stories such as *Star Trek*'. Commenting on his work with Furst: 'We tried to build each set so that it reminded you of something you had seen but weren't quite sure what it was.' The director wanted to move away from genre conventions because he felt they acted as a kind of 'straitjacket' (Neil Jordan, *The Company of Wolves* DVD commentary).

The filmed version of *The Company of Wolves* appropriates a variety of different folk-legends, fairy tales and myths, both oral and written, and shows an intelligent awareness of the ways in which fairy tales have been a tool for the acculturation of children for their prescribed social roles (see Lieberman 1986). The way in which the tale of Little Red Riding Hood has transmogrified over time is instructive when approaching the surfeit of meanings offered up by the film. Variations on this story can be found in ancient Egyptian, Greek, Roman, Celtic, Teutonic and Native American mythologies. In its original oral incarnation the folk tale marks the social initiation of a young woman, and celebrates her coming of age. It is also, importantly, a warning. A common story in the Middle Ages has an 'ogre, ogress, man-eater, wild person, werewolf, or wolf' attacking a child in the forest or at home (Zipes 1993: 7). The story functions socially as an admonition to deter children from talking to strangers, or allowing them access to their dwellings. In some versions of the story, when the little girl gets to Granny's house the wolf forces her to eat the grandmother's flesh and drink her blood, in a perverted ritual of transubstantiation. In all the early versions of the tale Little Red Riding Hood outsmarts the wolf in a variety of clever moves, and escapes.

In some pre-Perrault versions of the story, the girl acquiesces to the wolf, strips and throws her clothes into the fire. Bacchilega (1997) mentions this in part to show how aware and scholarly Carter was in writing her own version of stories, especially in *The Bloody Chamber* (1979). This brings our attention to the historical layering that she and Jordan exploit in *The Company of Wolves*. Charles Perrault revised Little Red Riding Hood with moral purpose, and eliminated any references to cannibalism. Perrault's story, written for the court of Louis XIV, 'transformed a hopeful oral tale about the initiation of a young girl into a tragic one of violence in which the girl is blamed for her own violation' (Zipes 1993: 18–19). In keeping with most feminist literature on the subject, Zipes equates the act of being eaten with rape, and most certainly with violation. In Perrault's version the little girl and Granny are eaten by the wolf. They do not escape, nor are they rescued, thus depriving the characters of any measure of salvation or redemption.

In the later version by the Brothers Grimm the child survives, but only because of the valiant ministrations of a huntsman, a strong male. Only he can save her from her own lustful desires, of which her red cloak – traditionally the colour associated with violent sexuality – is but an external manifestation. Michel Foucault, in *The History of Sexuality*, writes about the Grimm's de-sexualisation of the story as both a mirror and a response to the contemporaneous society's wish to guard against the sexualisation of children (1980: 104). As Maria Tatar writes, 'Religious, rather than social, morality held sway in Europe well into the eighteenth century and inscribed its stern values on stories told by adults to children.' She goes on to say that although the tales have the pretence of being instructive, they are in actuality 'sadistic stories aimed at controlling behaviour' (1992: 29, 31).

The wolf, both in oral and written tradition is a sexual, lustful being. It is not coincidental that in Italian the word for male wolf is lupo, and lupa, the word for female wolf, also means vulva. Allegorically, as cited in a German text from the mid-1800s, *Der Werewolf*, wolves have been the natural symbol of night, winter and death, characterised as swift, lusty, hardy and bold with a desire for blood and hunger for the flesh of corpses. Ernest Jones writes in *On the Nightmare* that the wolf is 'specially suited to represent the dangerous and immoral side of nature in general and human nature in particular' (1949: 132).

The wolf is also associated with fertility and phallic symbolism, and thus affiliated with creation. Significantly, werewolves were not associated with evil until the end of the fifteenth century. In medieval times werewolves were looked on with positive feelings, and even sensations of awe, as beings capable of integrating both the wild and cultural elements, beings at the intersection of nature and civilisation. The archetypal side of the wolf figure is embraced by Marie-Louise von Franz as a way to remain in touch with profound and ancient archetypes:

> We say the animal is the carrier of the projection of human psychic factors. As long as there is still archaic identity, and as long as you have not taken

the projection back, the animal and what you project onto it are identical; they are one and the same thing. You see it beautifully in those animal stories which represent archetypal human tendencies. They are human because they really do not represent animal instincts but our animal instincts, and in that sense they are really anthropomorphic. (1997: 36)

This alludes to ancient rituals in which one lived in the wilderness in order to be returned and recuperated within the social order. Little Red Riding Hood can be viewed as a sort of female *bildungsroman*.

Keeping the history of the tale of Little Red Riding Hood and the wolf in mind, we can turn to the film, *The Company of Wolves*. It begins with a framing story of a bourgeois family – mother, father and two daughters – as they arrive at their bourgeois country home. We are then drawn into the dreams and nightmares of the sleeping adolescent and youngest daughter, Rosaleen. Her dreams, or conscious and unconscious imaginings, form the material of the film's narrative. The setting of her dream world would seem to be contemporaneous to the time in which Perrault was writing, the end of the seventeenth century. The dream time is elastic enough to allow a diabolical figure played by the ever-demonic Terrence Stamp[3] to arrive at one point in a gleaming white Rolls Royce. Most importantly, though, it is the time of 'once upon a time', the universalised time of storytelling and fantasy.

Rosaleen as the dreamer sees herself as strong, fearless, powerful and special, dreaming a dream that enables her to have control over the story and the fictive world in which it takes place. It is manifestly an anxiety dream of a young woman searching, in psychoanalytic terms, for the integrity of her psyche; questing for identity, independence and sexual fulfilment.

Rosaleen's first dream places her antagonistic sister (and rival), Alice (Georgia Slowe), in a magical forest. Giganticised replicas of the stuffed animals and dolls we have viewed in Rosaleen's room in the film's framing story loom menacingly around the frightened sister. In an expeditious enactment of wish fulfilment, the sister is violently dispatched by a pack of wolves. Following the girl's funeral we are introduced to Granny, who says, 'Your only sister. All alone in the woods and nobody there to save her. Poor little lamb.' Rosaleen replies, 'Why couldn't she save herself?' The dream-Rosaleen is tough, independent and unsentimental, but is nonetheless heavily influenced by the superstitions, folk tales and admonitions of Granny. If the film is about the quest for sexual identity, Granny comes to represent one side of an archetypal view of the sexual. For her, the sexual is the demonic, given a real existence in the film that is brutal, fearful and evil.

Granny relates a tale to Rosaleen, establishing the narrative pattern in which the main dream is segmented by narrated stories of characters within the dream. Bacchilega points out that 'the film's story-within-and-against-other-stories technique not only successfully represents the process of working through an image to undo the distortions of dreamwork, but also performs the lively multiplicity of the storytelling process in a variety of ways' (1997: 67). She describes the structure of *The Company of Wolves* as a 'Chinese box narrative', similar to *The Butcher Boy*, *The End of the Affair* and *Breakfast on Pluto*. It is a kind of narrative labyrinth which is mirrored structurally in the literal labyrinths in *Mona Lisa* (the London underworld), *Interview with the Vampire* (the realm of the vampires), and the watery maze in the drowned town of *In Dreams*.

Granny tells of a newly-married husband who, just before consummating his marriage, excuses himself to answer 'the call of nature'. What he means by this becomes clear when he forsakes the marriage bed to rejoin his wolf-companions in the wilderness. It is an example of the way in which, for Granny, sexuality is inextricably bound up with bestiality, with the evil of the natural world and with the irreconcilable split between nature and culture. Before Granny is devoured by the wolf she says, 'Get back to hell, where you came from,' to which the wolf/man replies, 'I don't come from hell, I come from the forest.' But for Granny they are one and the same: the primeval, the unknown, the fearful. Granny constantly cautions Rosaleen when walking in the woods never to stray from the path, a common interdiction in folk tales. The path signals the safety in obedience and virtue, whereas the forest signifies the dangers of defiance, and most especially of wantonness and sexual desire. The main narrative thrust of *The Company of Wolves* is about female development and the erotic feminine. However, as Bacchilega points out, fairy tales are also filled with jealousy (1997: 31). This especially can be seen in the relationship between the girl and Granny, whose stories seem meant to scare Rosaleen about her emerging sexuality. (Jordan, in his DVD commentary, talks about Angela Lansbury's unique ability to appear both 'grandmotherly' and malefic at the same time.)

The second view of sexuality on offer to Rosaleen comes from her mother who is associated with natural phenomena and the cycles of nature, as opposed to the superstitions and fears of Granny. For the mother, wolves are dangerous because they are predators, nothing more. Rosaleen witnesses her parents making love, and asks if her father has hurt her mother, to which the mother replies, 'No, no, not at all. If there is a beast in men, it meets its match in women too.' Granny, on the other hand, tells Rosaleen, 'Men are nice until they've had their way with you, then the beast comes out.' Rosaleen, poised on the brink of womanhood, must choose between these competing attitudes to determine her sexual and social roles, and even, as it turns out, her species.

The dream-Rosaleen is intent on pursuing the Amorous Boy (Shane Johnstone), and dares to stray off the path while being courted ; she runs playfully from him until she reaches a huge tree. Rosaleen smiles knowingly, and fearlessly begins climbing the large, erect structure. A coiled snake hisses from amidst the branches. A long shot reveals the enormity of the tree, with the red-cloaked Rosaleen perched high on its trunk.[4] As she ascends she reaches a nest, where she discovers several eggs and a hand mirror. Rosaleen looks at herself in the glass with a pleased expression, then opens a tin of deep red lipstick and daubs the lipstick sensuously on her mouth. There is a cut to Rosaleen's smiling face reflected in the mirror, as one by one the eggs hatch to reveal not new-born birds but tiny, doll-like babies (reminiscent of Renaissance portrayals of the Christ child). The girl reaches out to touch her new-found treasures.[5]

In the next scene a country lad, still searching for Rosaleen, comes upon the supine, bloodied carcass of a cow, its calf standing by its side. A shot of a panting wolf

Rosaleen (Sarah Patterson) embarks on a quest into the world of experience

with blood streaked about its jaw is intercut. The boy screams 'Wolf! Wolf!' and runs to alert the villagers. We next see Rosaleen peacefully walking through the forest, stroking her 'baby' (taken from the nest in the tree), while another shot of the wolf is intercut. The village is in uproar when Rosaleen returns to her desperate family, but she calmly shows the 'baby' to her mother, who smiles. A tear rolls down the 'baby's' cheek.

The sequence is laden with significance, most unmistakably referencing the tree of knowledge, with the archetypal images of loss, innocence and entry into the world of experience. Rosaleen falls, like Adam and Eve, into what Northrop Frye called 'the order of nature as we know it'. He writes:

> The tragedy of Adam … resolves, like all other tragedies, in the manifestation of natural law. He enters a world in which existence is itself tragic … merely to exist is to disturb the balance of nature. Every natural man is a Hegelian thesis, and implies a reaction: every new birth provokes the return of an avenging death … this crucial moment … is a moment of dizziness, when the wheel of fortune begins its inevitable cyclical movement downward. (1957: 213)

Rosaleen's entry into the world of experience and adulthood – what Frye would call the ironic mode of tragedy – is a movement away from the ordered, protected existence of the parental home, as well as the safety of 'the path'. It is a point of no return, for as the wolf/man is neither wolf nor man, Rosaleen is neither girl nor woman. Rosaleen's lipstick is likened to the blood on the wolf's mouth, yet the wolf poses no apparent danger to the young girl. While a tear is shed for her loss of childhood, Rosaleen's entrance into the erotic – the emergence of appetite (for example she, like the wolf, can be a predator; she wants the giant phallus, not a mere lad), the masturbatory stroking of her lips with moist fingers, the spectre of childbirth, her mother's natural acceptance of her daughter's *rite de passage* – does not, within the context of this dream world, provoke fear or anxiety. The menstrual imagery of the tree scene – Rosaleen's red lipstick – is also typical of the references to 'first blood' so pervasive in fairy tales. Sleeping Beauty is cursed at birth to prick her finger on her fifteenth birthday; Rapunzel is locked away at age twelve in a tower; both near the age of their first menses. In this extract from *The Bleeding Tower* we have a litany of prototypical fairy tale images that deal with menstruation and the archetypal cast of heroines and goddesses who inhabit them:

> ...the Great Goddess is being used to suggest the eternal feminine life cycle ... the new moon (the White Goddess of birth and growth), the full moon (the Red Goddess of love and battle), and the old moon (the Black Goddess of death and divination); virgin, nymph, crone, the three aspects of the Great Goddess. Most heroines of tales are presented to us first in their white or virgin state. After they fulfil conditions of seclusion and trial and ride off with the prince, they are associated with the colour red, or nubility; and all have a brush with transformation or death, which brings them in touch with the black.
>
> Snow White herself is first innocent, or white; she meets her apparent death from eating the red side of the poisoned apple, analogous to menarche (or sexual knowledge, like Eve's); she goes into the 'seclusion' of death, although the dwarfs will not bury her in the 'black' ground; and she is revived by a kiss on her red lips, signifying marriage and nobility...
>
> Red is the most prevalent colour in the stories and frequently appears as a rose. The rose or any flower is a dominant menstrual image in literature and folklore. A flower is also an image for the hymen. Because old beliefs associated the menarche with the breaking of the hymen, these correspondences persist. Thus, the briar roses that grow around Sleeping Beauty's castle and cause the death of the would-be penetrators may be allusions to the fear of defloration prevalent among primitive peoples and their association of defloration with the dangerous properties of menstrual blood. (Delaney *et al.* 1988: 137–9)

Another staple of the fairy tale is cannibalism, and it is crucial to our understanding of *The Company of Wolves*. Marina Warner has a short chapter on Goya's 'Saturn Devouring His Children' (1819–23). It is a fascinating observation of the ogre, sexual appetite, moral taboo and the violence of incorporation (either incestuously or cannibalistically – though obviously the latter is a symbol of the former). The theme is tackled in the first part of *No Go the Bogeyman* entitled 'Scaring is Cannibalism' and Warner uses one of the best-known stories, that of Dionysus's birth and Kronos/Saturn devouring his child in Greek myth as a springboard into a lengthy look at this gory topic:

> Cannibals magnify the normal hyperbolically ... and the issue of survival through eating spreads across this dark and bewildering place ... Food – procuring it, preparing it, cooking it, eating it – dominates the material as the overriding image of survival; consuming it offers contradictory metaphors of life and civilisation as well as barbarity and extinction. (1998: 12–13)

There is an interesting recounting of Ovid's *Metamorphoses* and literature's first were-wolf, Lycaon, the cannibal chef who boasts he can feed Zeus human flesh, but fails and is turned into a werewolf as punishment; condemned to become 'an omophage, one who eats only his own kind'. Warner goes on to say that 'an almost identical story lies behind the punishment of Tantalus in the Underworld: he similarly dares to challenge the gods' wisdom by serving a cannibal feast. And for this crime, he is sentenced to perpetual hunger and thirst, as Lycaon is condemned to be a werewolf and lust insatiably after blood' (1998: 36–7).

A most contemporary concern is expressed in the tale of Polyphemus, a cannibal who eats both little boys and little girls. He is sexually indifferent to the gender of his prey. This figure has mutated into a threatening monster who goes beyond the instructive use of intimidation and warning for children. He is now rematerialised in contemporary culture as a child abuser and paedophile. Polyphemus condenses widespread fears in contemporary society that focus today on sexual, rather than mortal, danger – although one can follow the other.

The sexual innuendo of the predatory bogeyman has become far more insistent since Perrault deftly introduced it into the tale of Little Red Riding Hood, and this change of meaning colours the whole range of images in stories about eating and being eaten since Perrault, whose wolf sheds his overt bestiality and becomes, according to Jordan's film, 'hairy on the inside'. Already, Warner points out, Perrault's wolf 'had become a seducer, a stalker of young girls, a metaphorical consumer of virgin flesh' (1998: 37). Angela Carter, though, took it a step further when she warned that young pretty girls ought not be surprised if 'some greedy wolf consumes them, elegant red riding hoods and all … [There are] wolves who seem perfectly charming, sweet-natured and obliging, who pursue young girls in the street and pay them the most flattering attentions. Unfortunately, these smooth-tongued, smooth-pelted wolves are the most dangerous of all' (in Warner 1998: 37–8).

Rosaleen, off through the woods to Granny's house, meets with the wolf/man in his guise as a handsome huntsman. We know he is a wolf/man because, as Granny has warned, 'his eyebrows meet in the middle', and he has a foreign accent, often an indication of romance or danger. In a meeting fraught with sexual tension, Rosaleen flirts openly with the wolf/man. They joke about 'the remarkable object' in his pocket, a compass with which he will find the way to Granny's house in a wager with Rosaleen. As in the traditional story of Little Red Riding Hood the wolf/man wins the race and makes a meal of Granny. Rosaleen then enters the house, but completely rejects the masochistic and deadly identity that is given to the girl in the Perrault story. Rosaleen wears the red cloak, the emblem of her sexuality, but unlike her counterpart in the fairy tale Rosaleen can put on or take off her cloak, like a mask. This performance, a masquerade of sorts, is one of the most important tropes in the work of both Carter and Jordan. She can choose both her identity and her destiny. In fact, once she accepts the alluring advances of the wolf/man, the cloak is thrown into the fire in a heightened gesture that acknowledges her own desire. The huntsman is transformed into a wolf in an unmistakably sexualised transformation scene. Remarkably, Rosaleen displays little fear at the sight of the morphing, sweaty body as it bursts through his clothes. (Jordan chose Mischa Bergese for the part of the huntsman because he was a dancer, and had a dancer's body with the muscular articulation that could enact the fluctuating shape of the werewolf.) Perhaps most radically, in terms of both the story of Little Red Riding Hood and the image of the wolf, Rosaleen is neither raped, devoured nor otherwise hurt by the wolf – in fact, it is she who wounds him with his own weapon.

After gently caressing the wounded wolf, Rosaleen is apparently transformed into a similar creature with the metamorphosis occurring off-screen. Tellingly, it is only her mother, the character closest to the natural world, who recognises the wolf as her daughter and implores a group of gathered hunters not to shoot. Rosaleen leaves with the wolf/man to integrate into her new society, the company of wolves.

Rosaleen chooses to become what Noël Carroll in *The Philosophy of Horror or Paradoxes of the Heart* describes as one of the defining characters of the horror genre – the impure, the interstitial being, somewhere between woman and wolf (see Carroll 1990: 46–7). If dragon-slaying is part of the ritual quest of the mythos of romance, in this case Rosaleen opts to join the dragon. She strays from the path, choosing the pleasure principle over the reality principle, choosing what is pleasurable and sensual over duty and responsibility. Giving Rosaleen this choice disrupts the conventions of the fairy tale and maps out another way to view the stories, as a literal way to construct (her)self.

Rosaleen and her new acquaintances leap through the forest, jumping over the doll's house and huge toys first viewed in the dream of the older sister's death. The camera moves over the sleeping Rosaleen in her bedroom as the pack of wolves begin rampaging through the hallway and stairs of the family home; only now the home seems abandoned, overgrown with cobwebs, strewn with blowing leaves as foliage sprouts amidst the furnishings. The wolves crash in slow-motion through a portrait of a lady. The pack runs upstairs to the door of Rosaleen's room. She wakes, startled, then terrified, the hand mirror – the source of pleasure in her dream – on her pillow, her lips reddened by lipstick. She clutches at her bedclothes and moans as the wolves mill outside her door. In an instant, a wolf breaks through her bedroom window, tumbling over the toys we have seen in the dream, as Rosaleen screams in terror. A voice-over speaks from Perrault's *Le Petit Chaperon Rouge*, over the end credits: 'Little girls, this seems to say/Never stop along your way/Never trust a stranger, friend/No one knows how it will end/As you're pretty, so be wise/Wolves may lurk in every guise/Now as then 'tis simple truth/Sweetest tongue has sharpest tooth.'

It is unclear whether or not this waking terror is yet another episode of Rosaleen's dream or if, in fact, the dreaming and waking worlds have collapsed into one another. Considering the genre, perhaps it is a point of hesitation, an intersection between the worlds of reality and imagination that would make it, according to Tzvetan Todorov's definition, a perfect exemplar of 'the fantastic' (see Todorov 1973: 24–40). The family house is overgrown with elements of the natural world, now resembling the forest more than the home. The common Gothic motif of opposing two settings – the cultural, institutional and the common (such as the castle, the school, the church), with the primitive, the intuitive, the dark and the unknown (the dungeon, the dark forest, the labyrinth) here breaks down (see Bunnell 1984: 82–3).

Layers of civilisation are stripped away in seconds as the aristocrats are changed into wolves

If *The Company of Wolves* is an exploration of Rosaleen's psyche in terms of gender, social and sexual roles, what kind of identity has she discovered at the film's end? If the film is about Rosaleen's awakening sexuality, it can also be seen to be about the terror that sexuality holds. Rosaleen enters the world of experience – and teeters on the fulcrum between angst and pleasure that underwrites the process of growing up. Earlier in the film, the dream-Rosaleen tells her mother the story of a pregnant witch, depicted clearly as a figure from the underclass. The witch confronts the aristocratic father of their soon-to-be-born progeny on the day of his wedding to a woman of his own class. The party is elegant; the table sumptuously set with fine china, crystal and linen; the assembled guests are exquisitely attired. In a ritual gesture and common Gothic motif, the witch breaks a mirror, which distorts what it shows us. The guests turn into a pack of ravenous animals, 'wolfing' down their food, irrupting from their fine garments. Layers of civilisation and social propriety are stripped away as they are loosed into the wilds. Rosaleen tells her mother that the wolves would come at night and sing to the witch and her baby. The mother asks, 'What pleasure would there be in that?' to which Rosaleen replies, 'The pleasure would be in knowing the power she had.'

This scene also demonstrates Jordan's predilection for the dark carnival which Bakhtin writes about. It destabilises social norms, 'opening the way for licentious misrule, generating what might be called festive horror, a genre in which carnivals' material bodily principle … its base of promiscuous carnality, blasphemy, scatology and ritual degradation is translated from a comic social discourse into a pathological one' (in Morgan 2002: 135).

Is the sense of power or fearlessness so anxiety-provoking for Rosaleen when she is awake that it must be relegated to her dream self? The ending of the film may be seen as the reflection of the terror she finds in becoming a woman, and in finding herself deprived of the sense of power she experienced in her dream. Rosaleen dreams of transgression, of an escape from repression; she dreams of joining an untamed society, the company of wolves. (Originally, Carter and Jordan wanted Rosaleen to dive into a watery floor, which opens to receive her, but their budget could not accommodate this special effect.) Is the ending then the tragic fall, the calamity that must result from a woman's transgressive desires? Or does the sweet and powerful sexuality of which Rosaleen dreams turn out to be a nightmare, an attack by the 'beasts in men' that Granny warned of? Although Rosaleen is shown waking in the film's final moments, clearly the landscape of her awakening is dream territory, and cannot be taken as a realistic narrative topos. Yet Jordan and Carter have chosen to end on this note of panic and horror. Does the film, then, finally endorse Granny's vision of the terror of sexuality? The fearful words 'Sweetest tongue has sharpest tooth' form the film's concluding line, and the last we hear of our protagonist is her terrified screaming. The sweet tongue is Rosaleen's dream of a mellifluous fusion of nature and culture, of powerful femininity and desire without reproach. The sharp tooth must then surely be the more painful reality into which Rosaleen must grow up. It is not a happy ending.

Within the distinguished company of filmmakers such as Jane Campion, Stanley Kubrick and Tim Burton and authors such as Italo Calvino, Angela Carter and Margaret Atwood, Jordan is one of the most mordant modern re-tellers of fairy tales. His employment of narrative is much different than simply a correction or parody of their supposedly outdated values; rather, he investigates what it means to listen to fairy tales, what it means to trust narrative, and what it means to follow their paths. His films often show the messy results of fairy tales, the awkward ways in which we interact with our shared store of narratives and the complex interrelation of past and future which make fairy tales such vivid material for impassioned pastiche.

Mona Lisa: the hybrid genre and the postmodernisation of the fairy tale

'Some of them want to use you, some of them want to be used by you.'
— Annie Lennox and Dave Stewart

In Jordan's 1986 film, *Mona Lisa*, as in *The Company of Wolves*, we witness the way identity, gender and cruelty form the basis of a reality in which characters may find or lose themselves. The family and childhood, accompanied by notions of ambiguity, suffering and misrecognition, once again provide the core material for *Mona Lisa*. The dangers of growing up and the search for wholeness are central to the film whose protagonist is George, a middle-aged innocent, in a role written for Bob Hoskins by Jordan and David Leland. We enter upon a dark world characterised by duplicity, corruption, perversity and violence. Goya's 'Saturn Devouring His Children' and the story of Polyphemus once again surface, as we witness the horror of paedophilia; young girls are lured into sex trafficking and used with impunity to satisfy the depraved appetites of the rich. The metaphor of cannibalism proves applicable to the film as well, as the lost girls are first tormented by their pimps and then, drugged and helpless, utterly devoured by the insatiable maw of the sex trade.

Yet, faced with this sordidness, somehow the main character, George, manages to retain his incorruptibility within the underworld zeitgeist in which his position is, at best, marginal. It is London in the mid-1980s, and George has just been released from a seven-year prison sentence – a sacrifice he made for his boss, the real perpetrator of the crime, Dinny Mortwell. Mortwell not only remained free, but has in the interim become the kingpin of the underworld, trafficking in sex and drugs. In the film's opening scenes, George brings a bouquet of flowers to his wife (Pauline Melville) and daughter, Jeannie (Zoë Nathenson). The result is a screaming match, the door slammed in George's face. He throws the flowers to the ground, stomps on them and shouts 'You cow!' at his wife, then kicks over a pail of rubbish on the street. There is a largely black audience watching the spectacle, and several of the men in the assembled group start to gather round George menacingly. One says, 'Who's going to clean that mess up?', referring to the trash in the street, but also, with no small irony, to George's failed marriage and violent ejection from his home.

Robbie Coltrane as Thomas, George's closest and it would seem only friend, materialises as if by magic upon the volatile situation, ushering George away from the scene. George has apparently failed to notice the shifting of race relations in London, and refers to people of colour as 'darkies'. Thomas ushers his friend to the sporty vehicle George left behind; it is in perfect condition. This, and the ability of someone of Coltrane's girth to enter the area without being seen, makes him a mysterious, wizard-like figure, Jung's prototypical Wise Old Man. George then looks in the car's rear-view mirror in the first of 23 such mirror shots. These shots serve many purposes, but certainly they act as a key figure to show the way in which George is fixed in a retrospective mode.

George's re-emergence into London is portrayed primarily through the character's literal point of view and/or the perspective of his consciousness. From the opening scene we see George as a solitary outsider in a bleak, working-class environment, yet he is never defiled by the venality of the sordid, inhumane world into which he must venture. As Jordan remarks, 'I had to model the city to make it part of [George's] brain … I created a version of London that people hadn't seen, because it probably isn't there' (in Falsetto 2000: 232). The streets and buildings of London become increasingly unrecognisable and foreign to George and to the viewer, satisfying Jordan's absorption with de-familiarisation.

The postmodern hybridity of genre is invoked and appropriated in *Mona Lisa*. The film has been called a 'neo-noir', and it does indeed contain a variety of stylistic and thematic gestures that are textbook cases of film noir. As Paul Schrader writes:

> The overriding noir theme: a passion for the past and present, but also a fear of the future. Noir heroes dread to look ahead, but instead try to survive by the day, and if unsuccessful at that, they retreat to the past. Thus film noir's techniques emphasise loss, nostalgia, lack of clear priorities, and insecurity, then submerge these self-doubts in mannerism and style. In such a world style becomes paramount; it is all that separates one from meaninglessness. Chandler described this fundamental noir theme: 'It is not a very fragrant world, but it is the world you live in.' (1986: 177)

While Jordan engages with the broad outlines of film noir in *Mona Lisa*, the viewer quickly comes to understand that the film is not located within a solitary generic

Film noir iconography: Simone (Cathy Tyson) and George (Bob Hoskins) try to evade a lethal enemy

niche. In fact, George's character, in his mortifying lack of refinement, is almost a lampoon of the typical noir hero. Certainly, a sense of loss, unclear priorities and self-doubt riddle George's existence. A hallmark of Jordan's work is the fragmentation of his characters' understanding of themselves which in turn leads to a rupture in the narrative configuration – including a jumble of disparate genres. A sense of displacement is fundamental amongst many of Jordan's characters, and George in *Mona Lisa* must confront the confusing debris of his once-familiar universe.

Jordan is far too eclectic a filmmaker to adhere to generic codes, the super-text as proscribed by Aristotle. Nor is Jordan involved consciously in the process of tracing the history of culture, although his films may very well perform this function. The director uses generic style and themes as it suits a particular work. A stunning example of the use of film noir iconography in *Mona Lisa* is a scene shot in two lifts moving simultaneously as the passengers try to evade a potentially lethal enemy. Not only does the lift (and staircase) attain iconic status in noir films, but it also partakes of the strong graphic qualities typified by the genre. Filming on location at night, side-lighting, cityscapes, the *femme fatale*, the qualities of entrapment, betrayal and perverse sexuality are some of the many noir traits found in *Mona Lisa*.

George is thrust into this seamy underworld which he must learn, little by little, to negotiate. He is yesterday's man, living in a state of perpetual bewilderment in the film's present tense. It is this unsavoury world that George must inhabit, and it is a world in which his values, such as loyalty, have little currency. George's astonishing act of fealty – to go to prison for a crime he did not commit – is a sacrifice for which Mortwell shows little care or recognition. Significantly *Mona Lisa* takes place in a typical noir world of perversion, betrayal and lies, in which one is used or uses others.

The film is also equal parts fantasy – Thomas fabricates his strange Pop Art plastic spaghetti (*à la* small-scale Claes Oldenburg) and mass-produced neon Madonnas – while continually inventing eccentric and magical mystery tales. As the film draws to a close there is a homage to *The Wizard of Oz* (1939) when Thomas, George and George's daughter, Jeannie, skip merrily, arm in arm, away from the dark world.

George is perhaps more fitting, in a surprising way, as a hero of romance. In his own way, he is noble, and acts as a knight errant for Simone (Cathy Tyson). She is the self-described 'thin, black tart' for whom George serves as a chauffeur as she travels from one assignation to another. Once again we find ourselves in the realm of mythopoesis. As Northrop Frye wrote, 'the mode of romance presents an idealised world: in romance heroes are brave, heroines beautiful, villains villainous, and frustrations, ambiguities and embarrassments of ordinary life are made little of' (1957: 151). In the mythos of romance, morality signifies a coming to terms with experience and necessity, something George learns during the course of his journey. Desire is an escape from necessity, and, for Frye, it has negative connotations. The world into which George stumbles is based on desire, and base desire predominates.

The essential element for the plot of a romance is adventure, and the major adventure is the quest. There are three main stages of the quest; the first is the perilous journey and preliminary minor adventures. The second stage is the crucial struggle in which either the hero or foe or both must die. In this stage confusion and anarchy, pathos and catastrophe reign, while heroism and effective action are absent. The final stage is the exaltation of the hero or his/her recognition. Normally there is a struggle with a ritual death before recognition may occur. The central form of the quest in romance is the dragon-killing theme. The hero arrives and kills a monster, and then he marries the king's daughter. One of the major quest themes is wandering the wilderness or the labyrinth, and finally arriving in Jerusalem.[6] An important quest object (something associated with the quest, and often having female sexual affinities) might be the holy grail, the Christian eucharist, or the miraculous food provider, the cornucopia.

Considering Frye's formula for the quest, one can easily see the perilous journey as the entrance to Mortwell's kingdom, George's job as Simone's driver and his various attempts to get his daughter to speak with him. The second stage is the most problematic. One can easily see the dominance of confusion and anarchy incised in the narrative of *Mona Lisa*; any efforts George makes to find Cathy (Kate Hardie), a 15-year-old junkie/prostitute, are ineffective. It is the nomination of the hero and his antagonist that is open to interrogation. Clearly (and somewhat improbably), George must be called the hero. But who then is the villain? The candidates are Mortwell, Simone (who keeps George in the dark as she involves him in her quest for her lover) and, if we want to broaden the construct, the villain is the sex trade and the organised crime that supports it. The recognition of the hero occurs in the Brighton scenes when George and Simone are chased by their nemeses Mortwell and Anderson (Clarke Peters). George's ritual death can be seen in his absentation from the criminal world and his rebirth as a true father to his daughter. The dragon-killing theme is essentially a repeat of the second stage of the romance quest, but here the action of slaying Mortwell and Anderson is clearly analogous to the killing of the dragon. Also, it is Simone, not George, who shoots them, thus endowing her with heroic qualities – an engaging modernisation of the quest. One of the most important quest themes involves wandering in the wilderness or through a labyrinth before ending the quest in Jerusalem (Frye 1957: 187). As the narrative concludes with this stage, once more we have a reconceptualisation of the family by Jordan, which now includes George, Thomas and Jeannie.

The final generic link is to the Gothic, a modality that pervades Jordan's entire oeuvre to a greater or lesser degree. In the scenes set in King's Cross, where George

Simone searches for Cathy in the Gothic labyrinthine passages of King's Cross

escorts Simone in her search for Cathy, the fog and darkness create a claustral environment. It is a *mise-en-scène* of asymmetrical arches and dimly-lit caverns (see O'Rawe 2003: 195). The dark claustrophobia is developed through the use of other settings: Mortwell's sex shops are labyrinthine; the spaces that George traverses while looking for Cathy are not clearly delineated; there is never a master shot that illuminates the space for us. Thus, the bar, the bedrooms, the peep shows and stairwells create a sense of disorientation.

Directly after the opening sequence, George, whose behaviour oscillates between that of a tiny tearaway and a yob, buys a rabbit for his boss, Mortwell. Thomas tries to warn him that things have changed, and his generosity will not be appreciated. George attempts to deliver the rabbit to Mortwell, but is brushed aside. This sort of misperception or unwillingness to comprehend a changed reality is typical of many of Jordan's characters, and George's response demonstrates his tendency to over-reaction at perceived slights. Mortwell assigns George to a low-level job as the driver of Simone, a high-priced call girl. It emerges that Simone, who has worked the streets and been physically abused by her pimp, Anderson, is now an elegant, smooth operator with rich clients. How Simone made her Pygmalion-like shift from street-whore to a refined woman with excellent diction and sophisticated tastes is never revealed. When she finds that cloddish George is to be her driver she says, greatly annoyed, 'Where did they get you from?' and George responds, 'Under a cabbage leaf'; an utterance that is one of many fairy tale tropes found in the film.

George and Simone are an unexpected coupling. George's polyester outfits are hardly appropriate for the high-class world in which Simone travels. If 'style' is paramount to the noir hero, our hero's taste for polyester leisure suits make him a fashion victim *par excellence*. George has style, but it is redolent of a certain kind of 1970s style lacking even a hint of good taste. Certainly it is not a style that will impact favourably upon his now debonair boss, Mortwell. Simone buys fashionable clothes for George, but even fitted out as a 'real gentleman' he is an unconvincing noir hero. He may be attired like a gentleman but he resolutely remains the little Cockney guy inside. This is another instance in the film where things are not what they seem: there is a gap between the characters' perceptions of themselves and how they are seen by others. When George asks Simone if anyone falls in love with her, she responds: 'They fall in love with what they think I am.' Similarly, when George hunts for Cathy in the squalid peep shows of Soho, he is shown to the room of a prostitute who says she is Cathy. Later, we find that her real name is May (Sammi Davis), and she is happy to perform as 'Cathy' if it pleases her client. One of the greatest misperceptions in the film is Simone's sense that she is in control of her life and profession because she no longer has a pimp. In one scene, George bursts into a hotel room and finds Simone in a leather bondage outfit tied to a bed; she may claim that as an 'independent' sex worker it is she who calls the shots, but she remains at the mercy of her clients' desires.

George exists in Simone's night world. He drives her silently through King's Cross, as we see hookers' faces ripple across his windscreen as watery, transparent images. Young girls are imprisoned by their need for drugs, and in servitude to their pimps. Here, spectral figures haunt the roadway, gliding past George and Simone in their car. These figures at times stop at the window of the car to solicit, their faces ghastly and gaping. The diurnal depiction of the area is equally threatening, if only because there is no cover of darkness to conceal the very real need of the haggard prostitutes to solicit their clientele in order to provide money for their next fix. George enters each X-rated 'cubicle of hell' within Mortwell's kingdom, traversing Soho's slummy streets as he gallantly hunts for Simone's Cathy. In the process, he almost loses his own life and soul. Nothing is what it seems for George: Simone (who is, incidentally, a striking double to Fergus's Dil in *The Crying Game*), the once familiar London into which he has re-emerged and, in many ways, his inability to understand what his place is in this new world, as he undertakes his quest, engenders his most serious challenge.

It is only George's innate innocence and goodness that allows him to endure the ugliness of this Dantesque representation of London. Each visit to a sex parlour is meant to represent a circle of Dante's Inferno (Neil Jordan, *Mona Lisa* DVD commentary). As George visits the sex shops, peep shows and porn film shops, we see that he is outraged and disgusted. Naïvely, he purchases an X-rated video, whose chief plot point has Simone performing fellatio on Anderson. George's clumsy ingenuousness makes it possible for him to show the tape to Simone. He seems blind to Simone's possible response to the tape – her outraged shame and violence when her degradation is on display. It is likened by Jordan to a rape scene as George forces Simone to watch something that causes her great pain. Simone prides herself on her dignity and control, and the tape offers visible evidence of a time in her life when she was just another victim. Most certainly, she does not want George to bear witness to her abjection. Her relationship with him is one of power in which she is the dominatrice, and the tape clearly undermines Simone's position.

The idea of mis-matched or impossible love is common in Jordan's films. George obviously falls in love and wants to protect Simone, but she is in love with Cathy. In

George bares his heart to Simone amidst the tacky storefronts of Brighton Pier

one scene, Cathy eats an ice cream after George has 'rescued' her. He asks if she likes ice cream, and she says, 'That's all I can eat. I can't take solid food no more.' George asks why – he knows nothing about junkies and their damaged digestive tracts. His confusion is recognised by Cathy who says, 'You don't know nuffin' do you?' Once we see Cathy with Simone it quickly becomes clear that she is with Simone only because the older woman is able to take care of her. Cathy says to George regarding her protector, 'That one, she really likes me', an impersonal remark, hardly a statement of a woman in love. Simone's inability to discern Cathy's feelings recalls Simone's now ironic observation that men fall in love with who 'they think' she is.

This sense of the illusory as well as the enchanted is also evoked by many elements of the film's décor, including Thomas's workroom; Mortwell's chair shaped like a huge hand; the white horse found whinnying next to a café the group has entered; the white rabbit; the 'cabbage leaf'; and the star- and heart-shaped glasses George purchases on Brighton pier: the film is filled with surreal, fantasy imagery. The 'real' Cathy is rescued by George as he watches her through a one-way mirror being painfully sodomised. He opens the door and pulls Cathy through, suggesting a perverse version of *Alice in Wonderland*. In the background we hear the old man who has paid for Cathy's services say, almost inaudibly: 'You're not supposed to like it.' The film's final shot shows Thomas, George and George's daughter, Jeannie, skipping down the Yellow Brick Road. As usual, Jordan's vision cannot be pegged to one genre; *Mona Lisa* blurs the boundaries of neo-noir, romance, Gothic and the redemptive-quest narrative.

Fairy tales: historical modulations

There is a potent invocation of the fairy tale in *Mona Lisa*, particularly the story of 'Beauty and the Beast'. This particular example of intertextuality is conspicuous when Simone buys George a new, classy wardrobe and makes a joke about the frog turning into a prince. More than a fleeting reference to the Grimms' tale, 'The Frog King', or 'Iron Heinrich' (which are grouped thematically with 'Beauty and the Beast'), the line aptly categorises the narrative trajectory that Jordan appropriates in the film. In the Grimms' fairy tale, a beautiful girl is initially appalled by a bestial male suitor but comes to love him; her love turns him into a handsome prince. Simone's supposed love for George transforms him from a crude, crass unthinking thug into a gentle, caring 'prince' with designer clothes. The twist here is that this transformation has not been performed to free Simone from the dark kingdom of Mortwell and Anderson, but for George to rescue Cathy, the object of Simone's affection. A noir twist is given to the fairy tale arc.

One of the most dominant fairy tale and structuring motifs is the mirror. The most prominent mirror in *Mona Lisa* is George's rear-view mirror which continually frames Simone. This distorted view of the mirror reflects the dissimulation of Simone and George's relationship. The framing of the mirror shot suggests da Vinci's great painting of 'La Gioconda' (1503–1506), one of the world's great beguiling women.

Mirrors in the film not only create multiple Simones (and her ability to 'glamour' mere mortals), but they also make for multiple Georges. As George descends into the London underworld (with 'In Too Deep', by Genesis, as musical accompaniment) he is constantly framed in mirrors which reflect the dilemma of George's intrepid but abhorrent search. Before his encounter with the false Cathy, he is framed in a broken mirror that presages his encounter with the shattered victims of child prostitution and drug addiction who inhabit Mortwell's parlours.

The notion of mirroring includes the doubling (or even trebling) of images. George's daughter looks remarkably like the two teenage prostitutes, the real and the fake Cathy. This physical resemblance is thematically buttressed by George's comment, while he and Simone cruise the prostitutes at King's Cross, that he has 'a daughter that age'. Furthermore, he takes both 'Cathys' out for ice cream – a not-so-innocent encounter on the one hand, and a fatherly activity on the other. The repetition of these meetings is interspersed with scenes where George walks his daughter home from school; the dichotomy between her and the two Cathys makes manifest George's emotional journey towards wholeness. He is repelled by the exploitation of children in the underground world, and this means that he must disengage himself from organised crime. It is a voyage of self-discovery – what he can tolerate and what he finds intolerable, giving George, in the end, an elevated moral stature.

Jordan has made a dark, urban version of 'Beauty and the Beast' which is centred on the Beast-figure rather than on 'Beauty', who is normally the central character in the fairy tale. Here is Maria Tatar's introduction to the tale:

'Beauty and the Beast' stands as a model for a plot rich in opportunities for expressing a woman's anxieties about marriage, but, in recent years, it has turned into a story focused on the Beast rather than on Beauty. As Marina Warner points out, 'the attraction of the wild, and of the wild brother in twentieth-century culture, cannot be overestimated; as the century advanced, in the cascade of deliberate revisions of the tale, Beauty stands in need of the Beast, rather than vice versa, and the Beast's beastliness is good, even adorable'. While eighteenth- and nineteenth-century versions of the tale celebrated the civilising power of feminine virtue and its triumph over crude animal desire, our own culture hails the Beast's heroic defiance of civilisation, with all its discontents. (1992: 29)

This could be a description of the intertextual appropriation of 'Beauty and the Beast' in *Mona Lisa*. Bob Hoskins' George, as the beast figure, with his leisure suits, lack of manners and golden heart, is aptly described as someone whose 'beastliness is good, even adorable'. If we admire George, it is in large part because of his 'heroic defiance of civilisation' in single-handedly taking on London's low-lifes. His true nobility, lurking beneath the crudity, is underscored in the way he lends himself (albeit with some confusion) to the task of locating Cathy.

To consider Simone as a purely 'Beauty' figure is problematic. She, like the 'Mona Lisa', Keats' 'La Belle Dame Sans Merci' (1884), 'Lamia' and the *femme fatale* figure, is a false beauty whose devotion to George is an illusion. Their process of mutual acclimatisation, however, is similar to the events in the tale. Beauty is initially horrified by the Beast's appearance and his stupidity, but is eventually moved by his kindness to see an inner beauty lacking in the other men in her life.

Further, the character of Simone is strongly linked to the Romantic view of the female. The idea of the diabolical beauty of the Medusa is a beauty 'tainted with pain, corruption, and death' (Praz 1956: 52). A passage from the song 'Mona Lisa' which is played many times in the film, aptly summarises Simone's difficult role:

> 'Many dreams have been brought/To your doorstep./They just lie there/And they die there./Are you warm/Are you real, Mona Lisa?/Or just a cold and lonely, lovely work of art?' (Ray Evans and Jay Livingston, 1950)

Simone represents the Romantics' attraction to the Sphinx-like beauty (half cat and half woman); she is the cold and unattainable female defined by Sacher-Masoch. The Romantics were also intrigued by the beautiful negress – the exotic, cold, dark woman. This woman becomes frigid, unfeeling, fatal and idol-like while the man pines with passion, and falls at her feet. Simone may also be compared to a vampire. Walter Pater, when writing about the unattainable dark figure says, 'like the vampire, she has been dead many times, and learned the secrets of the grave' (1998: 80). Simone 'glamours' George, but only so that she may find her lesbian lover.

The Company of Wolves and *Mona Lisa*, though very different, still share many of the same characteristics. The most interesting to contemplate is the ending of both films. I have articulated the way in which Rosaleen awakes screaming from her dream, surrounded by ravening wolves, and how her blossoming femininity is charged with ambiguity and even terror. *Mona Lisa* ends with Simone in a Brighton hotel room, having murdered Mortwell and Anderson; she looks upwards at a bright light in a contemplative pose. (The source of this light is not explained, and seems to exist for the purposes of portraiture.) She seems to ponder her action, what her fate might be and how she – who so prized her control, experience and shrewdness – has landed in this situation. Perhaps she even wonders if her rescue of Cathy was an empty action of romantic gallantry. Simone now realises that Cathy is with her because Simone can supply her with drugs. Is Cathy worth a long prison sentence and a life in tatters? (We think of how Fergus in *The Crying Game* takes the rap for Dil, and is incarcerated for at least eight years.) George, on the other hand, joins hands with Thomas and his daughter, and they begin to skip along a path, arm in arm. Even in a fairy tale world there are consequences that impact upon one's actions. It seems that no fairy or magic wand will help Rosaleen or Simone. Both female characters have experienced a catastrophic or untenable journey into the unknown, whereas George can skip off into the sunset.

It is not difficult to understand how Jordan views these women. I think he is sympathetic not only to Rosaleen and Simone, but also to what women in general must endure to exist in contemporary society. How can they save themselves from calamity? He clearly cares about these 'women in peril' as evidenced by their centrality in his filmmaking. His sympathy is at times complex and full of ambiguity, but nonetheless represents a facet of his filmmaking that has largely been misunderstood or at best probed superficially. It would be difficult to read his stories and scripts and not conclude that much of Jordan's art is deeply concerned with what it means to be a woman in the modern world. The director's stance regarding women is much the same as his attitude towards men. He is open to the myriad possibilities and shifting of identity that is represented by all of his characters, both male and female.

CHAPTER FIVE

Neil Jordan, Author: 'The Ache for Aliveness'

The Miracle and fiction writing: Oedipus Wrecks

'Jordan sees liberation and the flight of the circus animals as the release and not the diminishment of creative energies. However, like Yeats [*The Circus Animals' Desertion*], his use of the image is multilayered and includes the strange creatures of the imagination, the dark powers that would repress them, and the responses of the artist to both. Because of that complexity, their release is a beautiful and terrifying fantasy brought to life as well as a metaphor for the richness of the heart's liberation.'

– Kathleen Gallagher Winarski

After working in North America on two films, *High Spirits* (1988) and *We're No Angels* (1989), Neil Jordan returned to Ireland to regroup. *High Spirits*, starring Peter O'Toole in a hilariously overripe performance, was meant to be a light comedy/farce about the drunken owner of a run-down Irish castle, who, in order to salvage the family home, opens it to tourists as a haunted house. Jordan was met with great resistance by the studio, Tri-Star, who wanted 'to turn it into a silly, frenetic teenage comedy which centred on the American characters'. Jordan said, with admirable diplomacy: 'The casting of the male lead, played by Steve Guttenberg, was not really my first choice' (in Jackson 1991: 19). The studio vetoed the delicate and loving irony, as well as the fun Jordan had with the entertaining and hoary tales of Auld Ireland that American tourists expect. Eventually, the film was taken out of Jordan's hands, scenes were re-shot and the film greatly altered. The critic Pauline Kael asked Jordan if she could see 'the director's cut' to which he replied, 'What director's cut? There isn't one ... I was involved with these producers from hell' (in Falsetto 2000: 234). The filmmaker insists his version is in a vault somewhere. This discouraging event was followed by the only film Jordan made as a director-for-hire, from a script written by David Mamet, again for a major studio. He discusses the directing and writing aspect of the film:

> That kind of collaborative process didn't, and doesn't, appeal to me at all. The only reason I used the script for *We're No Angels* was because I admire David so much. But I wouldn't do anybody else's script.[1] Even though I know, from experience, that writing films on your own makes you lead a miserable exist- ence and does lead to cancer, I'm sure ... I had extensive arguments with Sean Penn. But then he argues with everybody. You just beat your head off that guy. He's a very good actor but he's 'professionally difficult'. (In Jackson 1991: 19)

Following these somewhat unsettling experiences, Jordan returned to Dublin. As Jordan explains, 'I made *The Miracle* to my own satisfaction ... When you make films, I think you should tell an audience what you feel' (in Thomson 1990/91: 8).

The story follows two teenagers around a seaside summer resort as they fabricate stories about the people they see walking on the promenade. Their language is playful and imaginative and outstrips their experience of life. The teenagers are played by two 15-year-old first-time actors, Niall Byrne as Jimmy and Lorraine Pilkington as Rose. They were chosen from amongst 300 school children in the Dublin area. The cast was rounded out by Donal McCann who plays Jimmy's alcoholic musician father, Sam, and Beverly D'Angelo, as Renée, an American actor starring in a third-rate musical production of *Destry Rides Again* in Dublin. Jimmy and Rose are intrigued by Renée, and begin following her about, making up stories about her past. Jimmy, beset by the agony of his raging adolescent hormones, becomes obsessed by Renée.

Jordan returns to very familiar territory in *The Miracle*. In many ways, the film represents a variation on the director's award-winning collection of short stories, *Night in Tunisia*, and his other works of fiction. The title story is echoed thematically in *The Miracle*; it is a story about a musician father at odds with the son who rejects any over- tures his father might extend.[2] As in *The Miracle*, the father would like his son to play in his band, which the boy reluctantly does for an evening. Jordan's fascination with the family romance and jazz are both found in *Night in Tunisia*, as is his preoccupation with budding adolescent love and most especially, their concupiscence.

In the following passage from Jordan's story, the father and son relationship is given particular depth and exploration, echoing Jordan's concerns in cinema:

> He would occasionally look and catch that look in his listening eyes, wry, sad and loving, his pleasure at how his son played only marred by the knowledge of how little it meant to him. And would catch the look in his father's eyes

and get annoyed and deliberately hit a bum note to spoil it. And the sadness in the eyes would outshine the wryness then and he would be sorry, but never sorry enough. (1980b: 48)

The father/son breach is given a succinct treatment in the story. Not unexpectedly, Jordan's own father may have provided at least some of the substance and inspiration for the director's work. He was an 'educationist', a teacher and mathematician who seems to have been fairly strict with his son. He limited the film-going of the cinema-struck Jordan *fils*, and forbade the reading of comic books. (Although he had his own private stash of comics.) Another convergence between Jordan's life and the story is that he and his father would play music together. Jordan played classical guitar while his father played the violin. Jordan is characteristically reticent when discussing his father, although he admits that he 'naturally' went against his father's wishes by refusing a career in teaching. (Jordan taught for eight years, and loathed it.) The father's frustration with his son's wasted talent is expressed in *Night in Tunisia*, and echoed in *The Miracle*:

> When he had finished he got up from the table and idly pressed a few notes on the piano.
> 'Why do you play that,' his father asked. He was still at the table, between mouthfuls.
> 'I don't know,' he said.
> 'What galls me,' said his father, 'is that you could be good.'
> He played a bit more of the idiotic tune that he didn't know why he played.
> 'If you'd let me teach you,' his father said, 'you'd be glad later on.'
> 'Then why not wait till later and teach me then.'
> 'Because you're young, you're at the age. You'll never learn as well as now, if you let me teach you. You'll never feel things like you do now.'
> He began to play again in defiance and then stopped.
> 'I'll pay you,' his father said. (1980b: 59)

The exasperation of the father in *The Miracle* resonates in this passage from the story. There is even a repetition in the film of the line 'What galls me is that you could be good.'

The densely poetic details of Jordan's writing are difficult to capture in film as this passage from another story in *Night in Tunisia*, 'Skin', makes clear. It is a story about a bored housewife. 'A housewife approaching middle-age. The expected listlessness about the features. The vacuity that suburban dwelling imposes, the same vacuity that most likely inhabited the house next door' (1980b: 52). She reads about Swedish housewives who mollify their boredom by driving to places in the country for trysts with strangers. The woman acts upon her fantasies by driving to a secluded area near the sea. A man parks his car nearby. The banality of the subject is conquered by Jordan's eloquent and deeply expressive writing:

But the sea must have touched her core with its irrational ceaseless surging. For what she did then was to turn back, back to the sea, picking high delicate steps through its depths, thinking: He sees me. He sees my legs, my tucked-up skirt, the outlines of my waist clearly through the salt-wet fabric. He is more excited than I am, being a man. And there was this pounding, pounding through her body, saying: This is what the sea means, what it all must mean. And she stood still, the sea tickling her groin, her eyes fixed on the distant tanker, so far-off that its smokestack seemed a brush stroke on the sky, its shape that of a flat cardboard cut-out. Around it the sea's million dulled glimmering mirrors. (1980b: 56)

This passage illustrates not only Jordan's romance with the sea, but it speaks to a more universal and mythic foundational core, relating to Yeats' construct of the *anima mundi*. The same story contains the following passage:

Her tweed walking coat was hanging in the alcove. Outside, rows of starlings laced the telegraph-wires. Motionless black spearheads, occasionally breaking into restless wheeling flights, to return again to their rigid formations. The same expectant stasis in her, her drumming fingers, like fluttering wings. She was a starling. The sudden, unconscious burst of disquiet. The animal memory of a home more vibrant, more total than this. The origin-track; the ache for aliveness. (1980b: 54)

The woman's characterisation as a bird and the reference to the 'animal memory' impels the story towards a more profound dimension. The housewife is released from the conventional banalities of her life and is situated, if only briefly, in the realm of the collective unconscious.

One is reminded of James Joyce in the carefully described poetic imagery as well as in the melancholic strain of Jordan's writing. Joyce's thirst for inventive possibilities of existence as well as his concern for the writing process are shared by Jordan. Jordan creates poetic effects in his films through a synergy of sound (dialogue and music), visual images and performance. The dream-like atmosphere in his films can be likened to the lyricism of his fiction, which in turn strongly invokes Joyce's conception of 'nighttime consciousness' versus 'daytime consciousness'. The following paragraph from *Night in Tunisia* illustrates how unfilmable the language of fiction can be:

He played later on the piano in the clubhouse with the dud notes, all the songs, the trivial mythologies whose significance he had never questioned. It was as if he was fingering through his years and as he played he began to forget the melodies of all those goodbyes and heartaches, letting his fingers take him where they wanted to, trying to imitate that sound like a river he had just heard. It had got dark without him noticing and when finally he could just see the keys as question-marks in the dark, he stopped. (1980b: 43)

One also finds in Jordan's early stories, and 'The Last Rites' in particular, the polysemia of postmodern fiction, the shifting amongst a variety of points of view. The story is about a young labourer who goes to his local bathhouse to commit suicide. The narrational perspectives are shared amongst a foreman in an asbestos factory, an old cockney, 'a young Trinidadian', as well as the young man (1980b: 12–13). We also witness significant changes of point of view (as well as temporality) in the stories within stories as in *The Company of Wolves*, *Interview with the Vampire*, *The Butcher Boy*, *The End of the Affair* and *Breakfast on Pluto*.

'Sand', another story in the compilation of *Night in Tunisia* features the confusion and agitation churning around gender and adolescent physiological changes. Accompanied by the hormonal mayhem of youth, a young boy founders in moral quicksand, as does Jimmy in *The Miracle*. The story is once again set in a seaside resort town. A boy swaps with an itinerant tinker – if he can ride the tinker's donkey, he will allow the tinker sexual access to his older sister. It is one of Jordan's strengths that he is able to capture the sinuosity of the real world and elevate it through poetry. This passage from 'Sand' exemplifies this poetic dimension:

> She was crying, great breathful sobs. 'You won't,' he asked. 'I will,' she said, 'I'll tell it all.' The boy knew, however, that she would be ashamed. He picked up her towel and her suntan lotion and began to walk. He had forgotten about his hate. He was thinking of the donkey and the tinker's flaking palms and his sister's breasts. After a while he turned. 'Stop crying, will you. Nothing happened, did it?' His hands were wet with the donkey's saliva and to the saliva a fine film of sand was clinging. When he moved his hand it rustled, whispered and sang. (1980b: 31)

The homoerotic sexuality one finds in Jordan's films (for example, *The Crying Game*, *Interview with the Vampire*, *Michael Collins*, *The Butcher Boy* in the form of the paedophile priest, and certainly in *Breakfast on Pluto*) finds its way into 'Seduction':

> I fell into the water again and I felt his arms around my waist, tightening, the way boys wrestle, but more quietly then, and I felt his body not small any longer, pressing against mine. I heard him say 'this is the way lovers do it' and felt his mouth on my neck but I didn't struggle. I knew that in the water he couldn't see my tears or see my smile. (1980b: 51)

Jordan's unabashed interest in the homoerotic is a signal aspect of both his films and fiction. As is true of many artists, Jordan likes to explore his wild side and investigate the imaginative possibilities of sexual couplings. In this one is reminded of Yeats' fascination with decadence, 'which could incorporate any amount of ostentatiously extreme political, religious, sexual and aesthetic attitudinising … the age found a concept and implied way of life so disturbing that it brought the decade to its strange crisis in the trial and conviction of Oscar Wilde for sodomy in 1895' (Brown 1999: 58–9).

The enduring themes of Jordan's written fiction and filmed work invoke characters who are haunted by loss, sorrow and loneliness. This same sort of melancholy arises in the most autobiographical of Jordan's fiction, *Sunrise with Sea Monster* (changed for North America from the more appropriate, but less titillating European title, *Nightlines*), and is coupled in this book with another of Jordan's fixations – older women. In the book, Donal, who falls in love with his piano teacher, Rose, is in his mid-teens; she is at least ten years older:

> She came regularly, on Tuesdays and on Thursdays … There were no rings on her fingers, which I knew was significant. Much more significant was the smell of her hair as it brushed off my cheeks, the feel of her breasts pushing into the small of my back. There was an eroticism there that was undefined, which I would always connect with the stark glory of a Bach prelude, which even now I could not call desire. It gave me balance and poise, completed me, or more properly, completed the house. That cold structure on the edge of the Irish Sea seemed warmer for it. I allowed myself to wonder would my mother have been like this, had she lived. (1995: 33)

The characters in *Sunrise with Sea Monster* seem to acquiesce in their sexual coupling without a sense of sinfulness or remorse. They relish the constant danger of discovery and even court it.

> So God expressed Himself as always, through silences. I came to accept them after a while, came to enjoy them, even: the pregnant silence between phrases of music, the occasional hush of her voice and now and then, as before, but infinitely more nostalgic, the feel of her hands on mine when she came to correct me. We came to relish our status as sinners, the melancholy of the truly damned. (1995: 50)

Rose marries Donal's father, and she continues her affair with her step-son. This sexual triangulation and transgressive Oedipal relationship within the family are common to many of Jordan's writings, and can be witnessed in *The Miracle* in the relationship of Renée, Jimmy and Sam (Donal McCann). In *Sunrise with Sea Monster*, the triadic sexual relationship between Rose, the son and the father cannot survive the death of one of the participants, the father. In the final analysis, and here the kinship with *The Miracle* is strongly articulated, *Sunrise with Sea Monster* is as much about the father and son relationship as anything else. Jordan writes:

> A silence settled between us that we knew was permanent. At night I dreamt of him, traversing the waves of the Clare coastline like a merman, in an element that perhaps would have suited him more than most. Rose slept beside me, frozen in her loss, her body stiff and unattainable. Now that he was gone he was all she could desire, and I was the cause of the absence that gnawed at her, as she was of the absence that gnawed at me. (1995: 173)

Returning to the collection, *Night in Tunisia*, the relationship with a much older lover achieves a special poignancy in 'A Love', in which the woman is suffering from cancer. (This situation is replayed as well in *The Past*.)

> I went behind you up the stairs. Your breathing was so heavy that it sang in my ears. And then we were in the room and it was so bare, there were two beds, a wash-hand basin, a Virgin and a cinema poster, so seductively bare. You asked me to turn while you undressed. My face must have shown my surprise because before I could answer you turned. And I watched you, I saw your clothes form a little heap around your feet, I saw your shoulders that were very thin and your waist that was almost fat now and your buttocks and your legs. And your skin told me you were definitely older. When you were in your nightgown you turned. 'Come on', you said.
>
> There was a knowledge burning through both of us, it was like the yearning that had been there years before, a secret, like blood. But it wasn't a yearning, it was a question and an answer. You knew that with every garment you took off you were stepping into a past self, a self that had that yearning and you could see from my face that I knew too. 'Come on', you said again.
>
> And I took off my clothes and I wore the nakedness I had worn for you, I was a boy then, and I took off your nightdress so you could wear it too.
>
> I didn't look at you, I put my arms around you, standing there, both of us were breathing, our chests touching. You stepped backwards towards the bed. 'Come on', you said. (1980b : 12–13)

The rhythmical repetition of the phrase 'Come on' structures the passage, and shows the great extent to which Jordan's fiction partakes of poetry. The observations of his lover's body, the delicacy with which he describes both her physical being and her shame in it, and her dormant but aroused longings for the lost something that sorrowfully can never be lived again are quite heartbreaking.

In 'Seduction', two prepubescent boys teem with sexual wonderment and excitement counterpoised by repulsion in the swirling vortex of hormonal aggression. The boys are fascinated by Leanche, whose voluptuous figure elicits glances from both men and boys. Leanche is also a 'loose woman' which greatly adds to her allure – from a distance. The character of Renée in *The Miracle* echoes this 'type'; she has no qualms about exhibiting herself for Jimmy's pleasure as she undresses for a frolic in the sea. She has a blasé, sophisticated and urbane attitude that stimulates Jimmy. Renée allows Jimmy into her dressing room, only to tease him by telling him to avert his eyes (a command he ignores), while she undresses.

With the idea of Renée's 'to-be-looked-at-ness' we see a favourite feature of Jordan's *mise-en-scène*, the mirror. There are at least six mirror shots in the film, most involving Renée framed in her dressing room mirror, in the great tradition of similar shots of stage divas in *Morocco* (1930), *All About Eve* (1950), *Opening Night* (1977) and *Todo sobre mi madre* (*All About My Mother*, 1999); these shots seem to speak not simply to the vanity of the characters, but also to troubled issues regarding their affective relationships and sense of identity. (We think of the stepmother in *Snow White* and her invocation, 'Mirror, mirror on the wall', made darkly manifest in *In Dreams*.) Many of these shots revolve around moments of character introspection, as Renée contemplates the harm that her desertion has wrought on the family. She says at one point that she ran off in order to find fame and fortune, and the doubling and isolation of her in the mirror shots as she applies or removes her character's gawdy make-up, enact a commentary on what she has found – an unfulfilling life of mediocrity and loneliness.

The most interesting use of mirrors in the film occurs in a scene in which Jimmy takes Renée into a fun-house of mirrors. This scene comes right before the sequence in which Jimmy accompanies Renée as she sings 'Stardust', and what we see is a conflation, in Renée's consciousness, of Jimmy and Sam. As she enters the hall, Renée looks for Jimmy. The next shot is a split-screen with three frames; one frame contains Jimmy, Renée is in another, and a dark figure who turns out (questionably) to be Sam is in the third. Renée is stunned to see her former lover, and abruptly exits the hall. Sam may or may not have been the figure in the hall; he is not aware at this point that Renée has returned. Renée may have only fantasised Sam's presence. This mirror sequence also establishes the film's primary doubling, father and son; it is a doubling that exasperates Jimmy, who in good Oedipal fashion initially perceives his father as a sexual rival for the woman he does not yet know is his mother. The tension between father and son can be viewed not only as a product of teenage angst, but as the hatred that only the double can inspire in a person. This scene provides an excellent example of Jordan's writing strategies as a screenwriter.

The hallucinatory image that Renée has of Sam is matched by the film's three dream sequences. Jordan views the dreamwork as essential to the characterisation, it 'is when the characters speak to themselves. They dream the truth before they understand it', as he points out in the press kit for *The Miracle*. In order to convey this cinematically, Jordan takes a somewhat oppositional approach to the more traditional representations of dreams in cinema. He filmed the movie's 'real' events slightly back-lit, using filters, and the dreams rather harshly to do the reverse of what one might expect, that is, disavow their oneiric quality. The first of Jimmy's dreams is one in which he fishes and makes a catch, only to find it is his father snagged on the fish hook, with terrified open eyes. In the next dream we see Renée dressed as a trapeze artist, while Jimmy holds her climbing rope. There is a cut to a burning photo of Sam, then a cut back to the circus. A shot of the flames licking Sam's body are intercut with Renée as she descends the rope. Sam is shown dead on the floor, his eyes staring (much like the fish in the first dream), and in the final circus image Renée and Jimmy stand together triumphantly. Maria Pramaggiore writes interestingly about this: '[Jimmy] has experienced the lack of a mother his entire life, yet when he discovers near the film's conclusion that Renée is his mother, he learns a new register of loss, the loss of a mother who is not dead. He must, in a sense, improvise the Oedipal conflict through that configuration' (1998: 285–6). In the final dream sequence – all of the dreams are Jimmy's subjective imaginings – curtains open to reveal Renée and Sam dressed in circus costumes, standing on either side of an elephant, their hands raised in jubilation. I would claim that this

Jimmy (Niall Byrne) and Sam (Donal McCann) captured during a momentary cease-fire in their stormy relationship

dream imagery presages Jimmy's acceptance of his origins; originary notions – where and who does one come from – are crucial to Jordan's work.

In *The Miracle* Jordan is also seizing upon issues of masculinity, as he does in many of his films. 'What is particularly Irish about *The Miracle* is that it deals with a specifically Irish kind of failure to understand women on the part of men. It grapples with the inarticulacy that the male character needs in order to keep going' (*The Miracle* press kit). It is Sam's 'performance' as a father and a lover that remains questionable. Kathleen Gallagher Winarski says: 'In spite of his drinking he has raised a son to be proud of ... and saves his son from a life like his. He hated his wife because the other thing, love, was too difficult. Things will be different for Jimmy; he and his father can now talk of love and hate and his beautiful mother' (1999: 106). This statement does not seem accurate to me; it is an overly optimistic assessment of the situation. The characters still have difficulty communicating with one another over the issues of friendship, love, parental concern, conflict and lust. They are things the characters try to talk about, but seem doomed to be eternally misunderstood.

Performance is one way the characters manage a degree of communication in *The Miracle*, but as with the other expressive elements of the film, the roles are often garbled, misperceived or indecipherable. Jimmy is probably the most complex example of the multifarious performances in the film. He plays with his father's band (under duress), but cannot abide the sort of middle-aged audience that he plays for; he is angry that the audience does not listen to him. Jimmy also acts out his sexual aggression with Renée, when he bullies and pushes her as he tries to comprehend who she is and her role in his life. It is unclear whether he and Renée actually consummate their relationship. When they are found together on the beach they raise themselves up and brush off sand. We might imagine that there could have been some sort of sexual congress, but the film remains silent about this issue. Some who have written on the film have taken the sexual consummation as a given: 'Arguably the real miracle is that Jimmy despite the trauma of losing his mother, having her miraculously reborn and then raping her … becomes an emotionally complete person' (Rockett & Rockett 2003: 116). Renée's complications as a performer are almost equal to Jimmy's. She is an American in Dublin playing a role in a theatrical adaptation of the film *Destry Rides Again* (1939), which had starred Marlene Dietrich. It is a reminder of her failure to belong to Jimmy and Sam's world. Renée is obviously attracted to Jimmy, but whether she sees herself in the role of a mother or lover is unclear. In the musical she takes a bullet for her lover, but this act of selflessness only points up the fact that she has never behaved unselfishly with her abandoned lover and son.

Renée is confused about what role to play with Jimmy; there is a strong push-pull element to their relationship. The meaning of the words 'mother' and 'lover' seem to confound Renée. She appears to be used to male attentions, and has difficulty refraining from flirtatious, come-hither conduct. Beneath this superficial behaviour, however, is a maelstrom of conflicted feelings. Is she attracted to Jimmy because of her maternal feelings for him? Or as she nears her forties, is she flattered by the attentions of a young boy? Is she displacing her love for Sam onto their son? These issues remain unresolved in the film, but they undoubtedly ratchet up the film's erotic tensions.

Sam makes his living as a performer of old standards, in a shabby seaside cabaret, but this only mirrors the bankruptcy of his role as a father. He would like to care for Jimmy, and does in certain moments, but their roles are reversed by Sam's alcoholism. Rose's performance is more light-hearted but, nonetheless, complicated. Clearly she loves Jimmy, but displaces her affection onto her performance as a storyteller: 'Too friendly to be lovers, too close to be friends, they lived in that twilight zone.' Because she cannot achieve gratification from her relationship with Jimmy (and the narrative pays less and less attention to her as he becomes obsessed with Renée), she devises a scheme to inveigle the Russian animal tamer of the visiting circus into a sexual relationship, in order to steal the keys to the animal cages. Rose also seeks affirmation of herself as an attractive, sexual woman. As each character becomes more confused by his or her role, they eventually rewrite them in order to free themselves from the uncomfortable confines of their characters' performances. The four characters are released to reinvent their roles, and rewrite a new ending to 'an old story'. Just as Rose lets the circus animals out of their cages, so must each of the characters find a way to liberate themselves from their assigned roles.

Jordan here deals with the contemporary family as divided, a place where things are in a state of deterioration. He says: 'I had the idea of using incest as an expression of rupture within a family, a prism where different aspects of what that implies are explored: mother-love, jealousy, sexual attraction' (*The Miracle* press kit).

As well as using fairy tale tropes and thematics in his films, Jordan is concerned with the construction of fairy tales, and the ways in which our response is activated by storytelling. He investigates the possibility of a discursive relationship with the representations in fairy tales and their remodelling in modern narrative forms.

There are two fairy tales that are especially important to *The Miracle*, and one of these is 'Donkeyskin' or 'Alleiruah'. Maria Tatar relates these two tales to the Cinderella story, but they travel in a somewhat different thematic direction than the classic versions of the story. Unlike 'Cinderella', where the villain is the wicked stepmother and the villainous trait is jealousy, in this variant group the villain is the father and the trait is incestuous desire. Here the father/king, after losing his queen, is sworn by his dying widow not to marry unless he finds a mate as attractive as she. The father subsequently loses his senses, falls in love with his beautiful daughter who so closely resembles her mother, and demands her hand in marriage. The daughter then sets conditions to be met before she will consent, conditions which she hopes will prove impossible. Eventually the father fulfils even the most extreme wishes; in the case of the two tales cited he must provide a fur coat either made from a donkey who excretes gold, or a coat made from every animal in the kingdom. He delivers the items and demands an immediate wedding. The princess runs away and becomes a scullery maid in another kingdom, undergoes a Cinderella transformation, and eventually marries the prince and lives happily ever after.

The most obvious link between these tales and *The Miracle* has to do with incestuous desire, most prominently that of Jimmy for Renée. In the Grimms' version of the story ('Alleiruah') the king's desire for his daughter is caused by a hallucinatory misrecognition of the daughter as the mother/wife. This taboo erotic misperception is the crux of the film's narrative and we remain in continual suspense as to when Jimmy will discover that Renée is his mother. But Jimmy's confusion is also apparent in Renée who sees a lot of her old lover in Jimmy and projects her desire for her old flame onto her son. This is apparent specifically during the 'Stardust' performance. After the performance, Renée, in a close embrace with Jimmy, asks him where he learned the song. He replies that his father taught him. The implication is that this was 'their song' in the halcyon days when Jimmy was conceived. Jimmy then asks her if he played the song well, and she whispers, 'too well'. It seems for a moment that Renée, like the king in 'Alleiruah', is conflating her past love and their child. The lyrics of 'Stardust' add another layer of meaning to the scene: 'Words fail, to tell a tale/Too exotic to be told/ Each nights a deeper night/In a world, ages old.'

Incestuous love is the old, old song too exotic to be told. In recasting taboos from father/daughter desire to mother/son desire, Jordan is exploring untrammelled territory in fairy lore. In discussing taboos in the tales, Tatar points out that 'there are virtually no male counterparts to "Donkeyskin" (mother/son incest seems to resist representation in folklore)' (1992: 106). Jordan is thus exploring a dark recess of the mind that has not been substantially addressed in thousands of years of folklore and fairy tales, although Oedipus is an obvious exception. Much of the film's discomfort factor can thus be understood as a sort of visceral reaction to this taboo representation. Tatar explains at least some of the reasons for the embarrassment one feels reading these tales, and by extension watching *The Miracle*:

> When interest in psychological realism is at work in the mind of the receiver
> of traditional folklore, the proposed marriage of a father/daughter becomes

too hard to accept. But it is only too hard to accept because it belongs to a different order of reality/fantasy from the 'Donkeyskin' disguise or the gold excrement of the other magical motifs: because it is not impossible, because it could actually happen, and is known to have done so. It is when fairy tales coincide with experience that they begin to suffer from censoring, rather than the other way around. (1992: 104)

Similarly, Jordan not only adopts fairy tale rhetoric that looks closely at human taboos regarding incest, he compounds the discomfort of it all by substituting an even more un-representable taboo – mother/son coupling. In this scenario we get a painful story of recognition, with its climax in Jimmy's faux rape, in his attempt to extort the truth from Renée. Jordan constantly crosses boundaries, and has always been drawn to imaginative extremes in human experience.

The second important fairy tale is, once more, 'Beauty and the Beast', which is appropriated in a somewhat tongue-in-cheek manner in the subplot of Rose and her animal trainer beau. Throughout this 'romance' Rose makes comments about her project of making the beast, a Russian animal trainer, human through her love: when this relationship is consummated, the beast is literally released from its cage; in fact many beasts are released from their cages. This is no deep appropriation here; the tale is used to script a running gag in the film. This is a character-driven film that never really settles on an overarching tone, so Rose's romance can be seen as a humorous take on 'Beauty and the Beast' or as a desperate attempt to get Jimmy's attention, or both.

While Jimmy, confused and upset, sits in a church, an elephant walks into the frame and immediately alleviates the sombre tone. A parade of animals stride along the beach promenade, with Jimmy leading the elephant. (The parade of animals was originally supposed to be part of *The Company of Wolves*.) It is quite a Felliniesque moment, and also a miraculous one. Frye in *Anatomy of Criticism* makes the point that tragedies end in isolation, while comedies end in integration. One feels as Jimmy joins the parade that he has achieved a measure of acceptance vis-à-vis his mother. He is no longer disengaged from the world by a state of angst. As Kathleen Gallagher Winarski says,

The Miracle is not about the abandonment of religion and community, but it is about the need to be free from the beasts of respectability. In Jordan's world, worse than uncontrollable passions are the beasts of conformity and repression. The final miracle is, of course, the film itself. Jordan brings to his lost paradise all the beauty, the pain, and the wisdom of life itself. (1999: 107)

The poetics of point of view: The Butcher Boy

'It'll be a bitter for this town if the world comes to an end.'
– Mrs Coyle (Jordan/McCabe script 1996b, draft: 64.)

'All the beautiful things are gone.'
– Francie Brady (Jordan/McCabe script 1996b, draft: 71)

There is a potent interface between the work of filmmaker Jordan and novelist Patrick McCabe. *The Butcher Boy* would present a particular attraction for Jordan, conceptualised as it is in the Ireland of the 1950s and early 1960s, the period in which Jordan grew up, a time governed by the paranoiac A-Bomb and anti-Communist hysteria. The repressive, largely rural, smalltown milieu characterised the era. It was a time when mysticism still paralysed much of the country, and many amongst the Irish remained in thrall to archaic religious beliefs and superstitions. In this vein, Jordan has said of his films, 'The constant concern is to do with realistic and surrealistic explanations of human behaviour and whether human beings answer to rational modes of thought or are inspired by things quite irrational and unknown to themselves' (in McIlroy 1986: 108).

We turn now to an examination of Jordan's inspired use of point of view and voice-over. The tools of narratology serve to describe the shifting registers created by the voice-over and the slippery and potentially unreliable ways in which characterisation is mobilised by the perspective of a pre-adolescent boy.

McCabe's creation of Francie Brady, in all his extravagant aberrance, harmonises perfectly with Jordan's continual interrogation of the limits and necessity of human reason. McCabe, who has been appointed the 'high priest of rural Irish dementia' (Lacey 1998: 50), shares Jordan's worldview in his concern for the liminal states between rationality and unbalance, and what the novelist terms the 'social fantastic' (FitzSimon 1998: 176). In essence, both Jordan and McCabe are extremely interested in exploring what it means to be human in this world, the contrast between what Northrop Frye would call the world of innocence and experience and with rhythm in

Renée (Beverly D'Angelo) and Jimmy grapple with an attraction that tests the limits of their mother/son relationship

the visual, aural and verbal sense. Jordan has been characterised on various occasions as a filmmaker who 'translate[s] jazz into film style' (Pramaggiore 1998: 274). McCabe is well-known (as is Jordan) for his concern with the rhythms of language. In the novelist's words: 'you see, the things that people say, ordinary human exchange, you know. "Not a bad day", "is surely", "how's it goin", all this kind of stuff that you hear, the rhythm of it, it's actually quite fascinating' (in FitzSimon 1998: 186). Both Jordan and McCabe are musicians, and the latter unabashedly admits the influence of Jordan's title story in *Night in Tunisia* on *The Butcher Boy* in terms of the father/son relationship, the importance of music in the household and the significance of the natural world (see FitzSimon 1998: 176). Beyond merely categorising the similarities between the two artists, or focusing on the various strategies that are typically utilised in adaptation (for example, compression and simplification of narrative events; the concentration of sympathy on the main character; the deletion or reduction of the roles of secondary characters, and so forth), I want to address the ways in which Jordan has reconfigured McCabe's prose style in filmic terms, his dexterous and creative use of narrative voice and vision to give expression to the feelings, thoughts and sensations of the protaganist, Francie Brady (Eamonn Owens in a phenomenal performance for a non-professional actor).

Jordan articulates Francie's consciousness through the device of the voice-over of the older Francie (Stephen Rea), which begins: 'When I was a young lad, twenty or thirty or forty years ago, I lived in a small town where they were all after me on account of what I'd done on Mrs Nugent.' The older Francie speaks from the 'Garage for Bad Bastards', evidently an institution for the criminally insane. The flashback structure serves to create two distinct vantage points (and more, as I will explain later), permitting the viewer complex access to the character of Francie, both as an older man and as the young boy around whom the story revolves. A closer examination of the voice-over reveals the numerous strategies that manifest Francie's perceptions. This following passage occurs directly after Annie/Ma (Aisling O'Sullivan) has returned home, having been institutionalised with a nervous breakdown:

> Back from the garage there was no holding Ma, talking nineteen to the dozen, whiz here one minute there the next and hadn't she bought the bogman record we heard playing in the café. And that's when the buns began. Uncle Alo was comin' home from his big job in London for Christmas. And the house started filling up with cakes and buns for the Christmas party. Cakes cakes cakes! Buns buns buns! My Ma was the bun woman.

In an ironic counterpoint to Francie's blithe narration, the sounds and images in this scene tell a very different and much more melancholy story of a desperately unhappy marriage. It is important to note that this scene follows shortly after Ma's attempted suicide, characterised by its anxious and sombre tone. The music that accompanies the suicide scene is mournful, and there is no ironic narration to distance us from Ma's desperate state of mind. It is a good example of the way in which Jordan has structured the film to keep the spectator off balance. As Jordan says, 'A rhythm was established in the telling of the story and the balance between the laughter and the horror gets faster and faster towards the end of the movie, so by the end you're horrified one second and you're laughing the next' (in Falsetto 2000: 251). On the soundtrack we hear the traditional ballad 'The Butcher Boy' playing, as the camera pans down the sleeve of the record on which the title 'Regular Irish' is displayed, accompanied by a sketch of a 'typical' Irish father and son, emphasising the De Valerian image of an Ireland of 'near Edenic wholeness, and stable family values' (Herron 2000: 176). As Ma maniacally whisks her pastry batter the camera reveals dozens and dozens of buns and cakes on every surface of the kitchen.

The voice-over continues: 'Well if I heard that "Butcher Boy" once, I heard it a hundred times, and if you said to me "would you like to hear it again?" I know what I would have said – "no thank you!"' The image track shows Francie lying upstairs in his bed, staring at the ceiling, his expression remote and dispirited. We (and Francie) hear the sounds of crockery breaking, as Ma and Benny/Da (Stephen Rea) engage in a heated war of words. The next shot shows Francie gingerly threading his way through the marital battleground of shattered plates and pulverised cakes. In the foreground, Benny, in an alcoholic stupor, assumes his customary supine position. 'The Butcher Boy' continues to play as the record revolves on a turntable littered with demolished pastries. The voice (Sinéad O'Connor) plaintively sings the words of the ballad, 'I wish I were a maid again/But a maid again I'll never be', addressing Ma's feelings of regret and despondency in her dismal and ultimately doomed marriage and life.

In this passage the voice-over functions in several ways. The elder Francie's voice-over creates a gap between his account of the events and circumstances as they are recorded by other aspects of the film's discourse. The voice-over declines to mention his parents' emotionally pitched dispute, his mother's distressing conduct or his father's state of inebriation. The older Francie, who is responsible for the voice-over, speaks the words as if he were the child in the depicted fiction. He has learned, as children in abusive homes often do, to live in an unhealthy state of denial; he must psychically accommodate himself to survive the bruising emotional landscape in which he resides. The lack of emotional sustenance or connectedness condemns Francie to a life where cruelty and mayhem are the most conspicuous characteristics. This is an example in which the voice-over conflicts with the fictional world created by Jordan's *mise-en-scène*, the intensity of the embattled couple's unceasing quarrel, the literal and figurative messiness of their lives, and the oppression and helplessness Francie experiences in the face of this chaotic world.

The scene shifts to the Christmas party, where Da is found, sodden again, barely able to raise himself out of his chair. Da is a mean drunk, incapable of tolerating the fugitive moments of happiness experienced by his friends and family. Da's rage inevitably detonates, as he lashes out at his brother, Alo (Ian Hart). Ma tries in vain to quell the tempest, but instead steers the scene from contentious words to physical violence. Da strikes his wife, whereupon the argument escalates. The camera pulls into a photo of Annie and Benny as young lovers, offering visible proof that happy times once existed for the couple. The reliability of this cinematic gesture is called into question and made ironic when it is disclosed that Da, even on his honeymoon, had to be dragged out of pubs, and treated his wife 'no better than a pig'. Thus the articulation of the narrative becomes like a series of Borges-like Chinese boxes in its ambiguity, much like the narrative structure found in *The Company of Wolves*. The voice-over continues:

> It was a grand party but to tell you the truth I was getting a bit tired. Singing's alright. Singing's grand but I think five 'Beautiful Bundorans' is enough for me thank you, not to mention two 'Old Bog Roads' and one 'Never Do a Tango with an Eskimo'. But sure you might as well be talking to the wall as trying to tell them it was time for bed.

Once his mother has been physically brutalised, the narrating Francie speaks: 'Ahem. Excuse me. Ah yes. It's me, Francie. I do believe I shall be off to Slumberdown Mansions if you please. I've had a rather long day, begging your pardon.' The fighting continues, and the voice-over says:

> Yes – I do believe I shall be off on my travels. Excuse me but did you happen to see Mr Francis Brady by any chance? I'm sorry old bean but I really wouldn't know. I hope he's not going travelling through the wastes of space and time with Algernon Carruthers.

Here we witness Francie as he retreats to Slumberdown Mansions in the face of domestic carnage into one of the many personae he adopts during the course of the film.

In a distinctly postmodern gambit, the world of Francie's consciousness is exhibited, beginning with the opening credit sequence. It is set to a version of 'Mack the Knife', a cracking steel guitar instrumental by Santo and Johnny (which was in turn cannibalised from the Brecht/Weill 1928 musical *Die Drei Groschenoper* (*The Threepenny Opera*), played over a pastiche of comic book superheroes poised for action intercut with graphic sound bubbles, such as POW! and BLAM! It is interesting to note that these comic book images occur in a time frame that is contemporaneous to the early work of Roy Lichtenstein, an artist associated with the Pop Art movement. The same sort of cartoon imagery was used in the *Batman* television series (1966–68) In both instances there is a desire to engage with the high art/low art distinction that has been of great interest to popular culture critics. This reference sets the tone for the excursion we take through Francie's frenetic world in which the distinction between internal and external is blurred. It is replete with extracts from American horror 'B' movies, and largely influenced by American television shows, including *The Fugitive* (1963–67) and *The Lone Ranger* (1949–57), as well as by the upper-class British stereotype of the well-mannered Algernon Carruthers. As Tom Herron points out, these British and American models are 'always out of [Francie's] reach' (2000: 172), perhaps most poignantly displayed as he and Joe (Joe Purcell) watch *The Fugitive* on the Nugents' television, from outside their house. As greater violence is enacted upon Francie's psyche his regression into an imaginary world intensifies. The important distinction to be made is that the older Francie is often unreliable, creating what

Mrs Nugent (Fiona Shaw) and son Philip (Andrew Fullerton, right) push Francie (Eamonn Owens) out of their home, deepening his status as an exile

Wayne Booth calls 'a confusion of distance' on the part of the viewer (1961: 311). We do not know whom to trust.

The younger Francie maintains the film's the point of view. He is the character through which we experience the story. This would be an example of an external point of view (see Branigan 1992: 103), where we see what the character sees, not strictly through his literal point of view, but from an inferred point of view. What has been termed 'dual voiced' narration (Hayman & Rabkin 1974: 95), which is the merging of the point of view character and the narrator's consciousness, here becomes trebled, amalgamating the voice of the director/writer, the older Francie and the boy Francie. (When I refer to the writer/director, I am speaking solely of Neil Jordan. In an article in the Canadian newspaper, *The Globe and Mail*, Jordan said, 'I paid Patrick [McCabe] money to write the screenplay … But he seemed not to grapple with it and just kept writing parallel works, telling the same story in different ways. So I said I better do it myself' (in Groen 1998: C3). Thus, I am acknowledging Jordan's authorship of the screenplay, although McCabe's name appears as co-screenwriter in the credits.)

When Gérard Genette discusses point of view characters and vision, he provides instances in which the narrator gives over the perceptual sphere to a character, but remains in control, which is precisely the case in segments of *The Butcher Boy* (see Genette 1980: 189–94). Consider the scene in which Francie's father visits him in the 'School for Pigs'. Father 'Bubbles' (Brendan Gleeson) ushers Da into the room, as the voice-over begins: 'There was Da in his Al Capone coat, "How are you father?" No, that's not a bottle of whiskey in me pocket. I know how to behave in a place like this. Sure wasn't I in a home like this with Alo all those years ago.'

Da surreptitiously takes a swig from his hidden whiskey bottle. Francie is bitter and upset. He has been placed, with the apparent cooperation of his father, in precisely the sort of church-run borstal that engendered Da's childhood misery. Francie remains on one side of the room as his father proclaims how much he loved Francie's now-deceased mother. Da reminisces about their honeymoon, the idyllic time in Bundoran (standing for a mythicised Irish haven) at the 'Over the Waves' boarding house. Francie not only flatly refuses to listen to his father's nostalgia ('Shut up, shut up about it…'), but to his father's incredulity, mocks him by invoking Da's recrimination to his wife: 'May the curse of Christ light upon you, you bitch. The day I took you out of that hole of a shop in Derry was a bitter one for me.' Francie remains turned away from Da, as he puts his hand tentatively on the child's shoulder and says very softly, 'I loved you like no father ever loved a son, Francie.' After so much psychic and physical abuse, Francie has no tools with which he might deal with this term of endearment, nor can he respond to the evident loneliness and need of his father. The voice-over declares: 'It was hard for him to say it, I could barely hear it. It would have been better if he drew out and hit me.'

This sequence calls into question the reliability of what we see and hear. Is the scene told through the older Francie's point of view, or is it told through the device that Wayne Booth would call the implied narrator (see 1961: 71–5; 151–2). This would not be an embodied presence, but a spectral figure guiding us through the narrative events. Booth charts the figures in a fiction by schematising them in an arc from the real reader to the real author. In between, on either side, are the 'ideal reader' and 'ideal narrator'. The latter two – readers and narrators – are abstractions, intelligent and infallible figures who would be the optimal reader of a book.

In this sequence, Francie takes on the classical Irish role of the exile, a figure who is 'incapable of entering the community … of those who have been touched by him' (O'Brien 2000: 44). Francie cannot negotiate the emotional gulf between him and his father; he protects himself from the inconsistency in their relationship, quite understandably, by distancing himself from one of the few remaining representatives of home. As George O'Brien writes, exile becomes 'a means of structuring the inner reality of … characters' (ibid.). The scene recounts what Francie sees, as well as his internal perceptions. Nonetheless, it is the narrating voice that hovers over the proceedings, governing the amount of information dispensed, as well as opening and closing the scene. The notorious 'poo' scene is one in which Francie the elder and his screen incarnation most famously trace a complex dialogue with one another. The child Francie has broken into the Nugents' house, and amidst the performance of other transgressive activities (such as smashing Mrs Nugent's cakes and scrawling 'PHILIP IS A PIG' in lipstick across the walls and family photos), creates a simulated schoolroom. The grown-up Francie, in voice-over, plays the schoolmaster. He begins his lesson: 'Today we are going to do the farmyard. Now can anyone tell me what animals we find in the farmyard?' The embodied, on-screen Francie plays both Philip and Mrs Nugent, and responds to the questions of his interrogator.[3] The scene climaxes when Francie as Mrs Nugent defecates on the floor, urged on by the 'schoolmaster': 'Now show us Mrs Nugent, you can do it! Excellent work Mrs Nugent!' The most radical aspect of this sequence is that not only are the two Francies, young and old, communicating with one another, but the younger Francie is also playing the roles of other characters, Philip (Andrew Fullerton) and Mrs Nugent (Fiona Shaw), intensifying the delirious tone of a scene that is both shocking and immensely comical. The older Francie plays the catalyst in the scene, taking on the part of the 'instructor' to his protégé, the child Francie who responds to the instructions provided by the voice-over. The latter in turn enacts both Philip and Mrs Nugent, both of whom respond to instructions provided by the voice-over. The humorous temper of Francie's actions, and he is always poised somewhere between the innocent and the malign, serve both to distance us from the explicit imbalance of Francie's mental state and to retard the moments of genuine lunacy that will mark the film's latter sections. Jordan's film significantly alters the point of view of the novel because he is able to embody the characters rather than have the reader imagine the scene created by McCabe's use of language.

In the 'poo' scene we have Francie's deranged consciousness to represent narrative action (as well as the film's discourse); in other words, for most of the scene we are ostensibly immersed in Francie's physical and psychic world until the 'instructor' dominates through his intercession in the events (although, of course, one might look at every event in the film as a complete fabrication of the elder Francie). That is what makes the film open to interpretation and analysis, the absence of many of the normative uses of point of view. In the novel, McCabe even gives us clues to determine what may have happened in the scene. A brief passage from the book provides an example: '[Mrs Nugent's] mouth was hanging open and she was crying again and pointing to the broken mirror and the writing on the blackboard I mean wall' (1992: 63). This sentence gives the careful reader the cues to determine what Francie was really doing during his fantasy sequence. A completely faithful adaptation of this scene might have been similar to Francie's post-apocalyptic fantasy, showing literal representations of his imaginative world without the intervention of the off-screen narrator to guide us through tonal alterations. (This is reminiscent of the fantasy kingdom of the claymation figures in Peter Jackson's film, *Heavenly Creatures* (1994).) But Jordan takes a different approach. Instead, he makes a significant shift in enunciation, and leaves us visually outside of Francie's mind. We are not seeing the scene through Francie's eyes, but mainly through the vision of the elder Francie; he holds sway over the proceedings. The access to the narrative is at its most complex and confounding in this scene. Addressing similar permutations, Stanley Kubrick discusses his own manipulation of point of view in *Barry Lyndon* (1975):

> I believe Thackeray used Redmond Barry to tell his own story in a deliberately distorted way because it made it more interesting. Instead of the omniscient author, Thackeray used the imperfect observer, or perhaps it would be more accurate to say the dishonest observer, thus allowing the reader to judge for himself, with little difficulty, the probable truth in Redmond Barry's view of his life. This technique worked extremely well in the novel but, of course, in a film you have objective reality in front of you all the time, so the effect of Thackeray's first-person storyteller could not be repeated on the screen.

Francie and Da (Stephen Rea) share a brief moment of tenderness

> It might have worked as comedy by the juxtaposition of Barry's version of the truth with the reality on the screen, but I don't think that *Barry Lyndon* should have been done as a comedy. (In Ciment 2001: 170)

While this does not exactly correspond to Jordan's manipulation of point of view, it still is helpful. Of course Kubrick is being somewhat ironic by saying that in film the spectator always has objective reality in front of him/her, or that the third-person voice-over is objective, but he (and Jordan) know that this is only one possible use of the camera. The juxtaposition of a point of view as depicted in the film's visuals, coupled with the voice-over point of view, creates an interesting tension between comedy and disturbing on-screen dementia. This can also be found in the molestation sequences with Father Tiddly (Milo O'Shea) or in those scenes in which the viewer begins to comprehend that Da is dead. In theoretical terms these scenes show the collision of three distinct narrative points of view, these being subjectivity (the diegetic young Francie), a second subjective point of view (old Francie) and an omniscient point of view (the camera). McCabe's novel offers only the subjectivity of the older Francie, and relies on an imaginative reader to construct the other two. It is apposite that Jordan does not focus on Francie's desire to 'be a Nugent', as McCabe does in his novel. McCabe goes so far as to have Philip say, 'He wants to be one of us. He wants his name to be Francis Nugent' (1992: 60). After this, Mrs Nugent unbuttons her blouse and gives suck to Francie from her breast. The nature of this scene may have been too literal for Jordan. The wanting-to-be-a-Nugent plotline was a dispersal of focus in terms of Francie's story.

The complex use of voice and vision gains in importance and profundity as Francie spirals out of control. He has no recourse to language, which would serve as a conduit to understanding the events that befall him. He has been raised in an atmosphere of inhumanity, and thus the completion of the cycle of brutality with the murder of Mrs Nugent seems pre-ordained. As Jordan has said:

> The relationship between Francie and Joe is all the more important because Francie loses his mother and father. Another thing you ought to remember, and what the film tries to show, is that children have no language, no expression for certain enormous tragedies, like the death of a parent. Of course, it's a loss, and they are desperately sad, but they can't really express it. But a mate betrays them, and they have the language and the justice of the playground, that's something they can invoke. Francie's anger sends him over the edge to destroy whatever took Joe away from him. But he can't destroy what took his father away, alcoholism. Or his mother's suicide. He can't really do anything much about that. But he can kill Mrs Nugent. (In Jaehne 2006: n.p.)

Both manifestations of Francie, young and old, return to the site of the boy's ostensible wound, the loss of Joe's friendship. Francie continually dwells upon Joe's betrayal of him – his acceptance of the goldfish given to him by the despised Nugent boy, Phillip. The voice-over dolefully cries, 'But what did Joe have to take it for? Why why why? Why didn't he say "Phillip, you can keep your goldfish?"' The goldfish and the Nugents, and Mrs Nugent in particular, become the locus of Francie's sense of irretrievable loss, obsessive hostility and, finally, murderous aggression. Jordan has said of Francie, 'He's the unaccommodated man. He's somebody who refuses to learn the rules of disappointment. He refuses to civilise his feelings because that would do his feelings an injustice' (in Falsetto 2000: 251).

The narrational voices in *The Butcher Boy* slip amongst a variety of registers and defy strict categorisation. The young Francie is the active agent within the film's fictional world, but he, in turn, is the vivid and engaging creation of the older Francie who narrates the film (see Lanser 1981: 265–7). In narratological terms, we can consider the young Francie to be the primary point of view character, while the disembodied Francie of the voice-over may be seen as 'a character of sorts' (Branigan 1992: 107). A claim can easily be made that the older Francie has a distinct personality which, although it often merges with that of the young Francie, maintains its own individuality. Stephen Rea discusses his performance of the voice-over in an interview, 'It was very tricky, because a kid's speech patterns are different from an adult's ... so I had to try and suggest that thirty years later I was that boy grown up. That's hard. I couldn't just imitate him otherwise it would have been stupid ... The thing I'm most pleased with in *The Butcher Boy* is the voice-over narration, which makes a big contribution to the irony of the film' (in Zucker 1999: 95). Rea does not acknowledge that he takes on the point of view of Francie as a child. I would emphasise that this strategy is not a structural trope, but a poetic one which is used to record Francie's unravelling world and his slide into deeper and deeper alienation, mania and, eventually, psychosis.

Perhaps the most powerful example of the use of internal point of view, where the privileged view is at its most private and subjective, occurs after Francie is discovered with the decaying body of his father. A needle is stuck in his arm by the doctor and as he goes under, rose petals begin to fall, first on him, then on his dead father. Francie is then found in a field of snowdrops, in one of the film's increasingly rare peaceful images, as the horrifying dénouement approaches. Francie rises, as Joe's head pops into the frame. Frank Sinatra's cover of 'Where Are You?' is heard on the soundtrack. Francie and Joe are now standing in the hills by 'their' lake; the lake explodes as if a nuclear bomb had been detonated. The shot then frames Francie and Joe as they walk through their town, now devastated by the bomb, covered with ash and strewn with the flaming wreckage of buildings. Bits of dialogue from previous scenes are heard as the boys pass various locations used in the film; charred pig bodies have replaced the human presence. The voice-over says, 'Thank God I had Joe. Me and Joe Purcell, the last two in the universe in this bitter, bitter day when the world had ended.' As the hallucination or fantasy draws to a close, a figure on a black horse rides into town. It is an alien dressed in a priest's cassock, who intones menacingly: 'You've unlocked something very, very precious Francie.' The pigs (Francie's nomination as a 'pig' is a particular trigger for his rage and sense of inferiority), the nuclear war and the invasion of aliens (who, in turn, reference 'the Communists') spectacularly conflate many of Francie's preoccupations and fears. In this instance, the voice-over narration is extremely limited, and the responsibility for the narrative is ceded to Francie's intense inner imaginings and the film's visuals.

There is a great deal more that can be said about the issues of 'who speaks?' and 'who sees?' in *The Butcher Boy*. The structure of authority in the text is a tangled web; the resonating voices of a human consciousness are articulated with great subtlety and expressivity. This discussion suggests the labyrinthine pathways that make Jordan's virtuoso adaptation of *The Butcher Boy* such a richly textured and provocative experience.

CHAPTER SIX

Dark Romanticism

Interview with the Vampire: haunted by loss

'Pour forth the cup of pain ... Pain is my element as hate is thine.'
                                    – Percy Shelley, *Prometheus Unbound*

'The best vitality cannot excel decay.'
                        – Emily Dickinson (in 'I Reason, Earth Is Short')

After the tremendous critical and commercial success of *The Crying Game*, Jordan was offered the opportunity to direct a screen adaptation of Anne Rice's hugely popular novel, *Interview with the Vampire* (1976). One can see why Jordan was drawn to the book's sense of loss, inner anguish and pain, an aggregate of sentiments which can also be used to describe *The Crying Game*. Furthermore, the filmmaker consistently uses dramatic situations played out in extremis: Lestat can be seen as Louis' antagonist, but it is essentially Louis' internal discord that provides the film's most powerful dramatic material.

The thematics found in *Interview with the Vampire* are Romantic: man lost in a fallen world, exiled from love; the source of evil and suffering in this fallen world; questions of origins and identity; and, finally, the anxiety about God's very existence. Unquestionably, Jordan's work draws sustenance from these notions. At the core of his filmmaking is a sensual engagement with materials, and ways in which he (and the spectator) can interact imaginatively with the given world of his cinema. The director's films can be apprehended on a plane that is not subject to rationality; Jordan is very much in touch with the Romantic precepts in which it is claimed that the mind has a faculty that enables one to see beyond the forms of the material world to a greater spiritual reality, and that there is a 'Transcendent Spirit' beyond 'earthly contraries of Self and other, of mind and nature, of subject and object' (Abrams 1953: 57). The triad that represents Romantic thinking is subject/mind/spirit, superseding nature and earthly matter. They believed in the correlation of the individual mind and the mind of the absolute; this in turn was where Imagination could be located (see Abrams 1953: 57–8).

The Romantic movement began largely as a response to the bloody events of the French Revolution which many of the Romantics championed. They believed, and Yeats would later echo this thought, that beauty could only emerge from terror. Similar apocalyptic imaginings can be found in art movements linked to the end or beginning of a millennium, and are agitated by millenarian and eschatological ideas, that is, society will collapse, and in its fissures a regenerative energy would create a new social order.

The early Romantic period coincides with the Enlightenment, when thinkers felt that the world could be understood only through the rational mind. The Romantics were indisputably anti-Enlightenment: they believed that the sublime, the state of awe found in beauty or terror, was the ultimate goal of human experience. A crucial distinction was made between terror and horror – terror became something that threatens one from without, a sublime power that transcends the self:

> Though the numinous emotion in its completest development shows a world of difference from the mere 'daemonic dread', not even at the highest level does it belie its pedigree or kindred. Even when the worship of 'daemons' has long since reached the higher level of worship of 'god', these gods still retain as numina something of the 'ghost' in the impress they make on the feelings of the worshiper … The peculiar quality of the 'uncanny' and 'awful', which survives with the quality of exaltedness and sublimity or is symbolised by means of it. And this element, softened though it is, does not disappear even on the highest level of all, where the worship of God is at its purest. Its disappearance would be indeed an essential loss. The 'shudder' reappears in a form ennobled beyond measure where the soul, held speechless, trembles inwardly to the farthest fibre of its being. It invades the mind mightily in Christian worship with the words: 'Holy, holy, holy…' (Otto 1958: 17)

The Romantics obsessed over having to choose between God's bountiful presence and his complete absence, which signified a world in which transcendence and enlightenment were absent. Jordan speaks of the ways in which his fall from Catholicism has left him bereft (Neil Jordan, *The End of the Affair* DVD commentary). This apprehension makes its way into *Interview with the Vampire* when Louis converses with the world's oldest living vampire, Armand:

Louis: Then God does not exist?
Armand: (growing angry) I know nothing of God or the Devil. I have
           never seen a vision nor learned a secret that would damn or save
           my soul.
Louis: Then it's as I've always feared.

Probably the most important distinction between Louis and Lestat is that Lestat no longer believes in God. Lestat is beguiled by the here and now, and does not care to seek redemption. He is determined to be '…the best devil there ever was' (McGinley 1996: 82). Louis is consumed by guilt and the knowledge that he can never in all eternity attain redemption. 'The Romantic … deals with the tormented condition of a creature suspended between the extremes of faith and scepticism, beatitude and horror, being and nothingness, love and hate, and anguished by an indefinable guilt for some crime it cannot remember having committed' (Botting 2001: 3). In essence, it is a vision of the unending pain of existence, where all ends with '…despair, pain and annihilation … [The Romantic] hero is ultimately torn apart by [his own] demons' (Botting 2001: 6).

Louis, however, is perversely confined by his Christian morality as much as by his sensitivity. Conflicts arise when, as a vampire, Louis passes judgement on the conduct of other vampires; he is rather punctilious and clearly feels superior to his *confrères*. When he utters lines such as, 'Forgive me if I have a lingering respect for life', or to Lestat: 'And to think you are all I have to learn from', his overly-civilised and pontifical values surface. After he burns down his elegant estate in the Louisiana countryside, he and Lestat find themselves in a grimy, dank cemetery vault. Louis says: 'We belong in Hell' and Lestat responds, 'What if there is no Hell, or they don't want us there?' – a significant question indeed. But Louis intones in voice-over: 'But there was a hell, and everywhere we moved I was in it'.

> 'The stylistic keynote of Romanticism is intensity.'
>
> – Margaret Drabble

Dark Romanticism or, as it is sometimes called, Negative Romanticism, deals with the 'exploration of dilemma, ugliness and evil and often the repression of despair and the exploration of perversion' (Day 1996: 112). It is the nexus of many Jordan's films: *Mona Lisa*; *The Miracle* (especially in the mother/son configuration); *Michael Collins* (in which the Cain and Abel story is invoked); *The Butcher Boy*; *In Dreams*; *The End of the Affair* and *The Brave One*. It is a term we associate with Byron, who bore his own mark of Cain: his club foot. He flaunted the social morality of the times in his openly incestuous relationship with his half-sister. Byron's wife was the main recipient of his cruelty; he threatened to strangle their child as soon as it was out of the womb.[1]

Interview with the Vampire is constructed so that we witness in Louis the development of the Byronic Hero who has more depth of thought and feeling – a hero who offers resistance to all institutions that organise society, such as the Church, or any other kind of overarching pietistic construct that determines social behaviour. Louis refuses Armand's offer of companionship, and takes his own path, creating his dark and lonely universe. His sentiments are uttered by Byron's Manfred:

> In Fantasy, Imagination, all
> The affluence of my soul ... I plunged deep,
> But, like an ebbing wave, it dashed me back
> Into the gulf of my unfathomed thought...
> I dwell in my despair –
> And live – and live forever.
> (2000: 297)

Manfred is very like the Wandering Jew, an isolated, nomadic character who was a staple in both Gothic and Romantic literature, and whose paradigm is found in Charles Maturin's Irish Gothic novel, *Melmoth the Wanderer* (1820). Louis' anxieties may be seen as the assertion of his individuality, not merely the whining voice of a depressive. His rebellion takes on a sort of Satanic glamour. He faces the challenge of eternal loneliness with elegance, and in the end one can admire Louis' commitment to withdraw, as in Byron's Cain: 'I'm sick of all/That dust has shown me/let me dwell in shadow' (2000: 916). One admires the struggle of a man wishing to maintain what remains of his mortal soul.

Another modulation of the Byronic hero, the Hero of Sensibility, is at base a humane man who is afflicted by a sense of isolation, powerlessness and desperation. One can see that Louis, who has accepted Lestat's Faustian bargain, is inexorably drawn into Lestat's maleficent world. Louis represents a vampire who is plagued with an overwhelming sense of guilt, loathing the bloody banquet of which he must partake in order to survive. From Byron's 'The Giaour' (which means 'vampire' in Greek):

> But first, on earth as Vampire sent,
> Thy corse shall from its tomb be rent:
> Then ghastly haunt thy native place,
> And suck the blood of all thy race;
> There from thy daughter, sister, wife,
> At midnight drain the stream of life;
> Yet loathe the banquet which perforce
> Must feed thy livid living corse.
> (2000: 232)

Louis, the 'immortal with the soul of a human', is profoundly engaged with his sorrow and in a perpetual state of anxiety regarding the monstrosity of his newly-attained state. It is clear that even as a vampire he is temperamentally incapable of enjoying the cruelty that delights his maker, Lestat. The key note for Louis is depressed passivity mingled with guilt. His sombre disposition and his struggle with existential questions are his most prominent traits, especially after the death of Claudia (Kirsten Dunst) and her 'companion' (played by Domiziana Giordano). Louis is destined to hopelessness; angst and remorse are his partners for his time without end.

From the opening chords of Elliot Goldenthal's eerie, brilliant and troubling choral theme, a helicopter shot guides us to a fateful destination, and we feel as if we are moving into the heart of the most profound darkness. Jordan – a director who has a deep investment in the mysterious shadow side of humankind, as Jung might say – has created a consummate rendering of a soul in torment. The interviewer's (Christian Slater's) first contact with Louis is distinguished by the vampire's stiff formality, especially in contrast to the interviewer's casual behaviour. When the interviewer asks if Louis followed him, Louis responds: 'I was waiting in that alley, watching you, watching me.' This is the foundation of a trope we will witness in the remainder of the film: a sense of being overlooked (see chapter three, 'Storytelling and Performance', for further explanation).

When Louis commences his story, we learn that he had recently lost his wife in childbirth. He says in voice-over: 'I couldn't bear the pain of their loss and I longed to be released from it.' In a melancholic pose, Louis kneels before a statue, and drinks wine from a bottle. His voice-over continues over a flashback of his character from an

Louis (Brad Pitt) broods over Lestat's proposition to join the vampire world: 'I'll give you the choice I never had'

earlier time, before he is 'made' by Lestat. We see him in a saloon, as he describes his state of mind: 'I wanted to lose it all, my wealth, my estate, my sanity.' He gambles with a ruffian who explodes at Louis' suspicion that the man is cheating. The man overturns the card table and points a gun directly at Louis. Louis bares his chest and dares the gambler to shoot him. The voice-over continues: 'Most of all, I longed for death. I realise that now, I wanted a release from the pain of living.' The scene is presented as if on a proscenium stage. We watch the action from a high angle, and retroactively discover that this is the viewpoint of Lestat as he watches the performance.

> 'It is only the passions, and the great passions, that can raise the soul to great things.'
> – Diderot

Also crucial to Jordan's portrayal of his characters in each of his films is their sexuality. Usual in Jordan's practice is the way in which he voids the demarcations between heterosexual and homosexual, and violence and eroticism in his films. These boundaries do not seem to exist for the director, or comprise an unconscious anxiety that impregnates his work. He is always looking for that area where traditional behaviour is disrupted. Sex, such as it is, is 'a terrifying thrill rather than pleasurable affection' (Day 1996: 183). *Interview with the Vampire* is replete with sexual imagery, and the seeds of the film's highly eroticised nature are sown early in the narrative. Jordan says: 'Vampires don't have sex, so you've got to be creative' (Neil Jordan, *Interview with the Vampire* DVD commentary). If one recalls the 'making' of Louis, we first see him and Lestat locked in an embrace as they fly towards heaven, conjoined in ecstasy. (Here Jordan alludes to the paintings of Tintoretto, with his powerful High Renaissance/Mannerist sensibility.) When, in a later scene, Lestat makes Louis (a vampire) by sinking his teeth into Louis' neck, their movements are strongly sexualised as they struggle on the ground. Louis is initially the passive partner, with eyes closed and a dreamy look on his face. He relinquishes himself fully to the moment of rapture before feasting hungrily on Lestat. Once sated, Louis lies in a recumbent position as drops of blood from Lestat's wrist drip into his mouth. The sinking of fangs into a victim is erotic, not only because of the relationship to sexual orality, but because it is a penetration of sorts. The experience so transcends the '…bounds of finite and moral that the individual has the sense of being threatened with obliteration when encountering it' (Day 1996: 183). The vampires in the film inhabit a liminal world of sexuality: 'The vampires are androgynes, but their androgyny is an expression, not of increased sympathy and widened identity, but of indifference to everyone but themselves' (Day 1985: 143). In the film, this colossal self-absorption ranges from Lestat's heedless butchery of his victims and the 'I want more' of Claudia the vampire child, to the silent self-contemplation and existential terrors that plague the everlasting life of Louis.

Satan was an icon for Romantic rebels in their struggle against an unjust society and even an unjust God (see Thorslev 1962: 22). Much of this struggle stemmed from the increasing secularisation that swept European society, and progressive thinking amongst leading figures of the intelligentsia, such as William Godwin, Mary Wollstonecraft, *et al*. No more was man enchained to institutional religious proprieties. William Blake was one of the first to see that Christianity had a deleterious effect on the spiritual growth of mankind (see Thorslev 1962: 111); morality became an individualised expression of one's own beliefs rather than a mandate.

Jordan has claimed that in filming *Interview with the Vampire*, he was effectively making John Milton's *Paradise Lost*:

> The central theme is Louis who makes this Faustian choice – he decides to give up his mortal life for some other kind of survival, but realises he's beyond the realm of human feeling. It's a very old theme – *Paradise Lost*, which I read as a kid. The whole position of Lucifer in that story, the way he was thrown out of heaven and denied any contact with the face of God, that's what happens to Louis. (In Mooney 1994: 68)

Although Milton predates the Romantic movement (usually situated between 1789–1824), most critics consider him to be the most important precursor of Romanticism. The story of the angels expelled by God after they participate in a rebellion tantamount to a palace revolt is well-known. Because of their abortive mutiny, the fallen angels cascade from heaven down into the dust of hell. A question often arises about the difference between Satan and Lucifer. According to Milton, Satan's name in Heaven was Lucifer – 'The Light Bearer', God's most beautiful angel; but after his fall he becomes Satan, the Hebrew word for 'The Adversary' (see Milton 2001: 7). In Milton's text, Satan was the most beautiful angel in God's eyes, but his pride leads him to think that he is too good to serve God. This feeling engenders his recruitment of other sympathetic angels and their ensuing rebellion. The rebels attempt to wrest control from God and the loyal angels, but the renegades are defeated. With *Paradise Lost* Satan assumes the stature of fallen beauty: 'splendour shadowed by sadness and death'; he is 'majestic though in ruin' (Praz 1956: 56).

In mapping out *Paradise Lost* and its relationship to the film, we can see the coalescence of Louis' character, and the deep schism that materialises because of the differences between Louis and Lestat. Louis is far more sensitive than Lestat, and appreciates the beauty of the mortal world. He is capable of being both tender and understanding, particularly with Claudia, and still hopes to find some measure of goodness in the world. A passage from the poem illustrates Louis' feelings once he has become a vampire. It provides the reader with an example of Satanic regret, which Louis exemplifies and which is as important as Satanic fury, represented by Lestat:

> Me miserable! Which way shall I fly
> Infinite wrath, and infinite despair?
> Which way I fly is hell; myself am hell;
> And in the lowest deep a lower deep
> Still threat'ning to devour me opens wide,
> To which the hell I suffer seems a heav'n
> (Milton 2001: 48)

Louis is aligned with the figure of Satan who, as the era of Romanticism progresses, becomes more and more that of a hero. In the resolution of this speech in *Paradise Lost* – once Louis' decision is made to join the vampires – Satan/Louis bids adieu to all things human: 'So farewell hope, and with hope farewell fear/Farewell remorse: all good to me is lost' (Milton 2001: 82).

Louis, in line with the Romantic concern for origins, has an insatiable desire to know and understand the workings of the strange universe he inhabits. He confers with Armand on the matter:

Louis: Who made us what we are?
Armand: Surely you know the one who made you.
Louis: Yes, but who made him? The source ... of all this evil.
Armand: You die each time you kill ... you feel you deserve to die. But
                does that make you evil? But since you comprehend what you
                feel is good, doesn't that make you good?
Louis: Then there's nothing.

Louis is the rebel who cannot embrace the world he has entered. As he says: 'What could the damned have to say to the damned?' He is the archetypal loner unsuited to the tribalism of the vampire world. Louis is forever reflecting on his feelings, thus isolating himself from his companions by his withdrawn, pensive bearing. Louis is marked as the Cain figure in the narrative (recall that in *Michael Collins* the story of Cain and Abel was also foregrounded as a mythic underpinning), and Louis is the wanderer, the social outcast, cursed and marked by God. In Louis' conversation with Armand, he, like the other fallen angels, doubts the very existence of God. His angst grows out of a very Faustian idea that 'sorrow is knowledge ... the tree of knowledge is not that of life' (Thorslev 1962: 167). This angst is at the very core of Romanticism: how does one live in a Godless universe, bereft of morality and fermenting in contempt? Louis' 'mourning and melancholia' (as Freud might say) permeate the narrative. He says (in voice-over) as watches his last sunrise:

That morning I was not yet a vampire. I saw my last sunrise. I remember it completely. And yet I can't recall any sunrise before. I watched the whole magnificence of the sunrise ... as if it were the first. And then I said farewell to sunrise and set out to become what I became.

A similar sentiment is expressed in *Paradise Lost*: 'O sun, to tell thee how I hate thy beams/that bring to my remembrance from what state/I fell, how glorious once above thy sphere' (Milton 2001: 81).

Louis' depressive self-flagellation arises from his loss of his wife and child, and again after he loses Claudia and all regard for life. Louis' brooding over his misfortunes is reflected by Satan when the latter says: 'This is the seat/That we much change for heav'n, this mournful gloom/For that celestial light?' (Milton 2001: 11–12). The happiness Louis experienced in his marriage has turned to anguish, much as his beloved

Claudia's death makes him inconsolable. She and her companion are locked in a stone minaret sealed with a barred grate that lets in the rays of the sun. Only their charred ashes remain, which disintegrate as Louis attempts to touch them. (Jordan used photos of victims caught near the epicentre of the bombing of Hiroshima to model Claudia and her companion's final state.)

Once Claudia with her 'golden curls' is gone, Louis settles on a solitary existence, refusing the partnership proffered by Armand. He loses all but his regret, as reflected by Milton: 'Why do I overlive,/Why am I mocked with death, and lengthened out/ To deathless pain? How gladly would I meet/Mortality my sentence' (2001: 249). *Interview with the Vampire* offers a meditation on the human hunger for destruction and violence, a fascination that harkens back to traditions of oral storytelling in pre-literate societies. Indeed, vampires are found in all cultures, ancient to modern. They take the form of succubi, demons who have sexual relations with humans and draw life from them. Similar myths abound in ancient Assyria, Africa, China and throughout Europe; the connections between life and blood were often the basis for ancient rituals. Because of the fear of the power of free-flowing blood, in some tribes women were separated from others during their menstruation.

Ernest Jones, in *On the Nightmare*, proposes a psychoanalytic interpretation of vampires. He explains the dread of their existence as a consequence of widespread plague, and writes that this mass panic grows out of feelings of love and hate, guilt and grief for the dead ones and partly out of necrophilia. He equates the belief in vampires with sexual repression and guilt. The occurrence of nocturnal emissions were believed to be caused by a vampire; this monstrous creature was responsible for the flow of semen. A long history prevails in which blood and semen are equated (see Jones 1949: 98–130), strengthening a reading of *Interview with the Vampire* as a metaphor for the AIDS epidemic.

'The transgression does not deny the taboo but transcends it and completes it.'
– Georges Bataille

'Extreme seductiveness is probably at the boundary of horror.'
– Georges Bataille

The Romantics were greatly concerned with the innocence of childhood. They looked dolefully at the past and realised all that is lost over the course of a human life; this sense of loss has a particular resonance in Jordan's films. In *Interview with the Vampire* Claudia, a pre-pubescent, is portrayed as the Fatal Woman, a conception of the feminine that is recognised as far back as Cleopatra. She can be seen as a Medusean beauty, a figure dear to the Romantic poets, her face framed by corkscrew curls (see Praz 1956: 36). Claudia could be the model in the poem by Algernon Swinburne, who bridges the Romantic-Decadent periods; in *Chastelard* (1867), Swinburne writes:

For all Christ's work this Venus is not quelled,
But reddens at the mouth with blood of men,

Lestat's (Tom Cruise) passionate rage

Sucking between small teeth the sap o' the veins,
Dabbling with death her little tender lips
A bitter beauty, poisonous-pearled mouth…
(2004: 108)

As with Byron, we have the conflation of cruelty and sex (or sin); this 'bitter beauty', in spite of her hearty appetite for blood, is able to elicit some sympathy from the viewer. Although Claudia grows more mature in many ways, she can never experience living in the body of a fully developed woman. Claudia is the lamia figure in the film, in reference to one of the darkest and most powerful of John Keats' poems, discussed in chapter two. In Keats' work moral instruction is indicted, as is the demystification of nature by the 'enlightened mind'. It is an argument at the heart of Gothic and Dark Romanticism; both movements were repulsed by the core values of the Enlightenment in which reason was paramount.

Claudia is the lamia *par excellence*. She is the *sidhe* in Celtic folklore, creatures with the ability to 'glamour', to appear in different guises to seduce and steal a mortal into their world of soulless perpetuity. Lamia were known to lure both youths and children to suck their blood. This figure was most commonly represented with the head of a woman and the body of a serpent in the Garden of Eden (a female viper can be viewed as the correlative of the female vampire). The vampire attack is commonly characterised by the hissing and baring of fangs, similar to a snake attack. The female vampire embodies the subtle guile of the serpent and the sexual powers of seduction possessed by Eve.

By now, it should be clear that we find ourselves in a world that is clearly one of mythopoesis. In *Anatomy of Criticism* Northrop Frye uses the symbolism of the Bible and, to a lesser extent, classical mythology as a grammar of literary archetypes. His principle notion is that the meaning or pattern of poetry is a structure of imagery with conceptual implications. Frye goes on to describe the symbols of the total apocalyptic and demonic modes, which may also be understood as the world of innocence versus the world of experience. He cites work by Jean Cocteau and Franz Kafka as artists in play with the movement between myth and irony. *Interview with the Vampire* can be seen from this perspective, although it falls heavily on the mythic side in spite of its ample use of irony. The vampires reside in a demonic world, not one that is in any sense realistic or displaced from the demonic. The imagery Frye ascribes to the apocalyptic demonic is the world of the nightmare, bondage, pain and confusion. The film takes place in a world of ruins, catacombs and instruments of torture (the multi-level catacombs wherein the vampires performing in the grand guignol reside; Lestat's vein-opening device, for example). For Frye, monsters represent the animal kingdom and the emblematic landscape is the desert, the wasteland and brimstone. Jesus roamed the desert, but returned to civilisation with his faith renewed; the characters in *Interview with the Vampire* are condemned to an eternity in a spiritual desert and one can argue that Louis in particular roams the vast universe of the wasteland.

There is displacement to the analogy of experience, which is a less totalising concept than the pure demonic, because the creatures inhabit 'dreadful night, ruins, and cemeteries' (Frye 1957: 150). A well-known and easily understandable example of the way this displacement works would be in the mythic world, Oedipus kills his father and marries his mother; and as we move towards romance, a knight kills his father-in-law and rescues a damsel. The vampires possess the Devil as their divine symbol, and the lost or damned soul is the condition they most closely inhabit. Again this may be explained by examples of the displaced demonic. In other words, we are no longer in hell, but in the world of experience. Failure, betrayal, frustration, isolation and anarchy would be considered as symbols of the displaced demonic (see Frye 1957: 131–3). The conditions of life in the demonic are eternal torment, perversion and captivity; the hero does not comprehend moral choices in his darkness, but is held responsible by some unknowable power for just such judgements (see Botting 2001: 6). The section of *Interview with the Vampire* that most closely corresponds to these ideas would be in the sequences following Louis' visit to Le Théâtre des Vampires. Louis is interred in a bricked-up wall beneath the theatre while Claudia and her companion are imprisoned in a minaret that will soon be flooded with daylight. Although Louis has no part in Claudia's demise, one can see that her death – in all its horror – would ceaselessly plague the already highly sensitised Louis for all eternity. He has not only been deprived of Claudia's companionship, but he is rendered unable to save the one person who has brought him some measure of comfort and happiness in his world without end.

Romantic childhood: lost songs of innocence

> 'Most people are only a very little alive; it is only when they are so awakened that they are capable of real Good, but that at the same time they become first capable of Evil.'
>
>   – T. S. Eliot

The Romantics also privileged childhood because of the feeling that children were in touch with higher spiritual forces (see Abrams 1984). Romantics made much of childhood as a time of innocence, an idyll free from the constraints brought about by adult responsibilities and the self-consciousness that signals a leave-taking from a child's natural, free behaviour. The images in William Blake's *Songs of Innocence* and *Songs of Experience* are formidable; the imagery in the former collection is laden with pastoral representations and the attendant Edenic connotations. The notion of origins is central both to the Romantics and to Jordan, and can be found in the line 'Little Lamb, who made thee?' (Blake 1978: 25). On a prosaic level, *The Butcher Boy* charts Francie's transformation from a Lamb to a Tyger, or the movement from innocence to experience. We find this search for origins in *Interview with the Vampire*, when Claudia asks: 'Who made us these things?', as well as in Claudia and Louis' perigrinations through Europe searching for other vampires. Jimmy in *The Miracle* longs to know his mother and why she deserted him. Vivian from *In Dreams* wants to re-enact his childhood with an improved family. In *The Butcher Boy*, Francie returns to mythical Bundoran in search of the place 'Over the Waves' where his parents spent their blissful honeymoon, only to be told (in spite of his father's contrary contention that 'there was no whiskey then') that Da had to be dragged out of saloons, and treated his wife 'no better than a pig'. The paedophile priest Father Tiddly fits Francie out in the garb of

Little-Bo-Peep and masturbates not so secretly before his mother/child substitute. A quite perverse Lamb of God may be construed in this scene.

The opening stanza to one of Blake's saddest poems is found in 'The Chimney-Sweeper', wherein the poet laments the child labourers spawned by the Industrial Revolution:

> When my mother died I was very young,
> And my father sold me while yet my tongue
> Could scarcely cry, 'weep weep weep weep'
> So your chimneys I sweep and in soot I sleep.
> (1978: 108)

The poem is written in the first-person, and in other passages the little boy dreams of escaping from his difficult existence to the Elysian fields. One cannot help but associate the poem with Francie, labouring in the butcher shop. It is a messy, blood-soaked environment in which the only activity is the slaughter of animals and chopping them to morsels. Blake chooses to endow his child-narrator with the inability to see into his miserable conditions, just as Francie remains detached and in denial of his own struggles.

In another poem, 'A Cradle Song', Blake writes:

> Sweet babe, in thy face,
> Holy image I can trace.
> Sweet babe, once like thee
> Thy maker lay, and wept with me.
> (1978: 110)

The invocation of the lost prelapsarian world and the innocence of childhood is expressed by Blake with brilliant simplicity; comparisons can also be made with Claudia in *Interview with the Vampire*. In *Songs of Experience* is the line from 'The Tyger', 'Did he who made the Lamb make thee?' (Blake 1978: 125). This line has aroused much controversy amongst literary critics, who have interpreted the tiger as Satan; Blake makes his descriptions of the tiger both alluring and fiendish. Again, the originary question is posed, and in essence Blake asks: how did Evil, or, for that matter, Good develop? In *The Butcher Boy* we have a scene early in the film of Francie and his then-best friend Joe stealing apples from Mrs Nugent's tree, and essentially everything starts to career out of control from this relatively innocent gesture.

The Romantic agony, the idea that innocence can never be regained once lost, finds its way in the lamentations of a character in William Wordsworth's 'Ode: Intimations of Immortality from Recollections of Early Childhood' (1807) as the narrator suffers from his 'earthly freight', and despairs of a Fallen world that has lost its 'celestial light' (2000: 300). Wordsworth, in 'Characteristics of a Child Three Years Old' (1811), evokes the 'placid lake' of the Romantic pastoral dream (2000: 334). In *The Butcher Boy* the lake will be the site of Francie and Joe's childhood games, but will later take on sinister connotations when the lake explodes in a mushroom cloud. There is no more gamboling in Arcadia for Francie, as the explosion leads him to madness and destruction. 'To H. C., Six Years Old' also contains the refrain:

O blessed vision! happy child!
Thou art so exquisitely wild.
I think of thee with many fears.
For what may be thy lot in future years.
(2000: 246)

The speaker of the poem then talks about the miseries that will beset the child in adulthood ('vain and causeless melancholy') and 'the times when Pain [was the] guest' (ibid.). Similarly, we are reminded that Francie was denied the opportunity to enjoy an unspoilt childhood.

At first glance, it may seem difficult to connect *Interview with the Vampire* to *The Butcher Boy*, apart from their connection to Romanticism. However, if we look at the archetype of the *puer aeternus* (the source of the word is unclear; it seems to have come from Ovid, but there is no certainty about this), he is the Peter Pan figure, the boy who wants to remain young forever. The *puer* in Jungian psychology is meant to describe men who remain, in essence, adolescents. They are attracted to the promise of eternal youth, and have trouble developing an ability to make commitments. The *puer* is often transfixed by the lifestyle of homosexuality, the sort of orientation that would, for some, preclude monogamy. Still he cannot commit, and often retains the ambiguity of bisexuality. Marie-Louise von Franz was one of the first to identify this narcissistic trait:

The man who is identified with the archetype of the *puer aeternus* remains too long in adolescent psychology; that is, all those characteristics that are normal in a youth of seventeen or eighteen continue into later life … He lives in a continual sleepy daze, and that too is a typical adolescent characteristic: the sleepy, undisciplined, long-legged youth who merely hangs around. (In Beebe 1997: 201)

Certainly, this would be an apt (if somewhat imprecise) rendering of Brad Pitt's portrayal of Louis. Every archetype has a shadow figure. Lestat is the creature lurking behind Louis, called 'the trickster'. But Louis refuses to acknowledge and/or embrace this dark side of himself, a side that would enable him to come to terms with his vampire nature. As it is, Louis cannot remain in contact with his shadow; he seems like an angel, one who always seeks answers leading to inner wisdom. An acknowledgement of his trickster side would make Louis a more whole person. The trickster is the figure that lures the *puer aeternus* into his Faustian bargain. Louis' passivity and seeming inability to take part in the social world he now inhabits is, at turns, infuriating, pathetic and completely comprehensible. When he is offered the companionship of Armand (even though the older vampire has obviously conspired to bring about Claudia's death), Louis declines a personal relationship that would undoubtedly be premised on a more mature level than his companionship with Claudia. He retreats, instead, to the isolation of solitary brooding, refusing a path that might have ultimately ripened into a more adult relationship.

Claudia is important here because she is 'an eternal child', and her face suggests that archetype in sharing both the angelic radiance of Louis and the demonic gleam of Lestat. The leading female figure in Louis' life, she represents, as a mirror image of his soul, the developmental level of his emotional life and makes it more evident that the pouting, flat-voiced Louis is stuck in the infantile psyche (see Beebe 1997: 201). Claudia's inability to mature can be compared to Francie's lingering in pre-adolescence. Just as Claudia will never have the intimacy of adult relationships, so Francie is fixated at a pre-pubescent stage of development.

The premature loss of the mother figure is also typical of the *puer aeternus*. The mother is lost early in the boy's life, and this sense of abandonment makes it difficult to form emotional connections. Claudia, Louis and Francie have lost a source of emotional comfort, warmth and meaning. The psychoanalytic term for such an internal catastrophe is object loss, which produces a restricting of the possibilities of personality, so that an emotional flattening and deadening takes place (see Beebe 1997: 205). When the vampires kill Claudia they also kill any chance for Louis' emotional fulfilment. As Armand says, 'They are decadent. They reflect nothing. They are nothing.' They do not offer Louis the consolation of emotional growth and development. This is mirrored by Francie, who remains fixed at a pre-teen age where he exhibits no interest in girls, and still plays cowboys and Indians, long after most adolescents move on to more hormonally-charged pursuits. Both Louis and Francie will never achieve a fulfilled consciousness, because they shy away from emotional contact. 'Louis finally presents a despairing, negative attitude whose claim to higher moral ground is rightly mocked by the queerly wicked Lestat' (Beebe 1997: 209); similarly Francie, largely by his astonishing level of denial, becomes not only emotionally disconnected, but shows no moral growth either. Francie's murder of Mrs Nugent is the outcome of a boy denied emotional nourishment and fulfilment at every turn. When Joe, Francie's only hope of salvation, denies him in public, he spirals into his murderous rage and finally achieves the notoriety and recognition he so craves. If Ma and Da can no longer be of any help to Francie, like Louis he remains paralysed in an undeveloped stage. Is Francie sane when he is released from the 'Garage for Bad Bastards'? Whether he is or not, he is certainly quite child-like, which is a depressing commentary on psychiatry, but also condemns him to the status of the *puer aeternus*.

CHAPTER SEVEN

The Gothic: The Moment of Collapse

In Dreams: 'The bastard's in my head'

'In [Irish] gothic realism, a familiar narrative pattern is redeployed as in *Melmoth the Wanderer*, *Carmilla*, and *Dracula*; the isolated individual who traffics with extra communal forces is destined to be consumed by them.'

– M. G. Backus

'Ireland is the only country on earth where, from the strange existing opposition of religion, politics and manners, the extremes of refinement and barbarism are united, and the most wild and incredible situations of romantic story are hourly passing before modern eyes.'

– Charles Maturin

Neil Jordan is a director whose films, even when not dealing in an overt way with Gothic themes, characters or setting, are marked by a Gothic spirit that is fraught with darkness and anxiety, tension and fear, all of which in the world of the Gothic become pleasure. The Gothic provides a counter-narrative to modernity, humanism and the Enlightenment. As William Patrick Day writes: 'Gothic is a fable of identity fragmented and destroyed beyond repair' (1985: 6).

There is a transformation from Romanticism as the disturbance moves inside, and starts to question identity, individuality, conventions of society. 'Gothic fiction can be said to blur rather than distinguish the boundaries that regulate social life, and interrogate rather than restore any imagined continuity between past and present, nature and culture, reason and passion, individuality and family and society' (Botting 1996: 47). In contradistinction to Romanticism, there is no sense of possible redemption, and the imagination is granted no power over events. The Romantics were very concerned with origins and identity, whereas the Gothic breaks down identity; the world is seen as a place of fragmentation and chaos, disorder and defencelessness, especially for women.

The Gothic is a menace to the human soul through an overabundance of imagination, transgressive behaviours, and the lurking power of evil and spiritual corruption that undermine the moral authority of the individual; this may occur either through natural or supernatural forces. The mind itself may be denied wholeness or the ability to communicate pain to others. Corruption, irrationality and wickedness dominate the Gothic imagination.

The Gothic is more hidden, less exteriorised than the Romantic. Terror for the Romantics came from without, but in the Gothic the destructive affect comes from within and is called horror. While the Romantics laboured to correct social inequities and pietistic thinking, in the Gothic one cannot even be certain about what is real or imaginary. The uncanny decomposes all boundaries and defines predominant social and moral laws. The Gothic subject is disconnected from his/her self as well as from society that surrounds them; limits and control are unknown to the Gothic subject, or are placed in great doubt. In speaking of the Irish Gothic, the idea of the disconnect between self and society undergoes an interesting turn.

David Punter writes about two of the principle figurations in Gothic literature, the monument and the ruin as emblems of the uncanny. However, he claims that in the Irish (and Scottish) Gothic, upon closer inspection, the monument 'reveals itself as a ruin, as a thing of shreds and patches, as a location where, even if coherence can be felt, it will always be on the other side of a great divide, never immediately available to a life lived in the present' (2002: 118). As in many post-colonial narratives, memory and a sense of coherent history are under the risk of elimination. In Irish and Scottish Gothic 'specific modes of ghostly persistence … may occur when … national aspirations are thwarted by conquest or by settlement, as they have been so often … the Gothic is especially powerful in rendering the complex hauntings in such confined histories' (Punter 2002: 105). Imagination and emotion are both disturbingly excessive and destructive, whereas for the Romantics they were a necessary stimulus to the act of creation. The irrational triumphs in the Gothic, and societal conventions are broken apart. At a most basic level, the Gothic questions sexual identity: what is masculine? What is feminine? Obviously, this causes a departure from the safety of the family unit. The Gothic thus ruptures the basic ideas we have about culture, civilisation and identity.

Jordan's 1999 release, *In Dreams*, ostensibly a serial-killer thriller, was greeted almost universally with disapproval. This was all the more disheartening after the art-house success of *The Butcher Boy* in 1997. One critic, while praising the visual qualities of the film, calls Jordan to task for 'a flawed storyline'. After pointing out numerous unbelievable plot points, the writer then says, 'it's clear that when the work was divvied up Robinson dominated the writing while Jordan concentrated on the direction' (Gray 1999: 37). In fact, the script written by Bruce Robinson (writer/director of *Withnail and I*, 1987) is a lugubrious dialogue-focused work, most of which was deleted by Jordan, who still generously gave Robinson a co-writing credit. Yet *In Dreams* is very much an integral part of the Jordan oeuvre. It deals with thematics that can be found throughout his work: the importance of myth and ritual; the structure and meaning of fairy tales; a deleterious view of the family; violence and its attendant psychic and physical damage; questions about sexual identity; misguided longings for an ill-fated love; interrogations of masculinity; an attachment to the dream world; characters haunted by loss; and the fragile boundaries between the rational and irrational.

The film opens with raging water rapidly engulfing a church-like structure; a statue of Jesus floats by. The water bursts through a window, and shatters the glass. Then, after an elliptical transition we see scuba divers gracefully wending their way through the pathways of a town that was flooded and submerged to create a dam. The subterranean swimmers are bathed in a blue light as they swim silently through the drowned town. Their torches create an eerie, otherworldly luminosity. From the outset, *In Dreams* is situated in an oneiric world that is at once ghostly and unrelenting.

The divers glide through a primary locale of the Gothic, the labyrinth: 'a place of all forms of excessive, irrational and passionate behaviour, the labyrinth is also the site in which the absence or loss of reason, sobriety, decency and morality is displayed in full horror' (Botting 1996: 83). It is a disturbing opening that positions us within the world of the Gothic, and its attendant sense of despair and anxiety. We know this town was drowned to create a dam, but what are the divers searching for years later?

The film's narrative traverses territory that is *unheimlich*; it negotiates a liminal space. The underwater town is the space of imagination, but at the same time it is an authentic place that was once inhabited by characters within the film's fictive world. The underwater town is interstitial; it resides at the intersection of the real and the imaginary. As unstable as it is, the framework of the world as we know it will collapse entirely during the course of the film.

We meet Claire and Rebecca, mother and child, as they run lines for a school recital of *Snow White*. Rebecca performs, in a clever anthropomorphic Gothic gesture, 'The Mirror' (she is wrapped in shroud-like material that prefigures the raising of her corpse from the lake). As well as introducing some of Jordan's themes, this opening provides a link to Claire's work: she is an illustrator and adaptor of children's books; we find her looking at her adaptation of the Grimms' fairy tales. The family is completed by Paul (Aidan Quinn), an often-absent airline pilot. The home tends to be a place of sanctuary in the Gothic, but here a host of narrative events sabotages this domesticity. The violation of the family house occurs in stages. Firstly, Claire has disturbing dreams and premonitions. It is obvious from her husband's irritated response, ('Oh Jesus, here we go again') that this is one in an ongoing series of episodes in which Claire has exhibited the power to dream or visualise events. Her apparent fragility is also contained in the exposition when Claire says: 'I guess I'm crazy again.' In this line we get some of Claire's backstory. Because of prior articulations of her 'second sight', the psychiatric establishment considers her delusional. To muddy the portrait of 'the happy family' even further, it is then revealed that Paul has been having an affair with a flight attendant in Australia, thus accounting for his long absences. He rationalises his behaviour by complaining that because of Claire's obsession with the covert metaphysical world, he must seek intimacy elsewhere.

Claire has been dreaming of a series of child murders, and in fact we learn in the opening moments of the film that another little girl has been killed. This prompts her husband to inform the police of her visions, but the officer in charge of the investigation treats the message as the jabberings of an unstable person, and in this he mirrors Paul's own quasi-scepticism. The weakness or absence of the rational is one of the defining characteristics of the Gothic. Each in turn – Claire's husband, the police and a psychiatrist – will disavow Claire's cognitive gift. Anne Williams writes:

> These family 'scandals' of Gothic criticism call attention to the importance of boundaries: the literal and figurative processes by which society organises itself, 'draws the line', declaring this 'legitimate', that not; this 'proper', that not; this 'sane', that not, rules and divisions that structure all dimensions of human life. Such 'lines' and 'boundaries' may be real – the cold, hard stone of the castle and cathedral … Such lines and walls both create the possibility of transgression and suggest the proper punishment for those rebels who cross them, who 'go too far': to be immured, incarcerated, imprisoned in the attics, dungeons, or secret chambers of the family or the state. (1995: 12)

We watch the children perform the section of *Snow White* in which the huntsman is supposed to kill the girl as specified by her evil stepmother; the children in the play gather round the huntsman with his knife held aloft, chanting, 'Please show mercy, please.' This spooky scene prefigures the action of the film, but unfortunately for the murder victims there is no mercy granted by the killer.

Paul leaves for work after the play, and in a harrowing scene Claire cannot find Rebecca amidst the gathering of gossamer-winged little girls. Claire comes upon the wings of Rebecca's costume on a boulder near the shore, and perceives instantaneously what has happened. Claire had foreseen another murder, but did not know the victim would be her own beloved daughter. At this point the film's antagonist/murderer has not been revealed, but he stealthily leaves clues for Claire so that she will interpret his actions. The lake (which now covers the drowned town) is dredged for Rebecca's body, and before it is even brought to shore Claire bounds into her car and drives at a great speed, smashing through an elevated guard rail into the water. This action initiates one of the film's most striking narrative tropes: Claire's willingness and desire to die.

In one of the film's later scenes, when Claire is incarcerated in a mental hospital, her dog barks outside for her attention. Claire climbs out of a window and follows the dog onto a crowded four-lane highway. A huge truck is quickly making its way towards Claire when it swerves to avoid her, slamming into numerous cars on either side. Claire remains unharmed under the body of the truck. This heightened scene,

Jordan directs children for the school production of *Snow White*

which seems extraneous to the main action, confirms Claire's status as 'a special one'. She is spared most improbably in the accident and housed safely under the truck that surely would have killed her. It can be seen as an act of divine or malefic intervention. Claire is spared in a most unrealistic way so that she can complete her mission and die – not peacefully, but as one absorbed into the omnipotent evil that guides the film to its baleful climax.

When Claire awakens six weeks later from a comatose state, she is upset that she has been brought back to life and to mourning. There is an ellipsis to Claire waking again in the hospital bed, as Paul sings 'Don't Sit Under the Apple Tree'. She asks why he is singing that particular song, and Paul replies that she has been singing it in her sleep. Importantly, Claire says: 'Someone was singing *through* me.' This confusion between the self and other becomes one of the film's major themes. Claire is sent home; hair shorn, wearing an androgynous denim jacket and trainers in contradistinction to the more girlish and feminine look she sported in prelapsarian times. It is not only her innocence that will be stripped away, but her life as she knows it. The film also challenges the paradisal notion of childhood as it focuses on children's lives cut short by violence.

As the film progresses, when her husband attempts to make love to her Claire is seized by a vision of the murderer who simultaneously kisses her, and whispers, 'I know you've been dreaming about me, because I've been dreaming about you.' As she fends off the kiss in her dream state, she vigorously bites her husband's lip in the reality of her waking world. The underlying idea of cannibalism and the 'Dead World' throws the film into an ever more apocalyptic arena. Cannibalism is portrayed in fiction as evil and barbaric, where all the values and myths of a culture are inverted; the cannibal meal is not seen as communion, but as fragmentation and torment. The spilling of blood does not replenish the land, it is not redemptive as human sacrifice as it is often thought to be; the ritual dimensions of slaughter and cannibalism are lost and empty (see Sharrett 1984: 266). This aspect of anthropophagy ties in effectively with the dark carnivalesque traits of the Gothic.

Paul leaves for work, and what proceeds is a waking nightmare for Claire. The house is the defining symbol of what is right and normal; primitive anxieties erupt in the face of its violation. Such an intrusion occurs while Claire is in her home. Firstly, she spills a bottle of red ink on her workstation.[1] As an illustrator, she designs on her computer, and without her intervention images of apples begin to fill the screen, cascading across the monitor. Claire is startled by the sound of a child laughing and a barking dog; she runs outside and finds a swing in motion, an apple placed on the seat, and a radio that plays 'Don't Sit Under the Apple Tree' of its own accord. Claire smashes the radio to bits, and turns to the woods to look for her dog.

When Claire returns home, she smells something burning in the oven. As she enters the kitchen, apples overflow on every surface of the room. Although meant for the benign purpose of making apple sauce, the apples are a trigger for Claire's mounting anxiety and loss of control. She stuffs the apples into the garbage disposal unit with great fury. The machine then regurgitates its contents, vomiting pureed apples on Claire and the kitchen, in a scene that recalls the unstoppable water of the film's opening scene. Claire races upstairs and finds her computer typing messages of its own volition; the monitor fills with a response to, or repetition of, Claire's utterances. In an effort to rid herself of this disturbance, she heaves the computer out the window. We next see Paul as he enters the house; the walls are covered with graf-

Annette Bening and Jordan confer about apples

fiti, sentence fragments painted either in blood, paint or red ink adorn the walls and mirrors of the house. Claire lays prone on their bed, barely conscious; she has slit her wrists. The refuge of the home has now become untenable for her. It is a place that holds no comfort; it is a house transformed by unspeakable malevolence and affliction. David Punter writes about this transition as a reflection of the Irish Gothic:

> If [Shelley's] 'Ozymendias' is a quasi-Gothic myth that has to do with the fallen grandeur of past civilisations while continuing to assert their relevance as a warning to the continuity of national progress, then the myth in Melmoth [the Wanderer] goes one step further, as one might expect in an Irish context, and undermines the entire sense of memory and interpretation on which history is based. Whereas in England even a removed and subverted notion of tradition can remain relevant, here in the Irish context … there is no bedrock on which to stand. The Gothic removal of history does not suggest analogies to past civilisations or cultures, but rather exposes a terrifying abyss in an occupied land, the looming presence of a nonverbal 'history' that might not be human or coherent at all, just as the issue of Catholic emancipation in Ireland hinged on the denial of human rights to the majority of the population. (2002: 120)

This quotation is highly evocative of the narrative of *In Dreams*, for Claire, particularly, has the overwhelming void stretching out before her. Once she departs from her home she loses her bond with life as she knew it. Her personal history, including family and work, evaporates; Claire's remembrance of and identification with her security and connection with normality is severed and she plunges into a chaotic world in which the words 'Mommy' and 'Daddy' no longer have a stable or coherent meaning.

Claire is now checked into the local psychiatric facility, her wrists bandaged. The psychiatrist, Dr Silverman (played by Jordan's *doppelgänger*, Stephen Rea) probes Claire, showing her photos of the scrawlings on the wall of her home:

Dr Silverman:	Did you write this Claire?
Claire:	(laughing edgily) Yeah, but somebody made me do it.
Dr Silverman:	But who cut your wrists? Did someone make you do it?
Claire:	(laughter which turns to pain) No, that was all my own work.
Dr Silverman:	But why Claire?
Claire:	(firmly) I wanted it to stop. Can you dream when you're awake, when the sun's shining? I couldn't take it anymore, I'm not that strong.

Herein lies a dominant Gothic mode of thought: it is no longer the quest for identity (as in Romanticism), the issue now becomes the loss of the integrity of the self, a world in which wholeness is impossible (see Day 1985: 75). Subjectivity and objectivity commingle, creating an indescribable horror.

Claire's self-mutilation ensues from the invasion of her identity by the 'Other'. Slitting her wrists is a way of rejecting the Other and its violation of her consciousness. The permeability of consciousness and the idea of crossing previously secure boundaries, is a thematic signature and a most frightening feature of the horror film. The idea of penetration, particularly since it is an invasion not merely of the body, but the mind as well, leaves Claire in a dehumanised and fragmented state that separates her from the human community. Claire is in some ways the ideal Gothic heroine, the Persecuted Maiden, and is also easily identifiable as 'Freud's hysteric'; 'her presumed passivity and lack of self-knowledge make her easy to diagnose' (Massé 2000: 234). It is then up to Claire to become her own analyst and analysand.

The invasion of the self by the Other is a primary image in the Gothic: 'everything contains and becomes its opposite, the self is found in the Other and the Other is in fact a face of self' (Day 1985: 22). At some point in the trajectory of the story, 'the threat is contained in the other half of one's self, and at a certain point, these two parts of a whole engage in deadly combat in which they maim or kill one another' (ibid.). This is precisely what ensues in *In Dreams*.

As Freud wrote in 'The Uncanny': 'We have characters who are to be considered identical because they look alike. This relation is accentuated by mental processes leaping from one of these characters to another – by what we should call telepathy – so that the one possesses knowledge, feelings and experience in common with the other' (1955a: 234). The suggestiveness of the mirror and its incarnation in narrative mirroring is a basic Gothic figure. The mirror is the site of distortion, lack of balance and, perhaps most importantly, unreality. Michel Foucault has interesting remarks about the mirror as a counter-site, in which the authenticity of the real world is contested by a space that inverts and challenges it (see Foucault 1970: 3–16). The site of the Gothic is characterised by its heterotopia: all structures and landscapes are constituted by spaces that are omitted from the utopic world, 'gothic machinery and the wild landscapes of Romantic individualism give way to terrors and horrors that are much closer to home, uncanny disruptions of boundaries' (Botting 1996: 156). The 'I' represented in the mirror is an absent I, thus dislodging a sense of the real and the rational. It is one further example of the way in which the boundaries in the Gothic cease to exist. It is a melding, again, of self and other, 'marked by the fact that the subject identifies himself with someone else, so that he is in doubt as to which his self is' (Freud 1955a: 234).

There is an extended sequence in Jordan's film in which Claire, now confined in a mental institution, becomes aware that she is inhabiting the same room as Vivian (Robert Downey Jr) (her Other), and starts to follow the same escape route he charted as a teenage inmate. Once again a labyrinthian structure – air ducts within the building's walls and ceilings – is centralised in the film. The scene is played out via intercut shots of Vivian in the past and Claire in the film's present tense. (This looks forward to the complex temporal structure in Jordan's next film, *The End of the Affair*). At one point Vivian, dressed as a woman, asks the policeman who has unwittingly picked up someone he believes is an attractive young girl, to drive him to the lake (and the drowned town). The cop asks 'Why are we here?' to which Vivian responds, 'This is my home.' He then shoots the officer. As water has such a potent archetypal association with women and birth, it creates a situation in which the *anima* and the *animus* merge. Vivian's maleness coalesces with that which is symbolic of the feminine.

The sense of doubling is made manifest not only in relation to Claire and Vivian, but with Claire and her own selfhood. She spends much of the film in a state of immense agony, emotionally and physically – for example, when she is forcibly strapped to a gurney in a rubber room. There are in fact very few scenes of incarceration in any film as painful to watch as Claire drugged not into oblivion, which she might welcome, but in a kind of quasi-anaesthetised stupor that only frustrates her attempts to communicate the agonising vision she has of her husband being slain. She is impotent with rage, and her pleas are taken as a sign of madness; it is the paradigm of heightened dramatic irony. She screams at the orderlies: 'The bastard is in my brain and now he's murdering my husband!' As Steve Bruhm writes, 'pain evokes an antagonistic relationship between the body and the self, at the same time as that it allows no distinction between body and self: I hurt and I am being hurt; I hurt myself' (1994: 9). So, once again, we have a sense that the distinction between inner and outer are conflated in a tortuous scene of mortification. The sensation of pain is a constant in the Gothic world.

> By collapsing the distinction between the imaginative inside and the spectator outside, the play (*Cenci*) ultimately obscures the boundaries between privacy and publicity … Beatrice [the female protagonist] can no longer distinguish between what is happening to her physically and what is conjured imaginatively. And with no distinction between the inside and outside, she is unable to find refuge from her affliction; she can retreat neither to a private world cut off from the tortures of the outside nor to a communal sharing of her pains. (Bruhm 1994: 89–90)

Claire's pain is all the more frightening when we see images of her shut away, unable to take action to save her husband. She is framed clinging limply to the glass door of the rubber room as the camera travels backwards; it is a devastating depiction of her isolation, sense of hopelessness and loneliness. One is reminded here of Vivian, abandoned by his mother to die in the drowned town, chained to his bed, lost and alone. Claire's empathy for Vivian's circumstances are spoken in a simple but enormously touching response to the psychiatrist trying to understand Vivian's penchant for evildoing; she says: 'Maybe he's lonely.'

Claire's fusion with death, as mentioned above, is shown beautifully in an intercut fantasy/dream sequence in which Claire, in a flowing red silk gown, walks in slow-motion through the deserted corridors of the hotel in which her husband has been killed. Red is once more used iconically, as a symbol of the fall, the apples, of blood, of Ruby the kidnapped child whom Claire will rescue. Here Claire is enveloped by deep despair and insupportable grief. Yet there is something graceful and serene in her carriage: she is the mistress of the house of the dead.[2] 'Deteriorated places, neglected buildings, discarded streets and facilities may reveal … a lack of common renewal, a

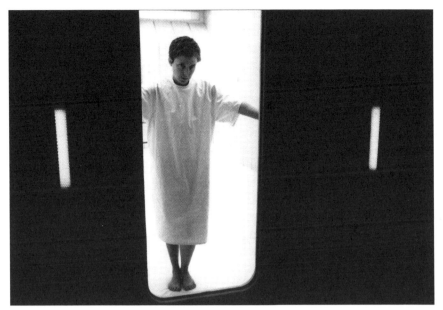

Claire clings to the door of the rubber room, unable to take the action that would save her husband

failure of the fertile, creative spirit. Such corrupted places are outcroppings of a social system's underground, unadorned areas of the communal psyche' (Morgan 2002: 185). The meltdown of Claire's identity and her alienation in a world no one can comprehend are critically important to the film.

In Dreams herein shows its face as part of the Irish Gothic. It has been called an 'impure' and 'heterogeneous' genre, and is divided into two divergent master narratives – the paranoid Gothic and Gothic realism. Within the paranoid Gothic sub-genre, the family unit is totalising and subsumes any criticism addressed to it. Once her family is slaughtered Claire's private world is one which is inhabited by guilt. Although Claire takes an active role in hunting down her adversary (recalling the popular detective/ androgyne figure of nineteenth-century Gothic), she clearly suffers from the pathology of masochism. As Freud states in 'The Economic Problems in Masochism' (1955c), the latter neurosis is the place where the libido and the death instinct meet head on. Claire mourns for her lost family; they are displaced by a bizarre family configuration of Vivian and another kidnapped child, Ruby (Krystal Benn). Vivian, who only appears physically in the film's final act, embodies a classic case of sadism, in which the destructive instinct, the drive for mastery and the will to power are the death wish turned to the external world. Claire is unable to externalise these drives, and therefore would be considered a masochist. In 'Beyond the Pleasure Principle' (1955b), Freud writes of the human instinct to preserve life through procreation by joining larger units. But this is coupled with a contrary instinct wishing to destroy those units and to return to an inorganic state, that is, death.[3] Vivian's wish to recreate the family unit is perverse in the extreme: 'the elements of biological inversion in the Gothic framework – the negation of all that is vigorous and life-beneficial [is an] extended trope turning on enfeeblement and deterioration – the absence of Eros' (Morgan 2002: 197). Freud also wrote in 'The Uncanny' (1955a) that the figure of the double revolves around a conception of self that is both sadistic and masochistic; and as William Patrick Day remarks, 'the Gothic world comes to dominate and control the protagonists, whatever their course of action, reducing them to the state of non-being, absorbing them into the other. The pattern of all relationships in Gothic fantasy operates on the dynamic of sadomasochism' (Day 1985: 19).

The Gothic and *In Dreams* support this contention in the gender-bending central relationship between Claire and Vivian in which dominator and dominated continually trade places, and where the masculine and feminine selves become indistinguishable, 'the haunted victim and the haunted persecutor ... each the other's obsession' (Fiedler 1997: 131). Vivian's sexual identity is emblematised by his long flowing locks and his lengthy, manicured nails, as well as his given name, which can be either masculine or feminine. Claire, a feminised presence in the opening sequences of the film, becomes sexually neutered during the course of the narrative. As Margot Gayle Backus writes: 'the relationship between sexuality (especially homo-eroticism), liminality, division, and repetition in ... Irish literary Gothicism' is commonplace in a 'heterogeneous selection of texts' (1989: 155)

Vivian's experience of family life involves his neglect and punishment by his mother, whose power still dominates Vivian's disturbed mind. (She left Vivian chained to his bed, and did not return to free him when the town was flooded. Vivian saved himself, but the trauma he experienced left him consigned to a psychiatric hospital.) Once Claire disturbs Vivian's inner sanctum, the 'Good Apple' cider factory, their relationship changes, and the level of danger and the potential for annihilation is elevated. When Claire tries to free the little girl, Ruby, Vivian anoints Claire the 'Bad Mommy' and puts her in 'Bad Mommy's' clothes, the same clothing worn by his own mother. (And which he apparently has worn too. Ruby says: 'When he plays Mommy ... you should hear how his voice changes.' She also says, obviously repeating something Vivian has told her: 'Daddies can be just like Mommies.') So the family romance that Vivian plays out turns on the woman, his woman, the stand-in for the uncaring, punishing mother of his childhood. To be a mother is to be monstrous. As Barbara Creed has written: 'definitions of the monstrous as constructed in the modern horror text are grounded in ancient religious and historical notions of abjection, particularly in relation to the following religious "abomination": sexual immorality and perversion; corporeal alteration, decay and death; human sacrifice; murder; the corpse; bodily wastes; the feminine body and incest' (1999: 252).

The representation of the mother figure in *In Dreams* is complex, and as with much else in the film is an inversion of the notion of the 'normal' mother. Claire's insupportable guilt over the death of her only child leads one to consider her qualities as a mother. The Earth Mother figure is crucial to fairy tales, and can usually be found alone in a habitation that is surrounded by woods; she also has a connection with animals (Dobie, her dog, in Claire's case). Jung has written about the dualistic status of the Earth Mother (which reminds us of Yeats' concept of the integrative and non-integrative woman):

[She] is associated with … maternal solicitude and sympathy; the magic authority of the female; the wisdom and spiritual exaltation that transcends reason; any helpful instinct or impulse; all that is benign, all that cherishes and sustains, that fosters growth and fertility. The place of magic transformation and rebirth, together with the underworld and its inhabitants are presided over by the Mother. On the negative side the mother archetype may connote anything secret, hidden, dark; the abyss, the world of the dead, anything that devours, seduces, and poisons, that is terrifying and inescapable like fate. (In Birkhäuser-Oeri 1988: 14)

In the storytelling of Christian origin, in which the Virgin Mary would be the mother paradigm, there is very little made of the more malefic side of mother figures. Fairy tales incorporate 'the dark points of the feminine principle or indeed the principle of evil' (Birkhäuser-Oeri 1988: 19) in the maternal figure. Here, the idea of 'Bad Mommy' is an interesting explosion of the obsessively 'good' mothers who protect and nurture their children. Claire has failed to save her daughter, in spite of her premonitions. In Jungian terms, Claire has, until this point, seen herself as a positive representation of motherhood. With all the ominous signals that collect around Claire's homelife, she encounters her dark side when she becomes 'crazy', but this does not exclude her perception of herself as Rebecca's 'good' mother. The more she fails to see how her darkness invaded her relationship with her daughter, the more evil, through the unconscious, will find a route to be released. Vivian's mother is perhaps more honest in that she has abandoned any notion of supporting her son even in the most basic way.

Vivian says as they enter the cider factory: 'We'll have pisketti for lunch.' He reverts to his child self, trying to recuperate the family that he lacked. Gaylyn Studlar has said that masochistic desire depends on separation, not consummation, and that to fill this desire, to achieve orgasm, means death (see Studlar 1988: 19); Claire's safety, although not her sanity, was ensured when Vivian was only a phantom presence. However, sharing a bed with him, although no sexual relationship is imaginable, now brings her closer not to orgasm but to the death spasm she will experience as the film climaxes. The two figures are locked in a mutual vortex of violent psychotic fragmentation in which Claire is willing to do anything to secure the safety of the child, obviously a displaced version of her own daughter. Claire, in a state of agitation and guilt, stops at nothing to physically and emotionally entrap Vivian and play upon his greatest fears. If we can see the three forming an ever-shifting triadic Oedipal arrangement, the lack is the sexual coupling of Daddy and Mommy, and instead the threat of castration hangs in the air, each half of the double terrorising the other physically and psychically. 'Rather than fertility, however, horror centres upon withering; rather than on renewal, it focuses on degeneration; rather than on an intrepid human vitality, it centres upon the eminently assailable human body and the deep-rooted anxieties it situates' (Morgan 2002: 85–6). Claire, dressed in Vivian's mother's clothes, begins tapping her foot, arms held akimbo, a scene of Vivian's past that Claire was privy to in one of her visions. It is a dangerous strategy, but as Vivian panics he becomes once again the little boy chained to the bed, and Claire is able to buy some time for Ruby to escape.

The ending of the film has Claire and Vivian battling it out. Their family is one of 'collapse, a broken, ironic version of fertility rite … radical destabilisation and disconnection. Ritual fragments are deeply significant to the horror aesthetic ordeal, labyrinth, the journey underground' (Morgan 2002: 88). Now outside on a bridge, Claire and Vivian are in a pitched struggle, each wielding their own weapon as the police helicopter hovers above, ready to shoot Vivian. Claire and Vivian fall into the lake of the drowned town and Claire dies, precisely as she foresaw in a dream; clearly, there are ritualistic aspects to her death in water. As she begins to float to the surface, bathed in a lambent light, she encounters her daughter:

Rebecca: Mirror, Mirror on the wall, who's the fairest of them all?
Claire: You are, darling.
Rebecca: No, you are.

Is Rebecca claiming that Claire's ultimate and most beautiful victory is her martyrdom and death? The conversation between the revenants continues:

Rebecca: Come with me.
Claire: Where darling?
Rebecca: Home.

It is an eerie reminder of the young Vivian's reference to the water as his home. It is interesting to note that in Jordan's shooting script *In Dreams* ends, disconcertingly, with this scene of Rebecca and Claire; we behold beatitude, comfort and signs of the numinous. In the finished film, however, Vivian, who survives the fall into the lake, is imprisoned for life for his crimes. He walks to his cell, and with the introduction of each new element of his environment, Vivian says, 'I can live with that.' He is complacent until he is shocked out of sleep by a corporeal Claire who says: 'Pleasant dreams', and violently bites his lip. Vivian looks in a mirror, and an off-screen hand reaches out and smashes his face against the glass. Suddenly words are incised into the walls and ceiling of the cell, reading 'Sweet dreams, Vivian', as the blood red inscriptions liquify and drip down the walls. Claire has now become the sadist, as she will control Vivian's life as long as he lives. Vivian begins to scream, and much like the scene of Claire's horrifying bondage in the asylum Vivian presses his face against the window, shrieking in terror; 'in death, the protagonist becomes not simply a victim, but fully a part of what tormented him. Death releases the protagonist from the last vestiges of human identity, and he becomes the embodiment of cruelty and terror' (Day 1985: 7).

It is striking how much the work of cultural philosopher and literary critic René Girard's seminal book, *Violence and the Sacred*, can illuminate and broaden one's understanding of *In Dreams*. His chapter called 'From Mimetic Desire to the Monstrous Double' contains a different formulation for the use of the word 'mimesis' than that of other scholars. He uses it to cover a whole range of things; it is a mechanism that generates the formation of personality, patterns of human interaction, belief systems and cultural practices. What he says is that we have to understand the relatedness of mimesis and desire, something that rarely comes into any theories that explain human agency. He deals with the way in which humans work and why we do what we do. One of the main points of his argument is that people are wrongly thought to desire spontaneously. In fact, human desire is mediated (or mimetic); people desire because of others, not because of their own preferences. Mimetic structure, for Girard, is the basis of human experience. These interactions are based on desiring in terms of others – what he calls 'non-instinctual' and sees as the starting point for both archaic and modern belief systems and emotions that form human society (1977: 146).

Girard discusses the role of violence in awakening desire, something we now call the pathology of sado-masochism because we believe that 'normal' desire is non-violent. What Girard calls 'the sacrificial crisis' is for him a universal phenomenon in which violence becomes the 'instrument, object, and all-inclusive subject of desire' (1977: 144). He opposes Freud's notion of the death instinct, which Girard calls 'a surrender to mythological thinking' (1977: 145), and something that takes us back to a belief in Fate, the gods, and other agencies who control human behaviour. The mimetic impulse is spurned, but this only strengthens the desiring person's wish. Therefore, Girard says, desire and violence are forever linked in the mind. These spiralling energies, rather than staying on the level of conflicting desires, become channelled into a ritual form. It is not good versus evil that is at the base of modern interpretations of the spirit of tragedy, but cycles. This cycle of alternation forms a relationship, fundamental to the relationships in tragedy; it is not the province of a single individual (1977: 149). Every act of violence, whether verbal (such as an insult) or physical, seems to be the ultimate blow, but actually it is only a step towards the next act of violence. Girard makes the evocative statement that 'desire clings to violence' because violence is the signifier of the cherished being, the signifier of divinity (1977: 151).

All of these alternations and cycles lead to what Girard calls the 'vertigo of violence'; reversal after reversal after reversal occurs, until the feeling of dizziness overwhelms the perception of reality. Their very souls and their being are seized in this irresistible, Dionysian whirlwind of violence that captures everybody in the eye of the storm. What happens is the creation of a phantasmatic state – it is not something people experience together, but a kind of bizarre, antic mixing together of elements which might normally be perceived of as separate (1977: 161). Once again, the notion of the dark carnival is invoked. Here Girard parts company with traditional sociologists. They try to classify this kind of grotesquerie as monstrous, with the participants as monsters. Girard sees these monsters as doubles, something that obscures the idea of difference. In the mental space that is created by simultaneous unity and difference, the opposing parties have unanimity only by acknowledging the monstrous double, which then becomes the object of violence. In this atmosphere of horror and hallucination at the peak of hysteria the monstrous double is everywhere at once; an act of violence is sanctified against this double – but the double is no longer distinguishable from 'the other': they are now one and the same (see Girard 1977: 143–68). The subject becomes caught up in the spirit of possession, and feels invaded psychically, physically

by a supernatural creature – a God/spirit/Demon who possesses one's soul. Possession is an extreme form of alienation – 'me and not-me' – in which one completely
absorbs the desires of the other; it is now no longer mimetic, but has internalised the
other (1977: 161–5). This provides a wonderfully clear description of the path and the
outcome of *In Dreams*.

Neil Jordan's overarching aesthetic strategy is to locate the fantastic and the
uncanny in an otherwise realistic setting. This aesthetic form then allows for the
uncanny to surface and to bring with it things like the diabolical form of the numinous
and the *heimlich-heimlisch* (the secretly repressed). Jordan marries the prosaic world
with the poetic, the physical world to the spiritual world, the world of the beautiful
to the world of darkness and terror. All boundaries are left in question. It is at this
crossroads that we find the films of Neil Jordan. Nowhere is this more evident than in
In Dreams, a work that is fully equal to his best films.

CHAPTER EIGHT

The End of the Affair: 'This is a Diary of Hate'

Adaptation and screenwriting

> 'Temperamentally, [Greene] was much like the central character, Bendrix – a lonely man, capable of great sympathy but with a sliver of ice in his heart. I feel lucky to have been his friend, but I doubt that I knew him – I don't think anyone really did.'
>
> – Paul Theroux

> '[It's] about Britishness, about rain and about God.'
>
> – Neil Jordan

To understand why Jordan was drawn to an adaptation of *The End of the Affair*, a *chef d'oeuvre* of one of the best British writers of the twentieth century, we must comprehend, at least to some degree, the tempestuous life of the book's author, Graham Greene. The book is a paradigm of what is called the 'second-phase narratives' of Greene's career: *The Heart of the Matter* (1948), *The Third Man* (1950) and *The End of the Affair* (1951) constitute a triumvirate of novels that witness Greene dealing with deeply personal matters; one also sees a diminished distance between himself and his protagonists as well as between the reader and the author. At this juncture Greene also introduces first-person narration to his work. Self-doubt and self-criticism emerge in these works in relation to the spheres of marriage, love, religion and art. Greene's book, while addressing many issues, is most certainly the portrait of an artist in crisis or at the very least in a state of apprehension about his work and life (see Hoskins 1999: 139–40).

The first paragraph of *The End of the Affair* reveals the questioning attitude that permeates Greene's work of the period:

> A story has no beginning or end; arbitrarily one chooses that moment of experience from which to look back or from which to look ahead. I want to say 'one chooses' with the inaccurate pride of a professional writer who – when he has been seriously noted at all – has been praised for his technical ability; but do I in fact of my own will choose that black wet January night on the Common, in 1946, the sight of Henry Miles ... or did these images choose me? (1999: 7)

This notion is echoed uncannily by Jordan in many of his interviews, when he raises the conundrum of whether a camera can reflect reality, or if it is his own feelings that create the filmed world.

Before Greene revised the book for a collection of his work, the main character, Bendrix, was presented as a venomous creature whose sexuality was permeated with malevolence; for example, 'The demon had done its work, I felt drained of venom' (1999: 65). One can perceive the Satanic lustre that tinges the character of Bendrix. A feeling of melancholia, even a sense of failure, percolates through the source novel and the film. Bendrix fails to save Sarah from her unhappy existence with her civil servant husband; he is unable to protect his soulmate from a highly preventable death. One assumes that Sarah has tuberculosis, which, if intervention is made, is not necessarily a fatal disease. It is difficult to assign blame for this neglect: Sarah herself, who has lost the will to live; Henry for not noticing; any number of characters who have heard her consumptive coughing long before she dies. Ultimately, it is Sarah who is the author of her own suffering, and it is her religious conviction (or delusion) that keeps her and Bendrix apart. And it is Sarah's death that can be viewed as a second sacrifice and renunciation of mortality that casts her, especially in the film, in a vaporous, almost saintly light. One can further understand *The End of the Affair* as an unconcealed portrait of Greene's own tortuous affairs of the heart. After a long and rather punishing courtship, Greene married Vivien (née Dayrell-Browning) in his mid-twenties. An agreement, insisted upon by the religious Vivien, compelled Greene to convert to Catholicism; being received into the Church did not, however, alter Green's penchant for prostitutes or a mistress on the side. Sarah, in *The End of the Affair*, is modelled after Catherine Walston with whom Greene had a twelve-year relationship. She was a society woman married to a wealthy landowner, Harry Walston, who was later attached to the Foreign Office. The descriptions and photos of Catherine confirm that she was a great beauty known also for her intelligence and charm. Catherine was undoubtedly a free spirit, an iconoclast who wrote: 'At the time I married [Harry] I decided that I would give it a try, and if I found anyone I liked better, I would leave Harry and marry X' (in Sherry 1995: 223). She was described variously as mischievous, vivacious and deeply religious. Malcom Muggeridge describes Catherine as '*sans merci* but so *belle*' (in Sherry 1995: 219). Clearly, Catherine's Catholicism did not hinder her inclination for love affairs during her marriage; she had no problem reconciling her amorous adventures with her religious beliefs. Greene's original dedication of *The End of the Affair* was 'To Catherine', an incautious affront to Greene and Catherine's social community, as well as an unabashed insult to Catherine's husband. The inscription was changed to 'To C', but remained 'Catherine' in the North American version of the book.

In Jordan's screen adaptation of *The End of the Affair*, he makes several important changes. Structurally, one of the biggest alterations involves the death of Sarah (Julianne Moore). In the novel, Sarah's death occurs two-thirds of the way through, and her diary is compacted into approximately thirty pages. Then the novel changes course and dwells on philosophy and religion, as well as the developing friendship between Bendrix (Ralph Fiennes) and Henry (Stephen Rea). Greene regretted killing off Sarah too soon in the story, and had no appetite to continue writing once she was no longer a character (see Lyall 1999). Jordan also found Greene's dénouement of the book wanting, so he kept Sarah alive until very near the film's end. He said in an interview, 'The basic dynamic of the character, Bendrix, is that the more he says he hates, the more you know he has loved. The thing I changed was exactly that kind of theoretical argument, that sense of philosophical argument towards the end of the novel which I think overwhelmed the characters and the story itself. I find if there is a fault in the novel it is that' (in Sheehey & Traynor 2000: 17).

The odyssey of Jordan's adaptation is interesting. He first asked fellow writer John Banville (winner of the Man Booker Prize for *The Sea* in 2005) if he was interested in collaborating on a screenplay of *The End of the Affair*. Banville wrote back in the autumn of 1994 that he agreed it would have been a productive union, and sent his first treatment of the script later that year. In an undated treatment called 'The Promise', meek Henry is recast as Santos, an older man, who is still a 'handsome, urbane, world-weary, and much travelled' diplomat who represents Colombia at the UN. Bendrix is a policeman of modest origin, Banville writes, 'Irish American, perhaps? He is intelligent, unexpectedly sophisticated, ambitious.' He is a senior officer demoted for stealing drugs from a bust and attempting to sell them. As the film opens, Bendrix is investigating Santos, thought to be fronting a money-laundering scheme for members of a Colombian drug cartel. Sarah is also of humble origins, according to Jordan, 'the typical WASP beauty', an opera singer who agrees to marry Santos so that he will sponsor her musical ambitions.[1] Bendrix becomes fixated on Sarah; he has the Santos apartment under surveillance. Bendrix and Sarah begin an affair, and he becomes enthralled not only with her, but with the world of opera. Santos learns of the infidelity and the surveillance and begins to play a 'cat and mouse game' with Bendrix.

The bombing from the source novel is retained in the treatment. Bendrix is believed to be dead, and Sarah makes a vow not to see Bendrix if God will let him live. This is really the only similarity between the book and Banville's treatment. Bendrix is warned that Santos is to be assassinated. It is the opening night of Sarah's opera career; an assassin aims at Santos, but Sarah, seeing the danger, throws herself in front of Santos and takes a bullet for him.

It is a difficult to imagine what was going on in Banville's mind when he wrote this. Even if the treatment eliminates the temporality (World War Two) and place (London) of the novel, both of which are acutely important to the tone of Greene's book, the casting of mild-mannered Henry as a drug lord seems rather preposterous. Banville was, by mutual agreement, released from the project, and a letter from 4 April 1996 suggests that the friendship between the two authors remained unharmed by the incident. Banville writes: 'Your economy and precision are apparent from the first lines. I think it will be a fascinating, dark and troubling movie. I look forward to seeing it in a year or two. Best of luck and do keep in touch' (from Jordan's personal archives).

A further alteration of the book is the rapid changing of time frames in Jordan's film. Where Greene uses this strategy perhaps four times during the course of the book (if we do not include Sarah's diary, in which she leaps from one time and space to another), in Jordan's work there are 18 temporal changes. He has said that one of the most difficult tasks he faced in setting up this formal device was finding a pivot point to cut from one time period to another (Neil Jordan, *The End of the Affair* DVD commentary). An illustration of a pivot point comes in an early scene of the film. It is 1944 and Bendrix and Sarah have been making passionate love on a sofa in a parlour. Immediately following their ardent sexual encounter, we next see Sarah and Bendrix tidied up, having drinks with Henry. An insert shot shows the tattered card of the detective agency Henry had mentioned to Bendrix. There is then a cut to the scene in which Bendrix meets with the detective. So two years have elapsed since Sarah and Bendrix had their affair – it is now 1946. There is no need to explicate the elision of time to the audience, they must work at putting the pieces of the puzzle together. The shot of the crumpled card helps us to associate Bendrix and the detective to one another.

Another significant difference is the use of dual point of view. We see the majority of the film through the eyes of Bendrix who speaks as a first-person narrator. Jordan underscores the shift in point of view once Bendrix has access to Sarah's diary, then for a time the narration continues from Sarah's perspective. What Jordan has done is to underscore this modulation by filming some of the same sequences twice, once from Bendrix's point of view and then from Sarah's. An example of this reallocation occurs when Sarah and Bendrix meet for dinner at 'their' restaurant, Rules, two years after Sarah has last seen Bendrix. The sequence begins with a shot from behind Sarah's head. The camera pans almost 180 degrees until it is behind Bendrix. Later in the film, we have the same scene from Sarah's perspective where the camera moves 90 degrees to display Sarah's actions. Jordan takes a less conventional approach in not duplicating the first camera movement in reverse, that is, making the movements symmetrical. Part of the director's originality is to see things in a way that brings variation to the two scenes, rather than replicating the scene from two literal points of view.

The explosion that knocks Bendrix down the stairs is also recapitulated by Sarah. In the first post-bomb scene, we follow Bendrix up the stairs into his bedroom; Sarah is in a kneeling position with her back to him. This is not his literal point of view, but nonetheless replicates, in a more generalised sense, what Bendrix would see. Sarah's reaction to the bombing is to run downstairs to her unconscious lover. (Just as Sarah screams Bendrix's name, Henry will scream for Bendrix when Sarah dies.) When we see the scene from Sarah's perspective, literal point of view shots are used, and the camera is positioned in a 180-degree reversal from the Bendrix sequence. Jordan has said, 'He walks upstairs and she leaves him and he doesn't see her again. His life is stopped there and then, you know? And when we meet him at the start of the movie he's like a dead man, a ghost of what he was, in a way, and he's haunted by the meaning of that event … all the characters are emotionally haunted' (in Sheehey & Traynor 2000: 17).

One of the strongest scenes in the film occurs when Bendrix and Henry have a drink together – the aftermath of this scene is written differently in the book and the screenplay. In the novel, the two characters speak, and Bendrix says,

> 'You were no more trouble to us than you'd been to the others.'
> 'There were others too?'
> 'Sometimes I thought you knew all about it and didn't care. Sometimes I longed to have it out with you like we are doing now when it's too late. I wanted to tell you what I thought of you. That you were her pimp. You pimped for me and you pimped for them, and now you are pimping for the latest one. The eternal pimp. Why don't you get angry, Henry?'
> 'I never knew.'
> 'You pimped with your ignorance. You pimped by never learning how to make love with her, so she had to look elsewhere. You pimped by giving opportunities. You pimped by being a bore and a fool, so now somebody who isn't a bore and a fool is playing about with her in Cedar Road.' (1999: 67)

Greene uses the injurious word 'pimp' no less than nine times. It is a use of rhetoric that gives us access to Bendrix's state of rage towards Henry, a most convenient target.

The final shooting script is simplified. Without going into a lengthy discussion about the differences between novel and film, my view is that most effective screen-writing avoids 'speechifying', unless it is a poor adaptation of a play, a courtroom drama or something that would call for long passages of dialogue. The script of *The End of the Affair* reads thus:

> *Bendrix*: You're a habit she's formed. You're security. You were no more trouble to us than you'd been to the others.
> *Henry*: There were others?
> *Bendrix*: Of course there were Henry. And are…
> *Henry*: Why did she leave you?
> *Bendrix*: I became a bore, Henry. Like you. But I wasn't born one. You created me. She wouldn't leave you so I bored her with my jealousy.
> *Henry*: You can't be jealous of me…
> *Bendrix*: You won, in a way. We'd come to the end of love. She could shop and cook and fall asleep with you, but she could only

	make love with me.
Henry:	She's still very fond of you…
Bendrix:	(angrily) One isn't satisfied with fondness.
Henry:	I was…
Bendrix:	And that made you her pimp. The bore of a husband who knows where his slippers are, but never notices his wife.
Bendrix:	(in voice-over) But we had another pimp, Henry. The War.

The goal of Greene's writing of the passage is to impart the intensity and brutality of Bendrix's rage as he attempts to provoke the already deeply-wounded Henry. However, Jordan's writing of the scene is extraordinarily succinct. In the film, we have the night scene of the two men on a park bench, as the rain pours down on them. We view Henry, obviously crushed, with the rain pelting his hatless head; because of the rain, it is unclear whether Henry has been crying or is simply wet. This powerful scene is inflected by the vividness of the actors' performances, the *mise-en-scène*, the lighting, the use of close-ups on the faces of each actor. When Bendrix says the word 'pimp', it is registered in Henry's physical bearing – it seems as if he has been struck in the solar plexus. All the hurt that collects around the offending word in Greene's book is transformed in the film to the equivalent of a body blow. It is also true that because of Stephen Rea's and Ralph Fiennes' exquisitely modelled performances, the film does not need a great deal of language to allow the viewer to comprehend the emotional intensity of the characters. Bendrix is mean and spiteful, and lacks compassion for Henry as in the book, but Jordan allows for a more nuanced apprehension of the characters.

The scene after Sarah's death is also treated differently in the novel and the film. In the book, Sarah agrees to go away with Bendrix and promises to call him when she is ready to leave. The novel elides eight days, and then Bendrix receives a call from Henry.

> 'Is this Bendrix?'
> There was something very queer about his voice, and I wondered, has she told him? 'Yes. Speaking.'
> 'An awful thing's happened. You ought to know. Sarah's dead.' How conventionally we behave at such moments.
> I said, 'I'm terribly sorry, Henry.'
> 'Are you doing anything tonight?'
> 'No.'
> 'I wish you'd come over for a drink. I don't fancy being alone.' (1999: 135)

In the earliest draft of the screenplay, the post-death sequence is treated in the following way:

Henry:	You'll have to help me Bendrix – I can't.
Bendrix:	I will Henry, I will.

> *Henry*:   I can't live in a world where she's gone, Bendrix.
>
> *Bendrix*:   I'll teach you to Henry. I know the world very well.

This makes Bendrix arrogant and smug, and lessens whatever sympathy the viewer might have for him. In later versions of the screenplay, the final line is changed to: 'I can help you', which becomes 'I'll help you' in the film. Even in that small change from 'can' to 'will', Bendrix emerges as a more compassionate person. He is not speaking from a superior position; Bendrix has no special powers that would enable him to care for Henry. The use of the word 'will' is more like a pact between complicitous friends, conjoined in grief. It endows Bendrix with a selflessness and humanity that is missing in the early versions of the screenplay. Gone also is the Luciferian hubris of Bendrix, 'His God was also Sarah's God, and I was going to throw no stones at any phantom she believed she loved. I hadn't during that period any hatred of her God, for hadn't I in the end proved stronger.' As Frank Kermode writes:

> Bendrix is … the hero Mr Greene has needed: a natural man who sees this God as a natural man would, an unscrupulous rival, corrupter of human happiness, spoiler of the egg; and a novelist who hates Him as a superior technician. Bendrix's book is plotted by God, a testimony to His structural powers. And we get for the first and only time the real Satanic thing, the courage never to submit or yield. (1973: 131)

Henry, as portrayed by Stephen Rea, is granted more dignity and more expressivity in the film (albeit in a minimalist way, with a few exceptions). Here is Jordan on Rea's performance:

> If you compare Fiennes as Bendrix to Stephen Rea's Henry – Rea's conception of that man, his character, was quite brilliant. He didn't want to play him as some dreary little cuckold – which he was in the book, Greene was quite cruel about the real Harry Walston. He was dressed with some style. If you look at his costume, it's got far more finish and style than Bendrix's has. Stephen presented him as a man who had actually vanished beneath the style, beneath the exterior. (In McCarthy 2000: 14)

In Greene's novel, Henry is a bit of a fool. In the scene where Bendrix meets him on the Common and they retire to Henry's house for a drink, Henry warms his hands by the fire. He continues as his sleeves start to scorch, until Bendrix says, deadpan, 'Your sleeve is burning Henry' (Greene 1999: 17).

I view Sarah as a pivotal character and a catalyst in the film, rather than the main character of the book as Greene has asserted at various times. When Bendrix and Sarah meet at a 'drinks party' at Henry and Sarah's home, Bendrix and Sarah are attracted to one another and leave the party to continue their private conversation. A small change is made in the film, which differs from the book and all three versions of the script. In each of the versions, Bendrix kisses Sarah, and she responds, 'I was wondering when you would do that.' In the film, we see Bendrix bend towards Sarah with amorous intent. But they hear Henry's voice in the background, and their activity is suspended. There is no dialogue. This is a tiny moment, but it supports the idea that Jordan wants to give the erotic journey of Sarah and Bendrix a more adult tenor. It is a case of absence being stronger than presence, or an action that ends prematurely and leaves the viewer to fill a narrative gap. We are privy to the development of an immediate bond between Sarah and Bendrix, so the question for the spectator becomes not 'if' but 'when'. Sarah's line: 'I was wondering when you would do that', seems more like something a character in a light-hearted romance or a musical might say.

When their affair begins, Bendrix's jealousy is so acute that once Sarah has made her vow not to see Bendrix if his life can be spared, he thinks of killing himself, and says: 'Hadn't she, at heart, hoped for my death, so that her new affair with X would hurt her conscience less … If I killed myself now, she wouldn't have to worry about me at all, and surely after our four years together there would be moments of worry even with X' (Greene 1999: 75). Sarah also writes in her diary, 'He [Bendrix] thinks I sleep with other men…' (Greene 1999: 92). Other scenes also mention 'the others', and this reference is still to be found in the final draft of the screenplay:

Bendrix: Which means you've done this before…
Sarah: I told you. All the others meant nothing. They were leading to you.

However, in the film there is no mention of 'others'. This invests Sarah in the film with a kind of purity and virtue, while allowing her to partake of the erotic. (In a sense she is replicating the behaviour of Catherine Walston; she can commit adultery but still remain an ardent Catholic.) Sarah makes love with Bendrix because she is profoundly in love with him, not because he is just another in a collection of lovers. Her sexual neediness, under the circumstances, seems quite natural. Their relationship is a *coup de foudre*, in which they speak their love for each other verbally and physically in their first private encounter, a precarious situation that takes place in Sarah's house and which is interrupted by Henry's return. When Sarah reaches orgasm, Bendrix worries that Henry might have heard something, but Sarah assures him that Henry would not know the sound. (Jordan consulted late nineteenth-century Japanese erotica as well as the *Kama Sutra* to create intriguing sexual positions for Fiennes and Moore; he wanted each sexual encounter to be different (Neil Jordan, *The End of the Affair* DVD commentary).)

The film seizes upon every opportunity that enables Sarah's character to be more beneficent. The screenplay includes a scene of Henry and Bendrix by the bench that contains a long dialogue scene cut from the film:

Bendrix: Smythe, Henry. With a 'Y'. My current replacement.
Henry: Why are you telling me this?
Bendrix: So you'll know. When he's replaced in turn.
Henry: What if you're wrong?

Sarah (Julianne Moore) and Bendrix (Ralph Fiennes) entwined in the Romantic trinity of sin/pleasure/death

Bendrix: I'm not wrong. I'm not saying she wished me dead, Henry.
               Just that it would have been more … convenient. Not quite a
               happy accident. More like an appropriate one. And you should
               go home now. Before you catch your death…

Again, this would have slandered Sarah's moral rectitude, even if Bendrix has it wrong. To implant the idea that Sarah has had a series of lovers would most likely vitiate the viewers' sympathy for her.

The Brighton scene also re-introduces Henry as the bearer of bad tidings as he breaks the news of Sarah's terminal illness:

Bendrix: How oddly we behave at such moments, Henry.
Henry: (like a schoolboy) You believe me, don't you? I have his letter.
Bendrix: Does she know?
Henry: She must suspect.
Bendrix: That's why she came away with me.
Henry: Perhaps it's her way old man. Of saying goodbye. She is so fond
               of you…
Bendrix: One isn't satisfied of fondness.
Henry: I was…

The last two lines are a repetition of the dialogue Henry and Bendrix speak during the post-pub rain scene, cut in the transition from final shooting script to film. This passage shows the ever-present danger in *The End of the Affair* of the film developing into a soap opera that Jordan adroitly manages to stave off. The knowledge that Sarah and Bendrix might have enjoyed each other for several years but instead come together, ironically, when she is about to die is prime territory for stale melodrama. But at its core what we witness is a tragedy – a life cut short, a burning passion turned to ash, each character, as in so many of Jordan's films, haunted by loss.

As a screenwriter, Jordan hones scenes until they attain an elegance and eloquence that makes the director one of the finest writers of dialogue working in cinema. A good example is offered in the first scene in a draft of the screenplay between Parkis (played in the film by Ian Hart) and Bendrix.

Bendrix:	The thing about jealousy, Parkis … is that it can only exist with desire. And whereas desire needs its object, jealousy invents one. You understand.
Parkis:	I think so sir…
Bendrix:	It's quite simple, Parkis. You're on a hunt for desire. Regard yourself as its servant.
Parkis:	The lady does seem to excite great emotion, sir.
Bendrix:	But the question is where.
Parkis:	Where, sir?
Bendrix:	Where is desire flowering now. Think of it as a river, Parkis. Of yourself as an explorer. You must find its source.
Parkis:	Of course, that's my job, sir.

In the film, Bendrix simply says, 'Try to think of it the way I do, Parkis. Jealousy can only exist where there is desire. Regard yourself as its servant.'

The film sustains a heightened aesthetic – in Michael Nyman's luscious score; Tony Lawson's effective editing; Anthony Pratt's evocative set decoration; Sandy Powell's costumes, and so on – but this aesthetic is also at one with poetry. Jordan's fiction writing has the same avoidance of talkiness, the same stripping away of the unnecessary, the sensorial pleasure of words and imagery chosen with the utmost feeling. As always in his work we see a fertile collision between realism and stylisation. Jordan is simply one of the best *dialoguistes* and *scènaristes* around. This is a distinction the French make – one who writes the words the actors speak and another writer who works on the story and situations. Although we do not tend to make that distinction, the functions can be very different. Someone may write beautiful dialogue but be unable to determine a workable path for the story, while a storyteller may not understand or have the proficiency to write good dialogue. Jordan can do both masterfully. He understands how to communicate without obfuscation and to find the particularities of the characters' language that show us who she or he is. It has to do with an uncanny understanding, curiosity and love of human behaviour in all its myriad forms. Jordan knows how to hold our attention in a scene through dialogue that may seem realistic, but actually is exquisitely sculpted. The director will strip a scene to its bones without losing its essential flavour, and then add the potent quality of elegance. We understand how the character feels before we understand how she or he thinks. It is perhaps one of the most difficult things about screenwriting: to write dialogue that sounds as if it was improvised on the spot. Jordan rehearses his cast mainly to hear his dialogue spoken, and then he rewrites it to suit the character. It is no accident that he is a writer of fiction; every word we read is selected with care, but again, there is a flow to his prose style that makes it arresting. One scene written for the film and that does not correspond with anything in Greene's book is the 'stocking' scene. It was hand-written in two drafts of the script, and then added to the film.

> *Bendrix*: (dressing Sarah) I'm jealous of your stocking.
> *Sarah*: Why?
> *Bendrix*: Because it kisses your whole leg. (He fastens her garters)
> *Bendrix*: (cont'd) I'm jealous of this button.
> *Sarah*: It's quite an innocent little button.
> *Bendrix*: Not at all, it's with you all day and I'm not.

In this emphatically seductive scene, one is reminded of the medieval French poems called *blasons d'amour*, in which a lover passionately evokes parts of a woman's body. One can find this in several films by Jean-Luc Godard, notably in *Le Mépris* (*Contempt*, 1963) and *Une Femme Mariée* (*A Married Woman*, 1964).

This analysis of *The End of the Affair* is centred on the writer/director's process, and allows the reward of working with a brilliant novel, a script treatment, three different scripts and the finished film. It is impossible to discern whether the passages discussed were simply left, as one would have said before the era of high-tech editing, on the cutting room floor. A scene might be found too long, too talky, unnecessary, dropped for any number of reasons. Looking at the multiple versions of *The End of the Affair* nonetheless brings us closer to the genesis of a consummate work.

Soul searching: the mysterium tremendum

'There is another world and it is this one.'
— Paul Éluard

One of the main changes between book and film relates to the miracle Sarah seems to cause. At one point in the film, Sarah finds Lance (Samuel Bould), Parkis's son, on assignment for his detective father, asleep on stone steps. She mistakes him for a lost urchin and gives him money for the tube, and kisses him on his cheek with the strawberry birthmark. The following dialogue is from the final shooting script, and is performed in the film as written in a scene at the site of Sarah's cremation:

> *Parkis*: Young boys, sir, they get these ideas, though I have to say even I can't explain it.
> *Bendrix*: Explain what Parkis?
> *Parkis*: On the day of her assignation sir, she walked to the tube. She thought he was lost sir, gave him a coin and kissed him on the cheek.
> (Parkis's son, Lance, comes closer; the birthmark on his face is no longer there)

Parkis: On his afflicted cheek sir. And over the weeks that followed, his
affliction gradually went away. I tried to keep him rational sir,
but he swears it was because of her.

This leads to another significant change in Jordan's adaptation of the book. In Greene's novel it is the 'Rationalist Preacher' Smythe, who has the affliction on his cheek. Sarah meets with Smythe in order to sort out doubts about her spiritual commitment. But Smythe falls in love with Sarah and asks her to marry him. She declines. To make the moment less hurtful, Sarah kisses him on his cheek. Later, completely to Smythe's astonishment, we learn that he has been healed overnight.

The novel has a second miraculous occurrence. Lance is very ill; Sarah visits and brings him a book she had as a child. That night in a feverous dream, Sarah promises Lance a present. After several days, the child is well again, and Parkis says: 'he told the doctor it was Mrs Miles who came and took the pain, touching him on the right side of the stomach … and she wrote in the book for him' (Greene 1999: 178). In one version of the script, 'Smythe … runs his hands expertly down Lance's back. Lance shivers.' It is suggested in this draft of the script that there is some power invested in Smythe's hands, as the boy is cured of his affliction by the end of the film. If this action had been retained in the film, it would cast doubt upon Sarah's already ambiguous ability to work miracles, and would mitigate her suffering and her embrace of Christ's pain, and perhaps prompt a greater ambiguity regarding the authenticity of Sarah as a miracle worker.

Sarah specifically makes the connection between the holy and the erotic. She says in voice-over: 'How cruel your knowledge seemed. You knew what I would say before I made that promise. You knew you'd keep me to it. You knew me the way his hands knew me when he touched another.' Sarah comprehends that things can exist without being part of the material world. She is in touch with a power greater than that of the quotidian plane of human experience. This distinguishes her from both her husband and her lover. As Rudolf Otto writes:

> [It] appears as a mighty propulsion towards an ideal good known only to reli-
> gion and in its nature fundamentally non-rational, which the mind knows of
> in yearning and presentiment, recognising it for what it is behind the obscure
> and inadequate symbols which are its only expression. And this shows that
> above and beyond our rational being lies hidden the ultimate and the highest
> part of our nature, which can find no satisfaction in the mere allaying of the
> needs of our sensuous, psychical, or intellectual impulses and cravings. The
> mystics called it the basis of the soul. (1958: 36)

The idea that a soul exists invites precisely the attitude one might expect of the consummate materialist Bendrix, who scoffs at the notion of spiritual meaning. The following from the film develops the crucial philosophical argument between Sarah and Bendrix:

Bendrix:	I can't live without you, Sarah.
Sarah:	Me too. Did you tell him, Maurice?
Bendrix:	Yes.
Sarah:	It's like a curse Maurice. You were dead. And I promised. Then you were alive again.
Bendrix:	You're afraid –
Sarah:	That if I break it, you'll be dead again? (he touches her face)
Bendrix:	That's me Sarah. My hand. (he kisses her again)
Bendrix:	My mouth. I'm alive. For the first time in two years.
Sarah:	Me too.

Sarah's acceptance of the spiritual allows her to see beyond the corporeal. They are in a church surrounded by statues of the saints and Jesus:

Sarah:	Do you believe in it Maurice? … Do you believe in things you can't see? (he looks at the altar)
Bendrix:	You mean Him?
Sarah:	I mean you. You see I've never stopped loving you. Even though I couldn't see you.

Sarah's death acquires the characteristics of saintliness: 'the ultimate fictive form of Sarah Miles "dying" suggests that an act of erotic self-immolation is about to be translated in terms of redemptive Christian sacrifice' (Thomas 1988: 18).

Sarah's relationship to God is also presented in a different register in the book and film script. In the novel, Sarah's arguments with God are more forceful than those found in the film. In one diary entry, she writes: 'You make me drive out love, and then you say there's no lust for me either. What do you expect me to do now God?' (Greene 1999: 100). In the completed film this line is dropped and instead Sarah's voice-over says: 'I'm beginning to believe in you God. And that's how you work. You empty me of love, then fill the emptiness.' In the novel, Sarah dares God: 'I'm not going to worry about You anymore, whether You exist or not … I'm going to make him happy, that's my second vow, God, and stop me if You can, stop me if You can' (Greene 1999: 116). In the film, Sarah is portrayed as a weak vessel, enveloped in remorse, both for leaving Bendrix and for failing to keep her vow to God. In Sarah's voice-over from the final version of the script she says: 'I am too tired to fight You any more. You've won and we have lost.' In the film this is transformed to: 'Is this coincidence, I wondered? Or the way life happens? And if this is life, am I stuck with it? But whatever it is I can't fight it. It's won and we have lost.' Sarah's character is more of a defeatist in the film. In the novel, at least she has the mettle to challenge God. As Sarah says when she sees Lance's strawberry mark in the film, 'What kind of a God would do that to a little boy?' In both script and film Sarah's voice-over says, 'Tell Him I'm sorry, I'm too human, too weak. Tell Him I can't keep my promises. I'm tired of being without [Bendrix].' By making Sarah a figure who is possessed of the dual characteristics of beatitude and imperfection, Jordan encourages a great deal of sympathy from the spectator. Sarah is like us, yet not quite; she suffers but she suffers exquisitely; she is elevated by her soulfulness and grounded in her eroticism – a potent amalgam.

Performance in The End of the Affair

> 'For a moment I was free of feeling … and it felt like happiness.'
> – Bendrix in *The End of the Affair*

The End of the Affair is a departure from Neil Jordan's previous films in many significant ways. Formally, it is his most sophisticated and complex work to date. The director/writer has fabricated a narrative structure that traverses the events of a six-year period, gracefully spanning and interweaving disparate temporal periods. Jordan has referred to this intricately structured film as both 'a metaphysical detective story and a visual, semantic emotional puzzle' (Neil Jordan, *The End of the Affair* DVD commentary). Jordan, who began his career as an award-winning fiction writer, was heavily influenced by *le nouveau roman*, and by Alain Robbe-Grillet and Marguerite Duras in particular (see McIlroy 1986: 112). Throughout his career, both as a writer and filmmaker, he has shown a highly developed sensitivity to the phenomenal existents of the world.

The invocation of *le nouveau roman* is highly relevant to the director's work with actors in *The End of the Affair*. One of the hallmarks of that literary movement is the writers' interest in the provisional, the contingent, the fleeting sensations of the moment. Additionally, there is no attempt to enter into the psychology of the characters, which is a key characteristic of *le nouveau roman*; one observes from a perspective with the character, having access to their external sensorial world, rather than as seen from an interior point of view. While Jordan's work is more psychologically attuned in its representation of fleeting sensations it is strongly linked to *le nouveau roman*. This activates what Jordan has called in any number of interviews 'sensual thinking', rather than abstract, intellectual thought.

Jordan said he watched two films repeatedly to prepare for the film: Robert Bresson's *Les Dames du Bois de Boulogne* (1945) and Max Ophuls' *Letter From an Unknown Woman* (1948). The impact of Bresson's style, although not fully realised in *Les Dames du Bois de Boulogne*, can be detected in Jordan's use of synecdoche at various points in the film, as well as in the highly rhythmical sound and image montage (such as the movement of figures ascending stairs, opening and closing doors, a typewriter clacking on the soundtrack). Perhaps the most powerful relationship Jordan bears to Bresson is what critic Hugh Linehan has called 'the intertwining of eroticism, death and an equivocal sense of the sacred' (1996: 19), and *The End of the Affair* is deeply connected with questions of belief and faith, issues that have never achieved such naked articulation in Jordan's previous work. Religion has a special resonance for Jordan, who says he is a non-believer, but was a believer as a child, and that his fall from Catholicism has 'left a hole in [his] life' (Neil Jordan, *The End of the Affair* DVD commentary).

In order to represent this freighted material, Jordan, for the first time in his career, worked only with professional leading actors of the highest calibre; non-professional actors and novices were not employed. The result is an exquisitely modulated chamber piece of profound beauty. The film takes places just before and during the Blitz in London, when people lived every day as though it could be their last (see Neil Jordan, *The End of the Affair* DVD commentary).

Jordan talks of resisting the temptation to 'broaden the film out', and wanting to 'make everything as small as it could possibly be' (*The End of the Affair* DVD commentary). The most succinct way to deal with his treatment of actors in the film is to examine several pivotal scenes in depth, as many of the strategies that are employed throughout the film can be found in these sequences. It is important to set up the prior circumstances of one of the scenes to be scrutinised: Henry has told Bendrix that he believes Sarah may be having an affair. He has the business card of a detective agency, but thinks it beneath his dignity or does not want to know the truth, and so declines to pursue the matter. Bendrix, whose passionate affair with Sarah terminated abruptly several years before, suggests that he go to the detective in Henry's place claiming that 'jealous lovers are far less ridiculous than jealous husbands'. Henry drops the matter, but Bendrix, who measures his love by the degree of his jealousy, visits the detective and instigates an investigation. Henry and Bendrix meet later in the rain that drenches most of the scenes in the film, and Bendrix suggests a drink.

The crucial scene to be considered commences in a pub, and begins as Bendrix inquires with seeming nonchalance about Sarah. Henry responds in an off-handed manner, but one can sense his discomfiture as he twists a tumbler of whiskey in his hands, gripping it far more tightly than necessary. Bendrix announces that he has taken matters into his own hands, and consulted the private detective; he now has all the documentation, photos and love letters that attest to Sarah's infidelity. During this section of the scene, Henry is appalled by Bendrix's 'infernal cheek'; his expression of consternation is largely made manifest through the extraordinary tightness of his facial muscles and the rigidity of his posture. Rea's voice is reduced to a whisper, an effective tool for the actor to communicate Henry's strangled emotion.

Bendrix's assault continues physically, as he places his leg across a stool, obstructing Henry's departure. He is provoked by Henry's passivity, and charged with anger that emerges as belligerent sarcasm. Henry, ever the meek gentleman, looks astonished but paralysed; his distress and indignation is held in by dint of habitual and capacious reserves of repression. His one action is to seize the incriminating evidence and ram it into the fireplace with a poker; it is a sudden and kinetic display of heretofore suppressed fury. As Henry rushes out of the pub Bendrix lowers his head, shouting after the object of his derision, 'I can always get you a carbon copy.' Now Bendrix's face becomes a study of conflicting feelings. Jordan has remarked that he likes actors who are able to communicate two entirely different things at the same time, and here Fiennes registers arrogance, malice, pity and gravitas all at once. The activity is internal, only a slight smirk is legible on his face.

Bendrix notices that Henry has left his hat on the table, thus providing an excuse for him to follow his victim. In an exterior shot, Henry is seated very stiffly on a

Henry (Stephen Rea) meets Bendrix (Ralph Fiennes) in the former's nocturnal wanderings

bench in the pouring rain. Bendrix apologises to Henry, who looks bewildered, lost, almost on the verge of tears, and terribly wounded. He physically recoils as Bendrix sits next to him. The rain streaks down his hatless face, making him all the more pitiable. Henry asks if Bendrix and his wife were lovers. Henry swallows hard in an effort to contain his rage, pain and confusion. He is near tears; a tremendous sadness and sense of betrayal suffuse his face. Rea again uses his voice to great advantage, employing the most minimal inflection, affecting a near monotone. His face is such a mask of mastered inexpressivity that each tiny movement and delicate change reveals the difficulty he has in stifling his feelings. His breathing is crucial as well during this interchange; overcome by emotion, he often stops breathing and must gasp for air.

The tone of the confrontation changes now, as Bendrix's cruelty and anger rise in pitch. It is at this point that he calls Henry Sarah's 'pimp'. As Bendrix says the word Henry reacts as though he has been punctured by a sharp instrument. He closes his eyes in unbearable misery and defeat. During this dialogue, the camera moves in close on Bendrix's face; he is thinking very deeply. But the key to Bendrix's thinking is that while remaining Ralph Fiennes, he is thinking as his character. Simon Callow puts this notion quite beautifully:

> I do believe there's a shamanistic aspect to acting … I profoundly disagree
> that acting should only ever be a reflection of life, a kind of mirror … I think
> that acting performance is life itself, it's a manifestation of life, it's an organic
> thing. It's a living, hugely complicated thing with its own ecology, its own
> biology … If it's working … it's a point of success when you cease to play
> the character and the character starts to play you. Then, something's really

happening; within the framework the author has created, the character must have its dangerous life. (In Zucker 1999: 45)

Jordan says of *The End of the Affair* that it was like casting Mitchum and Bogart in the same film (*The End of the Affair* DVD commentary). And what I believe he means is that often Fiennes and Rea are merely thinking and reacting in barely perceptible ways; they are not overtly expressing emotion. One can view the scene discussed above repeatedly and find new emotions in both actors' faces, always very subtly etched. The degree of understatement and the ability of both actors to convey the depth and pitch of their emotions is extraordinary. Rea utilises the smallest movements of his face and body and the constriction of his voice, to articulate the wounds to his selfhood. It is interesting that the little Rea does in this scene is quite different from the 'little' he does as Fergus in *The Crying Game*. Both are subdued, highly internalised performances; nonetheless each performance is informed by the given circumstances of the films' narrative. The physical expression, however limited, and the modulation of a quintes-sential spirit – call it soul or psyche – animates the presence of two distinctive char-acters, Fergus and Henry. Fiennes works primarily through the matchless intensity of his gaze, the translucence of his eyes that allow one to see into him, to the very core of his feelings. Fiennes has a truly amazing vulnerability and transparency, even while he appears to be doing nothing; his focus and concentration are fierce and total. We react to Fiennes' effort to express the inexpressible, that which can only be alluded to – call it the soul of the character. He has an almost uncanny ability to inhabit and embody his characters; that is what, at least in part, I think we mean when we speak of charisma; certainly it is great film acting. In describing what one sees in the performances in *The End of the Affair*, one is addressing a very essential conundrum, as well as acknowl-edging one of the pre-eminent skills of film acting: how does one communicate highly interiorised states? How does an actor make their deepest emotions visible?

There is one further scene I would briefly discuss, because it provides some of the most extraordinarily powerful moments I can remember seeing in any film and it speaks to Jordan's formidable work with actors. Sarah is dying, and Henry has asked Bendrix to live in their house, to be there 'when the time comes'. Henry watches over the dying Sarah, as Bendrix types in another room. We hear Henry scream Bend-rix's name. Henry embraces Bendrix, crying openly, and says: 'You have to help me Bendrix. I can't live in a world where she's gone.' The camera then captures Bendrix's face as he says, 'I'll help you.'

The moment reveals the depth of Henry's love for Sarah, his fragility and his capacity for profound feeling. It has an explosive impact, because of the degree to which Henry has suppressed his feelings during the course of the film, and the way his emotions now detonate with full expression in the face of his loss. Bendrix's eyes stare intently, the look on his face is somewhere between devastation and resignation. There is also, if only for a fleeting moment, a look of contentment. He is finally able to give of himself, without ego, or the expectation of reciprocity. The stigma of self-interest has been removed (much as the boy may have been miraculously cleansed of his birth-mark at the film's end). The actors, of course, do not say any of these things. But we, the audience, can feel what lies beneath the simple gesture of the two men embracing. That is subtext, and that is what great actors know how to communicate so brilliantly. The scene is intensely moving and unforgettable in its dimensionality. As in the whole film, the key is in the simplicity, and the utter conviction of the performances.

The importance of selfhood and its relationship to performance cannot be underestimated. No one can be anything but themselves, although they may filter the character through that self. Lindsay Crouse speaks with eloquence on the subject:

> The most difficult part of the art is the struggle to bring out the truth of your being, the fullest dimension of yourself … It's amazing how people will avoid using themselves in art, because we instinctively know that everything we do is a self-portrait. Acting is the art of self-revelation. We want to avoid that knowledge like the plague because of all the ambivalence we have about ourselves. We are not good enough … and if what we are doing is a self-portrait, everybody is going to see us. Oh my god, what will happen then? Technique is there to enable us to step forward and shine and remove all that fear, remove the tension, the self-consciousness, the defences, all the reasons we say we can't step out. But what a great example we set when we do. (In Zucker 2002: 14)

Jordan does not want to diminish the irreducible mystery that subtends human behaviour and existence in the world; instead, he wishes to display the kaleidoscopic array of feelings that make the human condition so enigmatic.

CHAPTER NINE

Fantastic Voyage: Recent Works

The Good Thief: chaos theory

> 'I kind of did it as an anti-American movie … I could have set this story
> in New York or Atlantic City, but I really wanted to see a European movie,
> like you used to see in the 1960s, where the whole thing didn't look like a
> machine. I went to France and met all these wonderful actors, who maybe
> only cineastes know.'
>
> – Neil Jordan (in Hoggard 2002: 2)

The Good Thief is a very loose remake of Jean-Pierre Melville's *Bob le Flambeur* (*Bob
The Gambler*, 1955). The director of the original, fascinated by all things American,
changed his name from Grumbach to honour the great writer, Herman Melville. As a
director, Melville was especially taken by the American gangster film; his most important work includes *Le Doulos* (*The Finger Man*, 1962), *Le Deuxième souffle* (*Second
Breath*, 1965), *Le Samourai* (1967), *Le Cercle rouge* (*The Red Circle*, 1970) and *Le Flic*
(1972). Daniel Cauchy, who plays Paolo in *Bob le Flambeur*, says,

> I have never known anyone who knew world cinema like [Melville] did. He
> was addicted to film and it showed. He has made movies under the most
> trying conditions because he really loved film. He had his own cinematic

style… sometimes slow paced … but it really brought something new to the period. He was the first by seven or eight years to shoot outdoors using a hand-held camera hidden in a delivery cart. (*The Good Thief* press kit)

Bob le Flambeur was shot over a period of two years, with Melville calling in his actors whenever he could find money to buy film stock. It is a highly personal film with largely unknown actors, a small crew and location shooting. This way of shooting was influenced by Italian Neorealism, and unquestionably exerted its influence upon the *nouvelle vague*. One of the more innovative elements of *Bob Le Flambeur* is Melville's use of sound; he incorporates fragments of songs, or what might be termed aural jump cuts, and eventually pieces entire songs together to invoke the sense of the active night life of Montmartre for the spectator. But Jordan takes very little from the original apart from the skeleton of the narrative; he has said, 'I began working on the script with a bit of circumspection, because I like the original movie a lot and I wasn't sure that I wanted to do something that was a remake of it' (*The Good Thief* press kit). *The Good Thief* is different to anything the director has done before, as he experiments with vibrant configurations of style. As the film begins we are dropped into the chaotic world of drugs, prostitution and, of course, gambling in the South of France.

The Good Thief has a four-minute post-credit sequence that contains a great deal of the expository information. It takes several viewings to fully comprehend the opening because of the extremely rapid montage – there are 68 shots in the first four minutes of the film. The scene contains remarkably inventive camera movements, editing patterns, sound, music, colour and *mise-en-scène*. The opening introduces us to five main characters: Bob Montangard or Montagna or Montana (Nick Nolte); Roger (Tchéky Karyo), a policeman; Anne (Nutsa Kukhianidze), a 17-year-old Georgian runaway with street smarts; Saïd (Ouassabu Embarek), an Algerian junkie and drug dealer; and Remi (Marc Lavoine), a sadistic pimp. The sequence introduces us to the locale (Nice), the club (Le Dice Club), where much of the action takes place, and the film's inciting incident, a shootout of sorts, involving Saïd and Roger.

The opening sequence is one of the film's defining moments. The camera follows the characters as they traverse space, enter different corridors or walk into off-screen regions. This kind of set-up is normally used to introduce a location and give it dimension, but in *The Good Thief* information is conveyed at the speed of light. The strobe-like effects, which we see at different junctures throughout the film, coupled with the hyper-kinetic moving camera intensify and complicate what might ordinarily be a more conventional opening. The stylistic gestures complement the film's thematic material and brings the coked-up environment of Le Dice Club vividly to life.

The colour scheme in the opening scene is sophisticated and inventive, with each room of the club bathed in a different colour, giving the location a unique appearance. The bar is blue (with a few pink neon lights), the gambling room is red, the bathroom is green, the hallway is orange, and there is also a yellow room that the moving camera passes, endowing the space with an aura of artifice. The film takes place in a world that lays no claim to realism. It is reminiscent of the use of artificial colour in *Angel*, although it is a good deal more prominent and technically adept.

Sound is another key element in the film's stylistics, though not always in ways that we have come to expect. The enchanting Maghrebi Arabic hip-hop song 'Parisien Du Nord', performed by Cheb Mami and K-Mel, opens the film. Significantly, the lyrics to the song are: '*Mi corazon, vous m'avez trahi*' ('My beloved, you have betrayed me'), which turns out to be the perfect theme song for many of the relationships amongst the film's denizens of the subterranean world. This song plays throughout the opening, raising and falling in volume as the space of the club is negotiated, creating a dynamic atmosphere, and giving the club aural depth. In terms of sound, there are many scenes where dialogue is muffled by other noise and music. When we are introduced to Bob, the down-and-out junkie gambler, he mumbles often incomprehensibly, adding to the chaos of the opening scene.

One of the most striking features of *The Good Thief* is the remarkably fluid cinematography of Chris Menges. Often the camera traverses the spaces of the film in a sped-up movement that helps to communicate the druggy unreality of Bob's universe. Time and space are both so distorted by the camerawork and editing, especially in the early sequences, that the viewer's sense of spatial coordinates is jumbled. It is difficult to know where characters are in relation to each other and what precisely they are doing.

Menges' camera seems to be hand-held, and is quite shaky, particularly during the following scene in which Saïd steals Roger's gun and holds it to the policeman's head. There are outcries in French and English as Saïd shouts in Arabic. Roger cannot understand what Saïd is saying. Bob, being Bob, understands Arabic and is able to translate. Saïd yells, 'I'll blow your brains out at the count of three. I may as well die here as in Algeria, if they send me back.' Bob casually translates. As the gun is about to go off, Bob stabs Saïd with a syringe, and the gun fires upward into the ceiling. Bob lackadaisically (as he's just shot-up) says, 'And I always swore I'd never share a needle.' Actions happen so quickly – the shots are short as the camera captures the action between Roger and Saïd from different angles – that the continuity of time and space is lost in this sequence.

An atypical editing pattern in *The Good Thief*, which has not been used before in Jordan's work, is the use of freeze frames to punctuate scenes. Jordan talks about how he used these pauses to create caesuras within particular narrative moments (Neil Jordan, *The Good Thief* DVD commentary). These 'punctuations' are effective as stylistic markers, and amongst many of the film's brilliantly-wrought set-pieces add panache to *The Good Thief* that is conspicuously different to the meditative Montmartre of *Bob le Flambeur*. Obviously, films made fifty years apart would reflect the technological advances and mindset of the two very different eras.

The film's set design by Anthony Pratt is also effective in illustrating the chaos of Bob's life. When Anne tours Bob's apartment in Jordan's film, she says, 'you come from money,' and Bob replies, 'old money'; he has *had* money. Bob lives in chaos: ice cream containers, a roulette wheel, a slot machine and dice are haphazardly strewn about his apartment, which is littered with paintings on the floor, on tables and perched upon chairs.

The kinesthetic camera movements and other visual stylistics plunge the viewer directly into Bob's world. They are more than stylistic constructions – they are striking in how they communicate the incessant, ceaseless motion and pandemonium of the nightlife in a resort full of petty criminals and assorted lowlifes.

The cacophony of accents from Eastern Europe, Ireland, Russia, Italy, Algeria, France and the US are at times barely audible. Jordan says, in his DVD commentary, that he wanted the disco/café scenes to replicate the sound one would hear walking around the space – fragments of sentences, music, ice clinking in glasses, and so forth – rather than a cleaned up soundtrack; very much like the 'dirty sound' of the films of Robert Altman and John Cassavetes. In addition, Elliot Goldenthal's score, which partakes heavily of jazz and the music of North Africa, makes a significant contribution to Jordan's stylistic explorations. All of these elements combine to make *The Good Thief* an outstanding representation of the multi-national, immigrant-based world of France in the new millennium.

Aside from *Interview with the Vampire* this marks the first time that Jordan uses a multiplicity of visual effects. There are freeze frames, intercut red leader, strobe effects and shots scattered throughout the film in which the camera is slowed down or speeded up. While the director's prior film, *The End of the Affair*, was deeply influenced by the need to 'keep everything as small as possible', and by very formal compositions (Neil Jordan, *The End of the Affair* DVD commentary), *The Good Thief* has an improvised feel with agitated camera movements. Action scenes are filmed in tight shots, withholding a sense of how spaces in the film are joined. Because of the construction of houses in the south of France, there is also a baffling lack of distinction between inside and outside (Neil Jordan, *The Good Thief* DVD commentary). Adding to the confusion, a scene often begins *in medias res*. We move from labyrinthine dark alleys to the particularly bright sunlight of the Riviera, to the pulsating, flashing lights of a disco in a moment's screen-time. Bob's universe not only lacks a centre, it is in constant motion; the movements act as a perfect correlative to his inner restlessness.

Performance in the mythic mode

At the centre of Jordan's stylistically unusual and thematically rich film is Nick Nolte's performance. As played by Nolte, Bob is anything but a Dostoyevskyian nihilist. As shabby and ruined as Nolte seems in yet another stunning, subtle performance, his behaviour is never less than noble. His embrace of excess, 'Always play to the limit, and damn the consequences', alongside his integrity and forbearance, endow him with a sort of rough grace. Bob's iconic stature is further embellished by his ability to discuss, in a witty manner, mathematics, theology, art history and rock and roll. This is one of the exchanges:

> *Bob*: Why are the French so unutterably bad at rock and roll?
> *Roger*: Beats me.
> *Bob*: I mean, look at it. We gave you Elvis, Frank Zappa,
> Jimi Hendrix, Bob Dylan. You give us Johnny Hallyday.
> Is that fair?

As argued earlier, issues of faith and the miraculous are eternal explorations in *The End of the Affair*. In *The Good Thief*, the film's narrative follows Bob from his state as a heroin-addicted loser to a transformation that is nothing short of miraculous. In what seems to be an act of divine intervention, Bob wins millions at a casino, and walks off triumphantly into the sunrise with Anne, the beautiful prostitute/crack addict he has protected and cared for. The film's finale presents an unsettling vision of redemption conflated with a strongly Electral subtext. The ending is particularly reminiscent of *The Crying Game*, when Dil visits Fergus in prison, where Fergus has '2,335 days' left of his sentence; it depicts yet another case of a fantastic, unattainable love.

Whatever one says about the stylistic explorations in *The Good Thief*, Nolte is its heart and soul. In some ways, *The Good Thief* is a film *about* Nolte, an actor who has fought his own alcohol- and drug-related demons. Nolte's life and work are charac- terised by a generous share of pain and self-destructiveness. These are paired with a devastating talent that permits him to inhabit a given character fully and intensely. Without Nolte *The Good Thief* would not have as much interest as it does. He is a nearly mythic figure who carries a degree of baggage from his life and other films, and there is no substitute for that kind of experience – he is the real thing. Melville wanted us to believe Bob was a legendary figure, but Nolte is Nolte and he bears his personal charisma on his face, in his movements and in his mumbly whiskey-and-cigarette voice above all.

Quite ironically, Nolte's famous drug bust accompanied by a mug shot with his hair wild and a look of discombobulation and anger, occurred very close to the release of *The Good Thief*. The mug shot appeared in the media in North America and much of Europe. Considering the role Nolte plays in the film, it is hard not to extrapolate on the melding of character and real life. It was the sort of incident that could be a publicist's dream or nightmare.

The face that Nolte has grown over the decades is magnificently creased and craggy; very like a bust by Rodin, it speaks unsparingly about his years of living on the edge. Nolte is one of the great American originals, a lone wolf and a force of nature who refuses to be restrained by rules. He has always been an anomaly in Hollywood. He began his career in earnest as a hunk in *Rich Man, Poor Man* (1977), a high-profile mini-series that could easily have catapulted him to stardom. But Nolte has had an uneasy relationship with the Hollywood studio system. He has attempted star vehicles such as *48 Hrs* (1982), *The Prince of Tides* (1991), and *The Hulk* (2003); but he has assembled a remarkable body of work in smaller independent films such as *Mother Night* (1996), *Affliction* (1997), *Northfork* (2003) and *Clean* (2004). Never entirely comfortable on studio projects, yet often appearing in films in which his work is supe- rior to the film itself, Nolte's career perfectly reflects the perennial conflict between the desire to create art in an industry ruled by commerce.

As our admiration for Bob grows, the film takes on an enigmatic character. We witness the redemption of Nolte, from the incoherent junkie and loser slouched on a bathroom floor as he is elevated to the status of a saviour and heroic quest figure. Because of Nolte's formidable charisma, we watch his resurrection, as fanciful as it may be, with delight. The viewer wants Bob/Nolte to win. As Paulo (Saïd Taghmaoui) says, 'Everybody loves Bob', to which Roger replies, 'That's the problem.' This film confers another layer of iconicity and complexity upon Nolte and his character. Jordan has, with the aid of Nolte, created a complex, multifaceted story that engages us on many levels. The director's experimentation with style coheres with the intrigue and multifarious relationships we are shown. The film is, in many ways, a celebration of Nolte's gifts as an actor; Jordan has taken the opportunity to explore his talents and experience. Although *The Good Thief* is concerned with many issues, both thematic and stylistic, it is Nolte's humanity that is at the centre of those concerns.

'Tonight you will be with me in Paradise'

The title of the film comes from the 'Gospel According to Luke'. The 'good thief' refers to a criminal crucified alongside Christ, who asks, 'Are you not Christ? Save yourself and us!' The thief then says, 'Jesus, remember me when you come into your kingdom.' And Jesus responds to him, 'Truly, I say to you, tonight you will be with me in Paradise.' At one point, Nolte as Bob, the alcoholic, junkie, thief, art connoisseur and father-figure to the characters of the shadow world, says to his nemesis and buddy, the cop, Roger, 'It always makes me cry when I hear that story.' Because Bob is an inveterate storyteller and manipulator *par excellence*, it is difficult to determine whether he is sincere or playing the fabulist. References to Jesus in the final shooting script were cut from the film, including the following exchange between Bob and Roger:

Bob:	Sometimes at night I'd wake up crying – lonely – I'd tell myself Jesus didn't have a father round him either, but that wouldn't do the trick. The only thing that worked was to crawl into her [his mother's] bed and have her tell me the story, not about Jesus, not even about Judas but about that good thief. Was he good at thieving, I'd wonder, or was he a thief that turned to good? Do you know what I concluded Roger?
Roger:	Maybe he was a little bit of both.
Bob:	You think so?

This dialogue reveals, quite poignantly, that there is a part of Bob who would like to think that though he has spent his life as a thief and a junkie, when he dies he will receive absolution for his sins. That is what *He* does.

Raoul (Gérard Darmon) is the thief who is recruiting Bob for the heist. Bob assures the assembled group that there will be someone who will betray them. Paulo, a lover of Anne's and a surrogate son for Bob, looks at Saïd and says:

Paulo:	You were right. There's your snitch.
Bob:	See how simple it becomes … When you embrace your own\ Judas?
Raoul:	So what does that make you? Jesus?
Bob:	Maybe I'm rising from the dead.

Bob (Nick Nolte) shooting up and hitting rock bottom

Bob begins the film shooting up on the floor of a nightclub bathroom. By the end of the film, he is an elegantly dressed millionaire, in what can only be referred to as a fairy tale finale that is redolent with references to *Beauty and the Beast*. The narrative movement of Bob through the film can be thought of in terms of Christian symbolism. Bob, like Christ, has many disciples – Roger, Paulo and Anne – who seem to follow him unquestioningly on his journey. There are dark forces who conspire against and harrass Bob in his quest, particularly the sinister figure of Remi (Marc Lavoine). The darkly lit, confining spaces of the opening scenes of Bob as a junkie/loser/gambler are similar to the entombment of Jesus. There is even a line in the film when Bob is about to kick heroin cold turkey in which he says, 'I feel a confinement coming on.' And certainly the film's ending, with Bob resplendent in (as he says) the 'rosy-fingered dawn', mimics the resurrection of Christ. It is the Ascension in *haute couture*.

The status of *The Good Thief* as a heist film is, at best, ambivalent. While most films in the genre focus on the details of the caper, such as Jules Dassin's *Rififi* (1955), the heist film *par excellence*, or Kubrick's *The Killing* (1956), which tends to foreground structure and the way the viewer receives the material, Jordan thwarts our expectations by cutting away at the moment crucial information is about to be disclosed. The director seems much more engaged in the mysterious concoction of computer genius Vlad, in a charming performance by director Emir Kusturica. He has designed an elaborate system to shut down the alarms in the gambling casino. We meet Vlad while he is playing the Jimi Hendrix version of 'The Star-Spangled Banner'. Blue laser lights mark the perimeters of the alarm system Vlad is hacking into. He talks to the assembled group of thieves about 'the beetle' he will place at the crime scene, meaning 'bug'. The electronics expert also shows computer generated three-dimensional plans for the heist. It is a visually inventive way for Jordan to reveal the mundane details of the operation. Very little screen time is spent either on the planning or execution of the theft. In spite of the prostitution, hard drugs, betrayal, violence, theft and murder, *The Good Thief* is not a dark, heavy film. The director's sense of humour is witty and wry. There is some facetious banter between Vlad and a security officer who frisks him as he enters the secure compound, site of the heist. Vlad is mildly annoyed and complains:

Vlad:	Don't you guys know me by now?
The Guard:	Procedure is procedure.
Vlad:	(slightly irritated) Oh. Procedure is procedure. Sounds like a techno band from Düsseldorf.

What grabs Jordan's attention are the personalities involved, such as a transsexual body-builder, Phillipe, now known as Phillipa; she unaccountably develops arachnophobia, and the spiders she must confront essentially bring the heist to a screeching halt. Melville's filming of the heist was very linear, and Bob is arrested at the film's end; although he claims *les flics* cannot prove anything. It is clear that the heist takes a back seat to the human and stylistic complexities which concern Jordan in this film.

The relationship of Bob to the French policeman, Roger, is interestingly ambiguous, and typical of many of the same-sex relationships in Jordan's films. Roger relentlessly follows Bob, ostensibly to investigate his shady schemes, but really to keep him out of prison. Their relationship, however, is more like that of a nanny and her charge, or close friends, or siblings who respect and protect one another. There is a subtle sense that Roger may actually have more of an erotic attachment to Bob. It is another presentation of highly ambiguous homo-social (or homo-erotic) behaviour that pervades Jordan's work, from his first award-winning book of short stories, *Night in Tunisia*, to films like *Interview with the Vampire*, *Michael Collins* and, of course, both *The Crying Game* and *Breakfast on Pluto*.

In the fictive world, Anne is the *lamia* figure, but one who is bewitched and bewildered. On the one hand she adores Bob (as do all the citizens of this chaotic world), but she also betrays him in a moment of drugged stupor. She says at one point in the film: 'Don't ever depend on me.' She is also Beauty to Nolte's Beast, and once again, as in *Mona Lisa*, we find the Beast by far the more interesting character. Anne develops a greater sensitivity, no doubt through her interactions with Bob, the magus. This is perhaps best exemplified by a conversation between Anne and her sometimes paramour, Bob's surrogate son, Paulo:

Anne:	(speaking of Bob) He doesn't want money, he wants what money can't buy.
Paulo:	What can't money buy?
Anne:	Beauty.
Paulo:	You're being mysterious.
Anne:	Beauty is mysterious.

In a dazzling final sequence that defies all logic, Anne and Bob, beautifully dressed,

Bob and Anne (Nutsa Kukhianidze) walk down the stairs of the casino into the 'rosy-fingered dawn'

and loaded with money, regally emerge from the casino and into the bright sunlight. It is here that Anne tells Bob a story of her origins.

Bob:	Want to talk to Paulo?
Anne:	No. Tell him he didn't live up to my ideal of manhood.
Bob:	Is there anyone who does?
Anne:	Yep.
Bob:	Who?
Anne:	My father. He was a circus strongman. He used to hang my mother from the highwire suspended from his teeth. Then one day his teeth broke.
Bob:	And?
Anne:	She got two false legs, he got two false teeth.

Then Bob concocts yet another version of his origins (we have heard several during the course of the film), as the sound fades out: 'You see, my mother was a rodeo queen. When you wrangle as many bulls as she did you get to recognise every kind of bullshit.' The fact that Anne has now joined Bob in his confabulations makes her the right partner for him, as a friend or lover. Their relationship is reminiscent of Bogart and Bacall in Howard Hawks' *To Have and Have Not* (1944). There is a running gag in that film: Walter Brennan, as Eddie, the liquored-up sidekick asks people he meets, 'Was you ever stung by a dead bee?' The characters dismiss Eddie as a bothersome alcoholic, and respond impatiently with logical answers like, 'How can a bee sting you if he's dead?' But when Slim (Lauren Bacall) is asked the question, she says, 'Yeah.' Brennan says, with a look of amazement on his face, 'What did ya do?', to which Bacall replies,

'Why, I bit him back.' This makes her part of the gang, an acceptable member of the Boys Only club that is part of Hawk's *weltanschauung*.

The Good Thief contains all of the director's trademark themes, albeit couched in an adventurous style. There is an emphasis on storytelling; permutations of the family unit; impossible love; homoeroticism; Oedipal subtexts; hybrid genre; the mythopoeic; the spiritual; and exile. The film is situated in a place (Nice) and in spaces that are unfamiliar or defamiliarised, as the club with its artificially multi-coloured rooms suggests. There is also an emphasis on the fairy tale quality as Anne and Bob (he, newly wealthy) walk into the light of the rising sun – all of their difficulties have been effaced, and their world is now one of glamour and paradisal glory.

Breakfast On Pluto: 'Love has reasons which reason cannot understand'

'If I didn't have my story I would start crying and never stop.'
– Kitten Braden

Breakfast on Pluto begins by introducing its main character and storyteller, Patrick 'Kitten' Braden (Cillian Murphy) as the opening credits roll to the pop strains of 'Sugar Baby Love' performed by the Rubettes. Kitten is dressed as a woman and pushes a pram containing a mixed-race baby who we later learn is the offspring of Kitten's friends Charlie (Ruth Negga) and her murdered lover, Irwin (Laurence Kinlan). Kitten walks beside a building site and receives catcalls and salacious suggestions from the Irish and English labourers as he pushes the pram. He responds to the provocation with no small amount of cheek, and his comments are directly addressed to the viewer (and the baby). Kitten begins to weave an extraordinary tale with himself as its central performer and star.

This credit sequence introduces our main storyteller and his possibly imagined or real life. There is never any corroborating evidence that Kitten's story is anything but one of many he tells about himself (just as Bob in *The Good Thief* offered different versions of his lineage). We never know if he is a reliable or a duplicitous narrator. It is important to remind oneself that Kitten is a writer, and that he, in turn, is the confection of Jordan and Patrick McCabe. Issues such as authorial distance, tone, character traits and development are crucial to *Breakfast on Pluto*, as is the unique position of the author to use the script as a platform for his own moral and ethical beliefs, convictions and preferences. Narrative elements such as time and space are also designed to suit the author's purposes.

Keeping the authorial privilege of Jordan and McCabe in mind, I will take most of the film to be a quasi-reliable portrait of Kitten's adventures. His voice is the presiding voice, although we are left in the dark about his true story. Kitten's diary and voice-over coupled with his Candide-like naïveté does nothing to engender an unconditional belief in his stories. Kitten's carefree, flippant style masks the grimmer reality he has experienced – abandonment, failed relations with men and the cruelty that is inflicted upon him by numerous characters. The opening shots not only introduce the film's main role and principle mode of address, but act to situate its present tense as the early 1970s in London. The bright hues and gliding, swooping camera moves of the beginning, which characterise much of the film, also indicate the key importance that visual stylistics will play in *Breakfast on Pluto*.

The film's opening song presages the central importance of the extensive, carefully selected songs which supply the viewer with the giddy delights that popular music often seems to communicate in movies (this is the first film in which Jordan has not used an orchestrated soundtrack as well as popular tunes). The music selection incorporates many of the era's popular (though not necessarily best) songs by such performers as Bobby Goldsboro ('Honey'), Harry Nilsson ('You're Breakin' My Heart'), T-Rex ('Children of the Revolution')[1] and Dusty Springfield ('The Windmills of Your Mind'). Music will play an important role in setting the film's whimsical, sometimes deliberately saccharine and almost always ironic tone. But these modest delights act as another escape for Kitten from the harsh realities and emotional chaos of his life. They are one means of coping with being gay in a small town in Ireland in the late 1960s through the early 1970s. The character's writing, and his inclination to retreat from unpleasant realities in the safety of the women's magazines he incessantly reads, provide an excellent fortification against the brutality of the world in which he lives. As two IRA yobs have their guns trained at his head, or as the British police mercilessly beat him, Kitten seems brave rather than beaten down as he sustains the pace of his witticisms.

Jordan has divided the film into 36 episodes with titles such as 'Saint Kitten', 'The Need for Glamour' and 'A Spritz in Time'. This structure is connected to the narrating device of the diary written by Kitten. We see the character writing of his experiences, and Kitten's literary ambitions represent an important part of his imaginative life; these scribblings also are the means by which he increases his self-awareness. The film (as in McCabe's novel) has an episodic, picaresque structure much like Sterne's *Tristram Shandy* (1759). Some films that are parsed into chapters with titles, such as Jean-Luc Godard's *Vivre sa vie* (*My Life to Live*, 1962), employ a style that has been called 'Brechtian' because it tends to mitigate against total involvement with the fictional universe of the film. Although the organisation and use of titles in *Breakfast on Pluto* are structurally similar to that of Godard's film, the purposes of the device are distinctly different for each filmmaker. In Jordan's film the chapter headings are used to push the story along, allowing the screenwriters a type of shorthand to move about temporally and spatially. The writers of *Breakfast on Pluto* do not seek an emotionally detached response; in fact the film operates in ways that intentionally elicit empathy. The play with narrative is another experiment in Jordan's frequent imaginative exploitation of form and style. (As with most stylistically or narratively interesting films, *Breakfast on Pluto* does not reveal itself in a single viewing – multiple screenings allow the spectator to grasp the range of meanings that inform the construction of the film.)

As the film proper begins, Kitten introduces two computer-generated robins as they swoop through the air and chatter to one another because 'birds always know everything that goes on in the town'. The film's strange post-credit sequence sets up the fairy tale-like mode of address. In the DVD commentary for the film, Jordan refers to the use of the robins and their aerial viewpoint as a kind of 'fableish' narration. The camera continues to swoop and glide to capture the robins as they fly through the air in a series of shots reminiscent of the opening sequence of Wim Wenders' *Wings of Desire* (1989), where two angels move effortlessly in and out of landmark buildings in Berlin. If we took the Wenders film and merged it, say, with a classic animated film by Disney (*Snow White*, 1937, for instance) it might begin to convey the sensibility of *Breakfast on Pluto*, at least in these opening sequences: an odd collision of the poetic with the whimsical, the realistic with the fabulous. Jordan constantly alludes to rational and irrational modes of thinking, and asks if human beings operate on a realistic or a delusional plane.

The film's narrative is excursive, and like Homer's *The Odyssey* the hero moves from adventure to adventure and traverses multiple locations. Michelangelo Antonioni's films of the early 1960s or Wenders' in the 1970s (for example, *Alice in the Cities*) are good examples of this excursive style. Antonioni's *L'Avventura* (*The Adventure*, 1960) begins with the disappearance of Anna (Léa Massari), and the remainder of the film moves the characters from place to place until the whereabouts of Anna are no longer mentioned. *Breakfast on Pluto* operates as a first person narrative; there are no other characters who assert their authority over the territory covered by Kitten's mostly linear story. The film flashes back to its first episode, with its Dickensian title, 'In Which I am Abandoned', and to a possibly imagined past that shows an infant in a basket deposited on the doorstep of the village priest, Father Bernard's (Liam Neeson) house, in County Cavan. The bell is rung as a woman deposits the basket and hurries away. The priest comes out, looks shocked and embarrassed, and surreptitiously brings the baby into the house.

In episode six, Kitten's tale of how he was conceived, entitled 'In Which I Am Mis-conceived', suggests a sensibility and pornographic imagery that might issue from a teenager. This narrative voice is very likely unreliable, as we see Father Bernard with his new housekeeper Eily Bergin (Eva Birthistle). When Father Bernard sees Eily scrubbing the floor, with her buttocks swaying back and forth in rhythmical movement, he licks his chops. When she realises that he is looking at her, she stands, looks down at his groin and sees that he has an erection. Eily points at this with a kitchen utensil and says, 'Dicky doodle down!' As Father Bernard takes Eily doggy style, she says: 'Frank Sinatra wouldn't do this, or Vic Damone.' In other contexts this may suggest a quasi-rape, but Kitten's point of view in the episode portrays Eily as neither upset nor anxious about the sexual activities. The scene is presented as the almost pornographic, imaginary view that might characterise an adolescent's understanding of sex. Both the priest and the housekeeper seem to be enjoying themselves enormously and the priest even gets extra rashers of bacon at breakfast into the bargain.

Although the film is narrated by Kitten in the film's present tense, this sequence provides an example of the writer as a trickster. Kitten is displacing his own over-attachment to popular icons onto his imagined mother, only changing the generation of singers to coincide with the decade of his conception (that is, Sinatra and Damone). The episode's portrayal of Father Bernard and his tryst with the housekeeper creates a situation not unlike that of *The Butcher Boy* – not surprising as Patrick McCabe wrote both source novels. The perspective is actually that of the mature Kitten, so we have an on-screen presence acting out the events of Kitten's diary. Kitten in all his manifestations (adolescent, singer in a band, the helper of a magician, and so forth) is refracted through the lens of a more developed consciousness. The sequence also has the imprint of a queer author writing about straight people making love. There is a melding of perspectives as the adolescent Kitten and the grown Kitten of the frame story describe the amorous relationship between his father and mother. This point is underscored by having the young Kitten dressed in clothing that is clearly too small on him, hinting at the gap between the teenage and adult perspectives.[2] The use of several points of view (a rather less complicated version of the Chinese box story structure found in *The Company of Wolves* and *The Butcher Boy*), maintains a level of uncertainty regarding the reliability of the narration, and allows the character to enter his own story as a naïf without the knowledge and experience that he will accrue as the film continues. It also galvanises the viewer's powers of observation and inference to comprehend the film's narrational strategies. Whether the point of view is judged unreliable or not, it will play a crucial role in our apprehension of the fictional world.

The film picks up Kitten's story and we see the child farmed out to a foster mother, Ma Braden (Ruth McCabe); Kitten's narrative maintains a linear time frame for the rest of the film. We see him as a young boy wearing a dress and high heels as his foster mother and step-sister walk in on him. His foster mother becomes angry, and scrubs him with a hard brush, as she forces him to repeat 'I am not a girl, I am a boy', which he does robotically, with little conviction. Kitten is presented as being aware of and comfortable with his sexual identity from an early stage in his life. Even as a pre-adolescent when we see him trying on his mother's clothes, he dreams of playing football in a silver lamé dress. Unlike many coming-out films with gay central characters, Kitten does not seem to be disturbed by his apparent difference to other children.

Time passes and Kitten grows into full-blown adolescence. We see a photo of Mitzi Gaynor on a magazine cover – an iconic figure for Kitten who imagines that his real mother looks, dresses and behaves like Gaynor. Kitten applies make-up in a mirror; he is now in full drag. Back at school, the head priest speaks with the boys about their changing bodies. He tells them that if they 'have any questions, of any kind, please write them down'. There is a box in which the schoolchildren place the folded papers containing their questions to ensure anonymity. We next see Kitten dragged out of the classroom, as he protests: 'But all I wanted to know was where I could get a good sex change?' These episodes continue the droll tone of Kitten's narration and do not suggest the anguish and pain that such transgressive behaviour most certainly would have engendered in the rural Ireland of the 1960s; Kitten is a fabulist who weaves tales about what he would have liked to happen in his life.

Kitten is about to leave town, and before he gets on the bus he swings his jacket round his head in a gesture of liberation. The character's transmission of his feelings clearly elicits a sympathetic response from the viewer. As is common in Jordan's film-making and fiction, there is no explanation of why Kitten is homosexual; Jordan refrains from probing his characters' sexual identities using the tools of psychology. Kitten is presented as the ultimate naïf, and the character is often placed in situations where he is mistreated or in grave danger. This, coupled with the film's non-judgemental approach to Kitten's plight, encourages a complicitous and congenial relationship to the character. Later in the film, we see Kitten writing his story of 'The Phantom Lady', and when questioned about his interest in this character, he says, 'If I didn't have my story I would start crying and never stop.' This is a crucial moment in the trajectory of the film in which Kitten's underlying sadness is revealed. This statement is essential to our understanding of Kitten and his deep feelings of grief, mistreatment and rejection; we apprehend the mask of imperturbable control he wears for self-protection. This is what Erving Goffman would call 'impression management', or the formulation of ideas about ourselves that desire to control the way others perceive us (Goffman 1959: 80).[3] Kitten's role-playing is essential to the film's narrative construction. This behaviour is evident in the many performances Kitten enacts throughout the film: as a misfit at school; as Billy Hatchett's (Gavin Friday) lover; as an Indian squaw in full regalia when he briefly sings with Billy and the Mohawks; as the would-be victim of a homophobic strangler (played by the suitably sinister Brian Ferry); as a Womble;[4] as a street prostitute; as the telephone lady questing for his mother; as 'the cross-dressing killer'; as a saviour of the world; as Bertie's (Stephen Rea) hypnotised subject and onstage helper; as a sex-worker in a peep show; as Father Bernard's confessor; as Charlie's buddy and confidante when she enters an abortion clinic; as the son to Father Bernard; as a father to Charlie's baby and as husband/wife to Charlie as well. This reconstruction of the family is critical, as the film begins and ends with Kitten pushing the baby in a pram. Once again Jordan is interrogating the meaning and social construction of the family unit, as well as dealing with the fluidity of identity.

One of the interesting aspects of the film is the way it deals with Kitten's sexual identity. Clearly the filmmaker approaches the character with great respect and sympathy. Although Kitten is harassed at every turn by his foster mother, the priests, the police, *et al.*, he retains his sense of humour and dignity, and rises above the melée. During the period in which the film is meant to take place, transvestism was represented in several contrasting ways in cinema. In the films of Andy Warhol, Paul Morrissey and John Waters, such as *Chelsea Girls* (1966), *Trash* (1970) and *Pink Flamingos* (1972), real-life transvestites such as Candy Darling, Jackie Curtis, Holly Woodlawn and Divine created characters that mainstream culture saw as objects of derision.

In the late 1960s and early 1970s many viewers did not see transvestites in such an affirmative light. Another approach was taken by Luchino Visconti in some of his heightened dramas of the era such as *La Caduta degli dei* (*The Damned*, 1969), which presented a transvestite (Helmut Berger) as the distorted product of the excessive, degenerate culture of Nazi Germany. Although not entirely negative, and meant as much to shock and affront the well-mannered, bourgeois audience of the art cinema as any film by Warhol and Waters, this view of transvestites continued to portray them as somehow disturbed or at the very least, not 'normal'. Ultimately, both the work of marginal directors like Waters and Warhol, and art cinema directors such as Visconti, was important in helping to re-define the way mainstream society viewed transvestites and gay culture, although it took years for these original, intrepid works to obtain value within mainstream culture. (How else could we countenance Nolte in a flaming red dress in Alan Rudolph's 1999 film *Breakfast of Champions*?)

Historically those films made Jordan's possible, but *Breakfast on Pluto* does not truly echo these specific works. The kind of persona in which Kitten feels most comfortable is a middle-class, well-mannered, well-spoken lady who loves romance novels and believes in true love. If there is a precursor to Kitten from the era it can rather be found in something like David Bowie's mid-to-late 1970s music videos, 'She'll Drive the Big Car', where Bowie would transform himself into the persona of a middle-class housewife. *Breakfast on Pluto*'s immersion in the glam rock era also echoes artists like Bowie, and it is no accident that Kitten yearns more for a middle-class existence, and a mother and father who love him. It is for this reason that he wants to recreate the 'normal' family unit at the end of the film. Kitten wants access to something he has never had.

The sense of abandonment felt by Kitten as he tries to find his mother has its ancestry in several Jordan films, especially in *The Miracle*. The exile in *Breakfast on Pluto* is also common Jordan territory. Kitten is an alien to his family, school, town and finally, his country, hence the appropriateness of Pluto in the film's title. Kitten does live in another world on another planet of his own making. We find the figure of the exile as early as the director's first film, *Angel*, as Danny wanders in the wilderness without family, friends or even his band mates. It is a deep issue in many of the director's subsequent films, and can be seen as recently as the character of Bob in *The Good Thief*, an exile from the US, and, in a sense, from himself as he obscures his feelings and senses with heroin, and the high of gambling.

As discussed in the chapter on dark Romanticism, originary concerns are a central thematic of the Romantic poets. William Blake writes in *Songs of Experience*, 'Did he who made the Lamb make thee?' (Blake 1978: 25). Kitten's quest for his mother is not merely a narrative device but the raison d'être of *Pluto* and the prime motivation for the character's journey, not only his physical journey to London in search of his mother, but his internal journey of self-awareness. The search for identity and meaning is at the heart of the film. The film argues that if we have no knowledge of where we come from, a gap in our psyche will remain unfulfilled. It will always obscure an essential part of the mystery of the self. Wholeness and unity can never be achieved unless this missing information is supplied.

In the section of *Breakfast on Pluto* entitled 'The Astral Highway', Kitten meets a biker (Liam Cunningham), the leader of a group called 'Border Knights', and as the assembled group smoke huge joints, Irwin (Laurence Kinlan), an IRA sympathiser, mentions what is happening in Northern Ireland. The biker responds, 'No politics, please. They jam the Astral Highway.' When asked why the bikers call themselves 'Border Knights', the biker replies: 'Because the only border that matters is between the one you left behind and the one that's up front. You think that when I ride my hog I'm riding around? I'm travelling from the past into the future with a Druid up my back.' How could one resist such a visionary? Kitten asks if it is a male or female Druid, and the biker responds, 'It doesn't matter. What matters is the journey. Do you know where it goes baby? "We'll visit the stars and we'll visit Mars, finding our breakfast on Pluto."'[5] Apart from the pleasures of Liam Cunningham's perceptive performance as a kind of Baudelarian stoner, the scene is important because it offers Kitten an alternative way of perceiving the world, one without the barriers and fixed identities he endures in his provincial home town.

The political realities of early 1970s Ireland are obliquely referred to as television images filled with riots and burning houses are shown in disparate environments. Although not commented upon, they are part of the frightening backdrop to Kitten's world, and set the stage for one of the film's first serious treatments of the era's politics. This section of the film involves a gun-running operation that includes Kitten's friend Irwin, and Kitten's lover Billy Hatchett, a frayed glam rocker. Billy puts Kitten up in a derelict caravan in which he believes he will find the romantic bliss and a space for the domesticity he has so longed for. This idyll immediately turns dark as Kitten accidentally stumbles on a major caché of guns hidden under the floorboards in the caravan. After a car-bombing incident in which one of his friends is killed, Kitten tosses the guns in a river, not understanding the serious repercussions of his gesture. In one of the film's more intense moments, two paramilitary thugs, with guns trained at his head, try to extract the location of their caché from him. They do not believe Kitten's account of dumping the guns in the water. Beneath the lightness of his being, we encounter the dark side of Kitten's existence. The sequence clearly highlights the shifting tones of the film, particularly coming as it does after the much more light-hearted material with Billy Hatchett and his tawdry musical revue. The play between the fantasy and darker territory is woven throughout, as it is in all of Jordan's films.

The 'troubles' are referenced later in the film when Irwin, whose involvement with a paramilitary group has steadily increased, is brutally shot execution style by two 'soldiers'. The script does not illuminate Irwin's character, and his death is exponentially less moving. The character affected most by Irwin's death is Charlie, Irwin's partner, who is pregnant with his child. Charlie is depicted as a carefree, fun-loving woman who falls to pieces upon hearing the news. Later, politics re-enters the film in the sequence in which a disco is blown up. Kitten, although he is a victim of the explosion, is horribly brutalised by the British police; the harsh realities of Irish/British politics of the time are invested with emotional force. That sequence is important because it plays a major part in Kitten's psychic breakdown, and leads to a period of street prostitution.

Kitten takes a boat across the 'wide and wild' ocean to London, and upon awakening the first thing he sees is John Joe Kenny (Brendan Gleeson) dressed in a Womble outfit. Kitten too becomes a Womble, which in its own way is fitting as Kitten seems to also live in a phantasmatic world; he perhaps recognises a kindred spirit in Kenny, whose bogus bonhomie in the Womble costume barely disguises a more vitriolic character who likes to drink and fight altogether too much. As with Kitten, Kenny (barely) masks his true feelings beneath an outlandish costume. His bitterness mirrors the failed ambitions and humiliations he must subjugate himself to when he performs as a cartoon character. This in turn reflects the anger of many Irish immigrants who sought work in London or Liverpool because of a lack of economic opportunity or the political unrest in Ireland, and were obliged to demean themselves in low-paying, mortifying jobs. What may seem like a humorous masquerade is, in fact, a cutting commentary on the treatment of Irish immigrants in Britain. Such indignities deaden the spirit of characters like Kenny, in spite of the gregarious geniality he displays on the surface. This role-playing can again be seen when Kitten finally sees his real (Irish) mother, who has acclimatised to life in England by losing her native Irish accent, something she may believe is expected of her in her adopted country. We never learn more than this about Eily; her thoughts and feelings are deliberately held at a distance from us as they are from Kitten, who never addresses her.

In the next turn of events Kitten meets Bertie (Stephen Rea), a third-rate magician who plays sleazy clubs in London. We watch as Bertie saws a woman in half, and soon Kitten takes the woman's place as Bertie's 'helper'. During a performance, Kitten is hypnotised, and told to find mummy. Pathetically, Kitten throws his arms around two patrons, a woman, and then a man. Bertie then says 'Go, look for mummy up here', and Kitten flings his arms around the giant speaker on stage, holding it with all his might. This sequence recalls a scene in Fellini's *Le Notti di Cabiria* (*Nights of Cabiria*, 1957), in which the innocent prostitute, Cabiria (Giulietta Massina) is mesmerised by a hypnotist, and told that she will meet and fall deeply in love with a man named Oscar. After the performance a charming con-artist (François Périer) introduces himself as Oscar, and proceeds to perpetuate the pattern of abuse that Cabiria suffers throughout that film. Cabiria's humiliation at the hands of Oscar leads to her final despairing act where she movingly pleads for Oscar to end her life by a roadside. In one of the great uplifting moments in the movies, Cabiria then displays her indomitable spirit of renewal when she encounters the smiling faces and singing of children and adolescents who once again move her spirit. In spite of the actions of men like Oscar, life is still worth living. Kitten shares with Cabiria a similar perseverance in the face of adversity, especially in the later scenes where he is beaten by police.[6]

As Bertie's assistant in his magic show, we see Kitten placed on a turning wheel preparing to have knives thrown at him. The first throw strikes him directly in the heart. The audience waits for Kitten to revive, and after he does not, they gasp in unison. Bertie, in the style of the Grand Guignol,[7] pulls the knife out with a heart affixed to it. Kitten wakes up as Bertie squeezes the heart as blood surges from it. The heart is bruised and broken, but the scene is handled with such good humour in its

Bertie (Stephen Rea) holds a simulacra of Kitten's (Cillian Murphy) bruised heart in his hands

depiction of the tacky stage show that the viewer cannot help but empathise with the two men; both have emotional wounds, and both want desperately to find the connectedness that a relationship would give their lives. Kitten and Bertie are running on parallel tracks, destined to remain apart – the liaison, like so many of the relationships in Jordan's films, is one of impossible love.

We do not know how much time has elapsed when we see Bertie and Kitten on a mist-shrouded pier. Bertie confesses that he has given up on the 'emotional side of things' and adds: 'But I could fall for a girl like the one over there', indicating Kitten, who is standing at some distance from Bertie. It is likely that he has harboured this secret affection for a long time. There is some hesitation and embarrassment until finally Kitten says, 'But you see the thing is, I'm not a girl', a direct quotation from *The Crying Game* after the 'revelation scene':

Fergus:	Do they know?
Dil:	Know what, honey?
Fergus:	Know what I didn't know? And don't call me that.
Dil:	Can't help it! A girl has her feelings.
Fergus:	Thing is, Dil, you're not a girl.
Dil:	Details, baby, details.
Fergus:	So they do know?
Dil:	All right, they do.
Fergus:	Don't. I should've known, shouldn't I?
Dil:	Probably.
Fergus:	Kind of wish I didn't.
Dil:	You can always pretend.
Fergus:	That's true.

Bertie tells Kitten he knew she was not a woman from the moment he met her (as does the viewer). Stephen Rea gives the small part a great deal of weight, in a portrait of a man who is a bit sad and creepy. He finds the real person, in pain, behind the stereotypes of older homosexuals who have spent their lives in the closet, unable to live an emotionally fulfilling existence. His face reveals the melancholy of a man stuck in a repetitive job that seems to have long ago lost its allure. Bertie is on the shelf, he is beyond his sell-by-date on the gay scene. His lips are pursed when he speaks, in a physiological manifestation of his repression. Bertie is burnt out and defeated; and now that he has let the cat (or Kitten) out of the bag and made himself vulnerable, he is rebuffed. Rea takes the time for his reaction to fully develop and Jordan lets him have a long moment of mute desolation. It is difficult to watch this scene of rejection, and one can see the sadness, embarrassment and shame in a single shot of Rea's face.[8] 'The camera loves to watch actors thinking', as Rea says (in Zucker 1999: 116).

The law in England decriminalising homosexual relations was only passed in 1967 (and then only for males aged over 21), so Bertie would have grown up repressed and, of necessity, cautious about his sexual affairs. Kitten represents a post-Stonewall generation of gay men, although growing up in Ireland in the 1950s and 1960s Kitten would no doubt share a good deal of Bertie's repressive and restrained attitudes to homosexuality. Jordan and McCabe manipulate the perspective of the era to allow Kitten a more contemporary view of his sexuality. The couple part in a moving sequence on a bridge that references the convention of earlier British melodramas, such as David Lean's *Brief Encounter* (1945), that end with lovers parting on a bridge or at a train station. But then Kitten lives in a melodrama, making the parting with Bertie entirely genre-appropriate.

In McCabe's book Bertie has a sexual relationship with Pussy (Kitten's name in the novel), and brings him home to his wife, Louise, who is undisturbed by this state of affairs. In fact, when Bertie leaves, Pussy and Louise form an *entente* (McCabe 1998: 93); Pussy sits on Louise's lap and she gives suck to him from her breast, the only sexual congress they achieve. The scene is reminiscent of the 'I want to be a Nugent' subplot in *The Butcher Boy*, in which Mrs Nugent similarly unbuttons her blouse to give her breast to Francie's hungry mouth.

We next find Kitten in a night club. A few moments elapse before a bomb detonates, wreaking havoc in the club. In a scene that is visually stunning in its use of slow-motion, a silvery disco ball crashes to the floor and registers the beauty of destruction that shadows many scenes of carnage and violence in Jordan's films. The sequence has an unreal, phantasmatic quality, in some ways reminding the viewer of the atomic bomb sequence in *The Butcher Boy*, where the holocaust reveals bodies strewn about the post nuclear, wind-swept landscape that is simultaneously horrifying and arresting in its beauty. As the disco scene continues, we see police rescue the wounded victims of the bombed-out club. Kitten is found prostrate, and laments, 'My tights are torn to ribbons', which is also the name of the episode.

In the next episode, entitled 'The Smile of a Cross-Dressing Killer', the narrative continues as police viciously beat Kitten, assuming as an Irishman he must be involved in the bombing. The police, especially P. C. Wallis (Ian Hart), are especially brutal, while Kitten treats the beatings with something approaching nonchalance and a good deal of humour. Again, the character resorts to his imaginative world to mask a grim reality that he could not otherwise survive. In spite of his brutalisation, Kitten does not want to leave his 'sweet little cell'; he wins over the police with his fey charm, and becomes something like a mascot to them. His desire to remain in prison seems consistent with the character's sense (and the reality) of being victimised and lacking wholeness – one can see why he would prefer incarceration to the hellish world outside the cell. The emotional savagery he would confront on the outside would be more difficult for the sensitive character to endure than a controlled, if very limited, environment. But ultimately Kitten rejects the identity of a victim. The refrain from Gloria Gaynor's disco hit, 'I Will Survive', could very well be Kitten's rallying cry.

We next see Kitten spin his most fabulous tale as 'Kitten Saves the World' in which he is dressed in a tight mini-mac and high boots – all in glittering purple lurex. This playful interval serves to lighten the mood as well as reinforce the importance for Kitten of retreating into the imaginary as a survival technique. He moves through the constructed fantasy space striking poses as if in a comic book, and punishing villains by vaporising them with a dusting of perfume. Obviously, this bespeaks his need to

Kitten in a sex shop show, in one of his many identities

feel powerful and in control, and in another nod to films of the 1960s, it wryly recalls and ridicules the cartoonish films of the era, often based on Italian *fumettis* (adult comic books). As Kitten disposes of his enemies with an atomiser, we are reminded of the female characters in such films as Joseph Losey's *Modesty Blaise* (1966) and Roger Vadim's *Barbarella* (1967), part of a cinematic trend whose female heroines used their sexuality in preposterous situations, and titillated the audience in what are undoubtedly sexist fantasies.

Once out of his prison cell, we see Kitten prostituting himself (again recalling the innocent Cabiria) and begin work in a sex show. He is in bondage of a different sort than that of his prison cell. We see him as the 'lovely thing', with ruffled dress, on a swing wreathed with flowers. Father Bernard enters the peep show and sits in Kitten's cubicle. Without realising who he is, Kitten asks the customer what he wants him (her) to do. He puts his hands suggestively between his legs and lubriciously licks his lips whilst staring at the mirror. The priest can see him, but Kitten cannot see the priest through the one way mirror, and the father impatiently demands that Kitten cease his lewd performance. Father Bernard, as if in a confessional, apologises for his mistreatment of Kitten and expresses a desire to make amends. The Father also apprises Kitten of his lineage. Upon realising who his client is, Kitten runs after him into the brightly coloured, neon-lit streets of Soho, made more chimerical through the painterly *mise-en-scène* and cinematography. The sequence in the peep show is set in perhaps the most fantastic space of the film; the décor is carefully constructed and the use of coloured filters evokes a strange, artificial arena begotten of an imagination unrestricted by reality (see Neil Jordan, *Breakfast on Pluto* DVD commentary). When Kitten runs out onto the streets of Soho, the use of neon and compressed spaces also recall the works of artists such as Dan Flavin and Bruce Nauman who have used neon extensively in their installations. The artificiality and painterliness of these scenes may also remind viewers of Kubrick's *Eyes Wide Shut* (1999), which also created an oneiric universe out of downtown Manhattan through carefully constructed décor and use of photography connected to the main character's (Tom Cruise) subjective experience of his universe.

The peep show sequence is also strongly reminiscent of a key scene in the latter part of Wim Wenders' *Paris, Texas* (1984) where Travis (Harry Dean Stanton) visits his ex-wife, Jane, played by Nastassja Kinski, in the sex shop in which she works. Travis acknowledges all of the foolish and insensitive things he has done, and talks about the pain and sorrow he has inflicted on his ex-wife. In *Paris, Texas* the characters use a telephone to communicate, and Travis also turns his back to Jane, thus inserting several layers of mediation. This gives the heart-wrenching scene more emotional distance than we find in Jordan's film, although the scene in Wenders' film is still disturbing and deeply moving.

Kitten is reunited with his Father and Charlie, with the new baby, in another of Jordan's skewed, reconfigured families, which also reflects the changing familial structures of the era. Father Bernard's church is torched, but we cannot tell if the perpetrators are people who disapprove of the family arrangement or (less likely) a paramilitary group. Kitten achieves his goal of seeing his mother, although he never introduces himself. We sense that perhaps she discerns something when she looks at him, perhaps a small degree of recognition. Kitten can now live his life without compromise or deception. The two robins return as if to say, 'And everyone lived happily ever after.'

The notion of transgression (in this case, of the family), whether related to kinship (incest in *The Miracle*), sexuality (*The End of the Affair*), gender (*The Crying Game*), the political (*Michael Collins*), the behavioural (*The Butcher Boy*), and the murderous (*Angel, Mona Lisa, Interview with the Vampire, The Butcher Boy, In Dreams* and *The Brave One*) is a key impulse in all of Jordan's films. *Breakfast on Pluto* fits this pattern of transgression, and further reflects Jordan's continued interest in stylisation versus realism, the off-kilter view of family, absent mothers, difficult fathers, characters who are haunted by loss, the psychic toll of violence, the quest for identity (sexual and otherwise) and the conceptualisation of masculinity. Kitten's search for wholeness, identity and love is central to the film's project and a hallmark of the director's entire body of work. *Breakfast on Pluto* thus becomes both a reiteration of Jordan's central thematic and aesthetic concerns, and a summation of his output as a film artist at mid-career.

In *Breakfast on Pluto*, Jordan has created a work that emphasises two of his main preoccupations: his love of music and the work of writing. Both are honoured in a carefully wrought aesthetic honed over a quarter century of filmmaking. The film also refers to a wide canvas of cinematic styles, filmmakers and cinematic movements that the director greatly admires. Jordan has always spoken with generosity of the importance of other filmmakers who helped shape his artistic sensibility, particularly Fellini and Kubrick. Jordan is a serious, highly original artist who persists in re-thinking and changing the parameters of his work as a filmmaker. He will undoubtedly continue to plumb many of the same issues that have invigorated his work for thirty years, both as a writer and as a director. The end of *Breakfast on Pluto* illustrates this consistency, and strikingly echoes the ending of *Mona Lisa*, made twenty years earlier. The two films both conclude very much like fairy tales, or renderings of fantasised wish fulfilments. In *Mona Lisa*, Thomas, George and his daughter go skipping off arm in arm into the sunset. At the end of *Breakfast on Pluto*, Kitten embodies the perfect *Ladies*

Home Journal reverie: a mum in a frilly dress pushing a baby in a pram. These stylised and surreal images challenge reality, and deepen the meaning of the director's character studies. Additionally, they demonstrate how deeply embedded subtext is to Jordan's storytelling and writing practice. They invite the viewer to contemplate the manifold nature of Jordan's artistic production.

CODA

The Brave One: 'There's Plenty of Ways to Die'

'Precisely because the universe in which we live is somehow a universe of dead conventions and artificiality, the only authentic real experience must be some extremely violent, shattering experience. And this we experience as a sense that now we are back in real life.'

– Slavoj Žižek

The opening paragraph of Neil Jordan's novel *Shade* begins:

I know exactly when I died. It was twenty past three on the fourteenth of January of the year nineteen fifty, an afternoon of bright unseasonable sunlight with a whipping wind that scurried the white clouds through the blue sky above me and gave the Irish sea beyond more than its normal share of white horses. (2004: 3)

Shade is narrated in part by a dead woman, Nina Hardy, interspersed with the narrative voice of the omniscient author. It is a ghostly presence that seems to haunt *The Brave One* as well.

The Brave One revolves around the life of a New York radio talk-show host, a storyteller, Erica (Jodie Foster), whose radio tag on her show 'I Walk the City' is 'The Street-walker'. The programme is comprised of her romanticised and sweetly sentimental commentary on her beloved New York, 'the safest big city in the world'. Throughout the credit sequence Erica's voice is over-dubbed from her different sessions in the recording studio, fragmenting her vocals. As noted in the chapter on storytelling and performance, the art of telling stories is a vehicle for the communication and sharing of human knowledge, understanding and feeling that is vital to Jordan's filmmaking process.

We first meet Erica as she and David (Naveen Andrews) discuss their upcoming marriage and the colour of the wedding invitations. Their talk is punctuated with their movements as they dance lovingly around one another, holding, hugging and kissing. The formalities concerning the wedding are prompted by David's mother, because, as Erica says: 'You have a family, David. I don't.' This fact becomes relevant once Erica loses David and lives in isolation from any community.

They stop as they walk their dog, Curtis, in Central Park and Erica claims that she wants 'the whole deal' as well, because 'it's not as if I'm going to do it twice'. David counters with: 'That's the nicest thing you ever said to me.' After they kiss they suddenly realise that it has got dark and Curtis is gone. Both of them call for the dog, but he fails to come. They leave the path – reminding one of fairy tale interdiction 'Don't stray from the path' – and enter one of the dark, Gothic labyrinthine tunnels that run through the park. We see the image of David and Erica on the shaky screen of a mobile phone. A man, Reed (Rafael Sardina) is seen holding Curtis by his leash. Reed starts to goad the couple: 'Hey, come on, don't you know there's a fuckin' leash law?' David tries to calm things down by being polite, but this has no effect. We realise there are three men, including Cash (Blaze Foster) and Lee (Luis da Silva Jr) who close in on David and Erica and beat them savagely with fists, bottles and metal pipes. We see the incident in a monochromatic image as it is recorded on the mobile phone. The thug holding the phone calls out at one point, as he smashes Erica against the tunnel wall: 'Hollywood time! HollyWOOD!' The images recorded on the mobile will be revisited at various junctures of the film as Erica remembers the attack. The scene of the assault is edited in a highly fragmented way, the rhythm is staccato, revealing only portions of the action and parts of bodies intercut with shots on the phone. This sense of mediation is important to the film; it gives it a quality of being overlooked, as if an invisible watcher is recording the events. It is an authorial intrusion of the type that we normally associate with art cinema (see Bordwell 1985: 211).

After the attack, we see Erica and David as they are wheeled on gurneys within the trauma centre of Columbia Presbyterian Hospital. Nurses and doctors insert intravenous drip tubes and shunts into their battered, blood-soaked bodies. Their clothing is cut away so that the hospital staff can attend to their wounds. Interwoven with the actions of the staff are abstracted shots of Erica and David's body parts as they make love.

We move away from the David and Erica story when Detective Mercer (Terrence Howard, in a complex and sensitive portrayal of a 'good cop') views a dead female in the same hospital with a bullet wound on her temple. The dead woman's partner, Murrow (Gordon MacDonald), claims that she has committed suicide, and even though her fingerprints are all over the weapon, it is taken for granted that her husband is the perpetrator. Detective Mercer later says, 'Women never shoot themselves in the face. Not in my experience.' Mercer then looks in on the comatose Erica; plastic tubing runs from her fractured, fragile body to machines. As the shooting script says, 'It's ugly, survival. Without passion – an odd way to hold on to a life.'

Erica awakens three weeks later from a coma to learn that David did not survive the brutal attack. After her stay in the hospital, she returns to her flat. The time frame is not clear, but one imagines that her physical recovery was protracted because of the massive damage perpetrated upon her. The sense of loss that percolates amongst the characters in Jordan's films dominates Erica's homecoming. Sarah McLachlan's honeyed voice sings 'Answer' on the soundtrack. Images of the fatal assault are again intertwined with shots of David and Erica making love, their bodies fragmented, reminding one of the lovemaking sequences in Alain Resnais' *Hiroshima, mon amour* (1959). The lovemaking in *The Brave One* and in the Resnais film emphasise the abstraction of body parts, and the beauty of the act of love suffused with a sense of melancholy and imminent loss. This abstraction of the body is similar to the way coitus is depicted in *The End of the Affair*, the only other Jordan film in which on-screen sex is depicted.

Erica's loneliness is palpable as she slowly adjusts to solitude and life without her partner. When she tremulously leaves her flat for the first time she is lit from behind, and framed with a canted angle that emphasises the vertigo and edginess of her fearful emergence back into her own life and the life of the city. There is a feeling that Erica and David shared 'Das Reich der Zwei', a kingdom of two, the term Kurt Vonnegut uses to describe the all-consuming, exclusive love of the main character in *Mother Night*, writing about his love for his wife (1961: 37). David and Erica appear to have a very small social network. Only Erica's friend, Nicole (Jane Adams), an art gallery owner, leaves a message on her answering machine during the time Erica remains housebound.

The first thing Erica does once she leaves her domestic space is to enter a gun shop in a shot ominously bisected by a security camera image in the foreground. The owner refuses to sell her a gun without the mandatory waiting period of thirty days. Her desperation is evident as she begs for the gun, but the shop owner is unimpressed. As she exits the store she is stopped by a gun dealer (Angel Sing). He offers her a pistol – a Kahr K-9, a popular choice for concealment and self-defence. The vendor offers her lessons on loading and using the gun and throws in the bullets for free.

We next find Erica ambling around the aisles of a convenience store. Suddenly, the Asian woman who owns the store is confronted by her raging spouse who says, 'So you won't let me see my kids?' A domestic dispute flares up; the man shoots his wife again and again as blood showers the photos of their children on the wall. Erica is hunched down in an aisle to avoid being seen, but she watches the action on ceiling-mounted surveillance mirrors. The man opens the cash register as Erica's mobile phone rings. Before she can turn it off the gunman hears it and starts walking rapidly towards her. Heavy breathing is heard on the soundtrack. There is a burst of fire from Erica's gun as she shoots wildly at the assailant through glass bottles on a shelf; the scene is filmed in slow-motion. She looks at the shooter's body and sees arterial blood spurting out of his neck; he is dying. With the finesse of a schooled criminal Erica has the savvy to eject the videotape from the store's monitoring device to avoid identification. The scene takes place in Spanish Harlem, and there is always a sense in the film that danger is imminent as Erica seeks out places where a woman would simply not go to alone, after dark. She lives in interstitial spaces, a twilight zone. Like the wolf/man in *The Company of Wolves* she goes between the world above and below. As the wolf/man says: 'I come and go between both.' And certainly Erica strays far, far from the path.

The Brave One grants the teller of the tale a wide berth for the creative deployment of fairy tales. The director chooses to focus on the more troubled constituents of this particular narrative form. Erica's lack of affect is contrasted by her outbursts of violence, and accommodates Jordan's penchant for probing the effects of trauma on identity, most commonly endowed with a basic sense of loss. Jordan's fairy tale-like narratives often mine the territory of traumatic social events as found in all of his films from *Angel* onwards. There is a feeling that his characters are often unable to return to normality in order to heal the source of their wounds. Jordan's storytelling arises from popular culture, and the vigilante film, like the horror film, expresses the social anxieties of the times. The film can be seen as a contemporaneous articulation of the fairy tale – but one which is registered in the key of apocalypticism.

The scenes of violence also demonstrate Jordan's predilection for the dark carnival which Bakhtin writes about. It destabilises social norms, '…opening the way for licentious misrule, generating what might be called festive horror, a genre in which carnival's material bodily principle … its base of promiscuous carnality, blasphemy, scatology and ritual degradation is translated from a comic social discourse into a pathological one' (in Morgan 2002: 135).

Misrule becomes, in *The Brave One*, millenarial thought, so prevalent in the post 9/11 world. The agents and events in the 'Book of Revelation', the notion of the 'last days', has always had a strong pull on Western intellect and imagination. One of the most important components and influences of eschatological thinking is polarity – the Manichean forces of light and dark with no middle ground. Creative energies are generated by the tension between Good and Evil. Millenarialism is generally preoccupied with violence as something that will destroy historical evil. It is swift and absolute like Erica's transgressive vengeance-fuelled actions. The 'end in the beginning', as Meyer Howard Abrams writes in *The Correspondent Breeze*, creates a circular movement. In Jordan's film this starts with unitary felicity as in David and Erica's relationship; then self-division, which marks Erica after the murderous attack; sin, established in Erica's nocturnal murders; then exile, wherein Erica experiences dissociation, and talks to Mercer about becoming a 'stranger' to herself and the world around her. Suffering is the next stage and is found in Erica's living hell in a post-David world. Finally there is a return in the cycle to initial happiness (see 1984: 225–7). The latter is left completely ambiguous in *The Brave One*, although it is admittedly difficult to contemplate Erica living a congenial existence after all that she has done and all that has been inflicted upon her. The Dark Romanticism at the heart of *The Brave One* is another manifestation of the director's links to that particular cultural and historical movement in which the visionary poets Blake, Wordsworth, Coleridge and Southey in England, and Hölderlin in Germany embraced the French Revolution as a crisis that inspired new hope, but also darkened the imagination. It is not too great a leap to nominate Erica as a terrorist. It is her personal *jihad*, when she decides to dispatch her 'evil' victims.

New York as a cityscape plays a large role in the film; the city is filmed almost always at night. There is an atmosphere that is strongly reminiscent of the way in which London is filmed in *Mona Lisa*, a version in both theme and style of Dante's *Inferno* (Neil Jordan, *Mona Lisa* DVD commentary). One could correctly consider *The Brave One* to be the progeny of the vigilante film, for example, Michael Winner's *Death Wish* (1974). Yet there is an oneiric quality to the photography in which the background of the shots is often out of focus and blurred, brightly-coloured neon lights flicker and rotating patrol-car lights figure prominently in many of the compositions. This sort of stylisation aligns itself more with the surreal than with the more realistic approach to the drama of *Death Wish*. Jordan's film is, like *Mona Lisa*, a rendering of a nightmarish, mythopoeic imagination of a city.

The presence of the camera insinuates itself into the space between the spectator and the actor; the cinematography is by Jordan's long-time collaborator Philippe Rousselot. The act of filming (and authorial intervention, as mentioned earlier) is emphasised to a greater extent than in any other work the director has made thus far. Shots are taken from behind curtains; through the wires of a construction site; through windows, guard rails on a highway, bookshelves; refracted through glass and mirrors; and perhaps most evocatively (if less than subtly) from behind tombstones in a graveyard. These shots are often lit from the rear and at times over-exposed, lending a spectral quality to the image. One of the mostly heavily mediated sequences is the violent beating in Central Park of Erica and David. The blurred chromatic mobile phone image is intercut with the film's 35mm images, and is repeated at various points as flashbacks.

Erica returns to her job against the express wishes of her boss, Carol, in an under-written role played by Mary Steenburgen. Erica begins her show, but has trouble speaking. While Erica starts to record she is photographed from behind bookshelves, which gives one the sense of surveillance by an unknown force and introduces the motif of the fragmented self which ripens as the film evolves. She says: 'This is Erica Bain and I walk the city. New York, like any metropolis is an organism that mutates...' Erica stops speaking; there is nothing but dead air. She starts again but only manages the first few words. Carol frantically asks if there is something else to cut to, and the engineer is about to pull the plug on the programme when Erica leans in towards the microphone and repeats her opening lines with great intensity, shot in big close-ups. Erica speaks:

New York, the safest big city in the world. But it is horrible to fear the place you once loved. And to see a street corner you knew so well and be afraid of its shadow. To see familiar steps and be unable to climb them. I never under-stood how people lived with fear. Women afraid to walk home alone. People afraid of white powder in their mailbox. Darkness. People afraid of other people. I always believed that fear belonged to other people. Weaker people.

It never touched me. And then it did. And when it touches you, you know … that it's been there all along. Waiting beneath the surfaces of everything you loved. And your skin crawls, and your heart sickens, you look at the person that was once you, walking down the street … and wonder will you ever be her again?

Her speech is intercut with shots of Detective Mercer listening in his car. This major transmutation in Erica's identity is a trope articulated throughout Jordan's work, starting with *Angel,* and is most strongly foregrounded in works such as *The Crying Game, In Dreams* and *Breakfast on Pluto.*

Another violent situation occurs where passengers are being harassed in a subway car. Erica sits off to one side in a nearly empty car. At the other end two toughs (played by Jermel Howard and Dennie White) are bullying the passengers. When the subway car enters a station everyone makes a quick exit, but Erica remains seated – collected and stone-faced. Erica at this point in the narrative has developed a carapace of hardness, just barely covering her still-raw wounds. As one character later says to the police, attempting to describe her: 'She was on lock-down. Kind of scary.' Erica is now a sort of zombie, a living dead person who feeds off those who are still alive. It is a survival mode that allows her to bear her personal apocalypse.

The two toughs cannot believe that Erica has stayed in the subway car. They look at her and say, 'The bitch is crazy.' One of the thugs approaches her, wielding a bladed instrument. He closes in on her, and runs the blade beneath Erica's chin, into the concavity of her neck and down to her chest, and says: 'Have you ever gotten fucked by a knife?' His body is suddenly hurled backwards by the force of the shot Erica has fired; blood splatters as the other thug moves towards Erica and she fires again. Erica's breathing is shallow and heavy as she exits the scene.

There are a number of shots that atomise Erica's face with swirling camera movements as she departs the scene of the crime. She goes to a club and vomits in the bathroom sink, then refreshes herself. Erica, perversely, returns to the area where we find Detective Mercer and his partner Vitale (Nicky Katt) investigating the crime. Mercer posits a theory: 'Maybe some average Joe decided he's not going to take it anymore, and I'm going to get me a gun and take matters into his own hand. Kind of guy you wouldn't ever notice.'

The following morning the headlines 'VIGILANTE' are splashed across newspapers. The idea of the vigilante can be intertwined with Renée Girard's concept of 'sacrificial substitution'. Implicit in this line of reasoning is the notion that all parties agree to a certain level of misunderstanding – a level of denial. Erica's shootings easily fall into the pattern of 'sacrificial substitution'. She is asked by her boss to open her talk-show to invite public commentary on the vigilante's activities. The comments run like this:

'As far as I'm concerned he's doing us a favour', to another caller who says: 'There's not a person I know who doesn't get some jolt of pleasure when they hear about a vigilante' and '… revenge makes us feel good'. There is a complicit sense that these human sacrifices are not murders, as well as a transgression of civil liberties, and the acceptance of this fact creates a consensus within the community. One victim, Erica's fiancé, David, is being displaced by another, but there is a tacit understanding that no one will mention this. Girard is also trying to remove the theological rationale for sacrifice, and to look at it as a social act; he wants to eliminate the 'God-told-me-to' aspect that is common to traditional sociological theory. Girard feels that we must recognise that religion has very little relevance in the modern world, and to say that sacrifice is an act of mediation between the sacrificer and a deity is merely an imaginary explanation. At base, Girard says, the way violence moves from one victim to another so easily ensures that the actual horror and senselessness of violence is hidden (see 1977: 1–38).

The relationship between Mercer and Erica develops after the second shooting. It is one of Jordan's great themes – erotic tension conflated with impossible love. Whatever Mercer's attraction for Erica is he cannot, once he comes to understand that she is the vigilante, think about having a relationship with her. His moral principles – which he will eventually abandon in order to help Erica's quest for vengeance – bind him to track down the vigilante, as expressed in this dialogue:

Mercer:	You know Erica, when I was a rookie, I used to give myself this test. If someone I knew had committed a crime, would I have the fortitude to put them away.
Erica:	What kind of someone?
Mercer:	Someone close to me. Like the best friend I could ever hope to have had.
Erica:	And?
Mercer:	I always hoped I would have had the courage, the dedication to say yes.
Erica:	And … do you?
Mercer:	I do. And it's important that you know that.
Erica:	I know that. It's what I admire about you.

Mercer is implicitly warning Erica that he will arrest whoever the vigilante is once the person is found. At this point he has very definite suspicions about Erica's involvement, and in a manner that is gentle and diplomatic, he is reminding her that whatever his feelings for her are, he must honour his duty to uphold the law.

The relationship between Erica and Mercer develops, and parallel editing is used to depict their congruity. Scenes of Erica in her apartment are intercut with Mercer in his. Both are insomniacs and they develop a pattern of late-night phone calls to reach out to each other in the night. Shots of Erica and Mercer together are often filmed so that each character shares the frame symmetrically, as in their long dialogue scene in the diner which is partially filmed from outside the window. A subtle halo is formed around the characters by the green neon lighting.

Mercer can be looked upon as Erica's 'fetch'. As discussed in chapter two, there is an ancient Celtic notion that alongside every mortal there exists a dark shadow-self, a doppelgänger or counterpart – the Irish word is 'fetch'. This notion permeates Jordan's work beginning with the IRA or Unionist assassins in *Angel*, who act as several versions of Danny's fetch. The fetch can represent many things: sexual, racial or cultural, amongst others. In many ways Erica is Mercer's fetch, a 'fallen angel', reminiscent of Louis in *Interview with the Vampire*, as one who inhabits the benighted niches of his mind. She is his moral fetch, the self-appointed executioner who exists in opposition to the detective's righteous respect for the due process of the law; his racial fetch – she is white, he is black. Erica has lost her lover to murder; Mercer has divorced. Erica's loss is by far the darker and more malevolent one. The detective comes to Erica's flat and says, 'Its pretty dark in here', to which she replies: 'I like it like that.' She exists now in the dark side, the place where menace, the irrational and the primal urges for violent revenge exist.

Erica's unleashed violence begins to be more of a quest to rid the city of pestilential individuals. One begins to understand that *Taxi Driver* (1976) is a kind of über-text for *The Brave One*. (It is of course ironic, intentionally or not, that Jodie Foster played a lost waif to Harvey Keitel's pimp in this Scorsese film.) As Erica walks in the dark, the driver of a parked car, Cutler (Victor Colicchio), says: 'What will fifty dollars do for you?' Erica replies: 'I don't know.' There is a young girl in a stupor hunched over in the back seat. The car attains the status of a twenty-first century Gothic claustral space, replete with hamburger boxes and candy bar wrappings. Erica says: 'You're looking for a party in the back seat?' Cutler responds: 'Oh yeah.' The girl, Chloe (Zöe Kravitz), bears bruises and cigarette burns on her arms. Erica speaks gently to the girl, and after Cutler finishes a drug-stimulated harangue, Erica says: 'You know what? Chloe and I are going to take a little walk.' Cutler replies heatedly, 'You ain't going nowhere.' Erica asks Chloe: 'You want to get out, don't you?' The girl replies in the affirmative. Cutler turns swiftly and burns Chloe with his cigarette. Erica places her gun at Cutler's temple, and he says, 'Uh oh, we got a supercunt here.' Erica warns him that if he does not let Chloe out of the car, ' I'll be the last supercunt you ever see.' Cutler lets Chloe and Erica out, but in a flash the car hurtles towards the two women. Erica stands tall as the car heads straight at her. She pumps three bullets into the windscreen which becomes spattered with blood.

Of all the characters in Jordan's repertoire, Erica most resembles two: Claire from *In Dreams* and Danny in *Angel*. The narrative patterning of *The Brave One* indisputably reflects its mythic origin, and certainly Erica is a mythological heroine of a sort. She is bound and determined to endure the horror of her emotional voyage of discovery, her precarious quest that calls up the most monstrous side of her being. She, like Claire, pushes the notion of the transgressive, embracing the connection between her impassioned rage which, when taken to the extreme, becomes a kind of madness. Both characters are in a state of abjection, which, as Julia Kristeva writes in *Powers of Horror*, '… disturbs identity, system, order. What does not respect borders, positions, rules' (1982: 4). The voyages taken by Claire and Erica lead them to a place of appalling depravity. Erica, in great pain, grows from a fearful, vulnerable woman to a particularly hideous self, as she becomes more and more capable of incorporating what Jung would refer to as her shadow side. In the end she attains a degree of unity, as Claire does, that can enable her to come to terms with the beast within. Erica follows the standard pattern of the hero's quest. But whether she experiences a symbolic rebirth – and as what sort of entity – remains in question. Consider the following conversation Erica has with Mercer:

Mercer:	Let me ask you a question – how do you pull it back together, after what happened to you?
Erica:	You don't.
Mercer:	I'm sorry. That was…
Erica:	No. It's a fair question. You … become someone else.
Mercer:	Who?
Erica:	A stranger.

In this she resembles the character of Danny in *Angel*. As in all of Jordan's work, moral, ethical and even physical boundaries are crossed and become indistinct. Like Danny, Erica loses her connection to the external world; she becomes a self-appointed executioner. She is avenging the death of her lover, as Danny is seeking revenge for the death of the deaf-mute girl, but their original motivation seems to dissipate amidst the truly fearsome things they do in the course of their journeys. Both characters by the end have lost a great deal of their humanity. Once Erica starts to stalk her prey she becomes, like Danny, as frightening as those she eliminates. On her quest she pursues one of the city's most vicious and notorious felons. He is Murrow, the man who, in the early hospital scene, claims that his wife has committed suicide, a story no one seems to believe. He is a character well-known to the police; Mercer describes him: 'He imports drugs, guns, people, whatever's in demand. Found three guys that had crossed him, hands superglued to a table, and expanding cement in their throats. I had his wife ready to testify against him when she is found with her brains blown out. Gun in her hand. Nothing adds up, except his lawyers. Now he's got custody of his stepdaughter and not for sentimental reasons. He knows she knows something and I hate to think of what he'll do to her.'

Erica tracks Murrow down and confronts him with his crimes. She suddenly grabs his tie and slams her forehead into the bridge of his nose. He staggers back, dropping the crowbar, his nose exploding with blood. A vicious battle ensues and Erica kills Murrow by smashing his head with the weapon he has dropped.

The physicality of Erica's violence against Murrow is more viscerally direct and less mediated than some other incidents in the film. He has done nothing to Erica, nor has Cutler, her prior victim. She has taken it upon herself to rid the city of evil, crossing a line from which she can never turn back. As Detective Bloom says to Danny in *Angel* about evil: 'It's deep. It's everywhere and nowhere.' Jordan is only superficially concerned with the escalation of violence in New York, or the use of personal weapons; he is more interested in the way violence corrupts the human soul. Yeats had his belief in apocalyptic terror and the mythos of sacrifice, ideas that are continually renewed in Jordan's films.

In some ways, *The Brave One* is Jordan's most tragic film. It is not tragic in the strictly Aristototelian sense but is a modern form of tragedy. It is not about the fall of a great, flawed individual, but about the loss of human feeling. Once Erica completes her ritual and kills the three thugs who murdered David and maimed her body and soul, there is no real sense of completion. Mercer will cover up Erica's murders; he reverses his earlier conviction that he would be able to arrest a criminal regardless of their personal relationship. But Mercer cannot remove her from her status as one of the damned. At the end of *Angel*, a film which bookends so well with *The Brave One*, one feels after Danny visits the faith healer that there is hope for his spiritual recovery. One feels no such hope at the end of *The Brave One*, perhaps Jordan's grimmest work. The last we see of Erica is a shot of her traversing the Central Park tunnels at night. In voice-over she says: 'This thing. This stranger. She is all you are now.' The shot grows dimmer until we are left with a black frame, as Erica is swallowed up in darkness. The end credits roll.

At the end of Jordan's novel *Shade*, when a funeral service is held for the departed main protagonist, Nina, a hymn is sung by those in attendance:

> There is a balm in Gilead
> To make the wounded whole. (2004: 272)

One hopes that Erica's inner wounds will heal. But Jordan offers no resolution, release nor redemption from the damage Erica has done to her soul. Yeats would say that it is only through terror that beauty is born and re-born. We are left without a response from Jordan.

NOTES

CHAPTER ONE

1   For those readers who wish to have a more in-depth account of this era of Irish history, I would recommend the following: Richard Dunphy (1999) *The Making of Fianna Fail Power in Ireland 1921–1948*, Oxford: Oxford University Press; Tom Garvin (1996) *1922: The Birth of Irish Democracy*, Dublin: Gill & Macmillan; Peter Hart (1999) *The IRA and Its Enemies: Violence and Community in Cork, 1916–1923*, Oxford: Oxford University Press; James Hogan (1945) *Election and Representation*, Cork: Cork University Press; and Bill Kissane (2005) *The Politics of the Irish Civil War*, Oxford: Oxford University Press.

2   Yeats in *A Vision* (1925) breaks down human experience into abstract and mechanical patterns – he writes of perspective and the modern eye coexisting with the subjective reality of the bodily and the spiritual life to which myth bears witness (see Brown 1999: 305).

CHAPTER TWO

1   'Yeats exploits mythology in *Responsibilities: Poem and a Play*. For it was in this work that the poet began to employ mythology in a sustained way, not simply as a source for metaphors, symbols and themes, but as an interpretative tool to account for contemporary events and experiences' (Brown 1999: 211).

2   It is interesting to note that in the same film, *The Crying Game*, Fergus's nemesis (Miranda Richardson) is named Jude, the patron saint of lost causes.

CHAPTER THREE

1   The story is this: 'Scorpion wants to cross a river, but he can't swim. Goes to the frog, who can, and

asks for a ride. Frog says, "If I give you a ride on my back you'll go and sting me." Scorpion replies, "It would not be in my interest to sting you since I'd be on your back and we both would drown." Frog thinks about this logic for a while and accepts the deal. Takes the scorpion on his back. Braves the waters. Halfway over feels a burning spear in his side and realises the scorpion has stung him after all. And as they both sink beneath the waves the frog cries out. "Why did you sting me, Mr Scorpion, for now we both will drown?" Scorpion replies, "I can't help it, it's in my nature."'

2   This passage from Corinthians I is used in Carol Reed's film *Odd Man Out* (1947). James Mason enacts the role of an IRA soldier (one presumes this to be so, although no paramilitary organisation is mentioned). He has been shot, and speaks the lines as if in a trance. One cannot help thinking that Jordan is paying homage to Reed's film.

CHAPTER FOUR

1   Useful examinations of the relationship between fairy tales and storytelling include W. Benjamin (1968) 'The Storyteller', in *Illuminations*, trans. H. B. Jovanovich, New York: Schocken; P. Brooks (1994) *Psychoanalysis and Storytelling*, Oxford: Blackwell; W. J. Ong (1982) *Orality and Literacy: The Technologising of the Word*, London: Methuen; M. Warner (1994) *From the Beast to the Blonde: On Fairy Tales and Their Tellers*, London: Chatto and Windus.

2   These elements are dominant subjects of much of the better recent criticism of fairy tales. See, for example, R. B. Bottigheimer (1987) *Grimms' Bad Girls and Bold Boys: The Moral and Social Vision of the Tales*, New Haven: Yale University Press; A. Carter (1990) 'Foreword', in A. Carter (ed.) *The Virago Book of Fairy Tales*, London: Virago; L. Sage (2001) 'The Fairy Tale', in *Moments of Truth: Twelve Twentieth-Century Women Writers*, London: Fourth Estate; M. Tatar (1992) *Off With Their Head!: Fairy Tales and the Culture of Childhood*. Princeton, NJ.: Princeton University Press.

3   Jordan had originally wanted Andy Warhol to play the role of the devil, but following the shooting of the artist by Valerie Solanas, Warhol declined a role in Jordan's film unless the production moved to New York.

4   The whole of the woods was constructed in Shepperton Studios. Anton Furst and Jordan found inspiration for *The Company of Wolves* from a number of sources including Gustave Doré's erotic drawings of the tale; the work of English painters Samuel Palmer and Richard E. Dadd, the latter a painter of dense and strange imagery, probably most renowned for killing his father with an axe and spending the rest of his life in a mental institution; and Francis Bacon for the flayed skin in the transformation scenes.

5   This scene bears a marked resemblance to a passage in Jordan's novel *Dream of the Beast*: 'I saw my monstrous head reflected there, ringed by a circle of eggs. Were they the swan's or the woman's, I wondered and lifted one of them out. The heat of my unruly paw was anathema to it, for the droplets of water began to sizzle and steam and a crack sped across the white surface. The sheaves of egg fell away and a cherub stood there, creaking its downy wings. One by one the other eggs split and cherubs beat their way to the ceiling. They settled into niches in the plasterwork. There was the sound of falling water' (1993b: 131).

6   Jerusalem is the city of God, or Heaven. Displacing from the world of total myth to a more realistic topos, one would say 'a beautiful city', or 'a fine building'.

CHAPTER FIVE

1   Neil Jordan entered into a collaborative effort once again when he filmed *The Brave One*. The final shooting script says: '*The Brave One* by Roderick Taylor & Bruce A. Taylor'. It then says: 'Revised by Cynthia Mort and Michael Seitzman'. The last attribution is: 'Current Revisions by Neil Jordan'. It is difficult to ascertain how much of the script was, in the end, the product of Jordan's revisions. Generally, in looking over various drafts of his scripts, the director seems very generous in sharing credit with his colleagues, even when he has done the lion's share of the work. However, in this case, this would be pure supposition.

2   An interviewer asked Jordan about his relationship with his father, he said: 'Any father ... was made

nervous by the fact that the things I was writing about were a bit shocking at the time, to him. There was quite a bit of conflict because of this so the whole thing of fathers in conflict with sons influenced me deeply ... the other points of identification had to do with music, landscape, atmosphere, Bray having been our holiday resort' (in Jackson 1991: 19).

3   It should be noted that in McCabe's novel it is Philip; in Jordan's film it is Phillip.

CHAPTER SIX

1   In Jordan's novel, *Shade*, we witness the most profound love as that which exists between the narrator and her half-brother, Gregory.

CHAPTER SEVEN

1   This action is reminiscent of Nicolas Roeg's film *Don't Look Now* (1973), when John Baxter (Donald Sutherland) spills red ink on the slides he is working with, and then loses his daughter in a drowning incident. The coursing ink is an omen of the blood that will be spilled later in the film. The match of the spilled ink and the dead daughters connects the films in a very concrete way.

2   A parallel may be drawn to Frankenstein's monster (Boris Karloff) in *The Bride of Frankenstein* (James Whale, 1935), when after the female (played by Elsa Lanchester) is constructed by Dr Frankenstein (Colin Clive) for the monster, she is repelled by him. The monster then proceeds to destroy the laboratory, with himself, the she-monster and the elderly mad scientist trapped inside. It is an apocalyptic ending, and before the monster dies, he repeats, over and over: 'We belong dead.'

3   See Peter Brooks (1984) *Reading for the Plot: Design and Intention in Narrative*, Cambridge, MA.: Harvard University Press. This book includes an illuminating and complex Freudian reading of the structure of the novel.

CHAPTER EIGHT

1   In Jordan's personal archives.

CHAPTER NINE

1   The use of music by T-Rex reminds the viewer of Marc Bolan's androgynous beauty which has a strong relationship to Kitten's physical appearance.

2   There is something quite Dennis Potter-like about this device of having someone who is clearly an adult play an adolescent. It reminds one of Potter's television drama *Blue Remembered Hills* (1979), and performed at the Royal National Theatre in London in 2004. The story has grown-ups dress in children's clothes and act as if they are children. Jordan takes this a step further by having the grown-up Kitten dress in clothing that is obviously too small for him, and calls attention to the fact that the story is told by the older narrator.

3   Erving Goffman (1922–82) was a specialist in micro-social interaction from the perspective of social psychology.

4   The Wombles. On-line. Available at http://en.Wikipedia.org/wiki/The_Wombles (accessed 17 May 2006). The Wombles are fictional characters created by British author Elisabeth Beresford, originally appearing in a series of children's novels from 1968. Wombles are pointy-nosed furry creatures who inhabit every country, although the stories mainly centre on Wimbledon Common, in London. Songwriter and producer Mike Batt wrote the series' theme tune, and later went on to perform and produce a number of successful novelty singles as 'The Wombles'.

5   'Breakfast on Pluto' is a song written by Don Partridge and Alan Young, performed by Partridge.

6   Jordan's fondness for Fellini, and *La Strada* (1954) in particular, is important. He says, regarding Fellini: 'It was the first time. Everybody has a first time, everybody goes to movies when they're young, but when you actually see a film where you suddenly say "my God there's more than eating popcorn here in the cinema", it kind of takes your breath away, and that did mine. There's probably a very basic

appeal for me in cinema, given my basic urge to tell stories. And if you see a medium where you can tell a story and it's open to all the elements that are available to fiction, to symbolism, to allegory, to development of character, to all the classic laws of literature, and as well as that you're dealing in sound and colour and shape and texture, it definitely is something with immense appeal' (Toíbín 1982: 15).

7   In *Interview with the Vampire*, Rea also plays the host and perpetrator of a ghastly Grand Guignol stage show.

8   This long-held close-up, devoted to characterisation, is almost never seen in mainstream feature films after the 1970s. The length of the shot reinforces Jordan's consummate respect for the actor.

FILMOGRAPHY

Feature-length films

Angel (1982)
Production Company: A Motion Picture Company of Ireland Production. In association with Bord Scannán na hÉireann/Irish Film Board/Channel 4 Films
Producer: Barry Blackmore
Executive Producer: John Boorman
Director: Neil Jordan
Screenplay: Neil Jordan
Cinematography: Chris Menges
Editor: J. Patrick Duffner
Music: Keith Donald
Cast: Veronica Quilligan (Annie), Stephen Rea (Danny), Honor Heffernan (Deirdre), Donal McCann (Bonner), Ray McAnally (Bloom)

The Company of Wolves (1984)
Production Company: ITC Entertainment, Cannon Films, Palace Productions, The Cannon Group Inc.
Producer: Chris Brown, Steven Woolley
Executive Producer: Stephen Woolley, Nik Powell
Director: Neil Jordan
Screenplay: Neil Jordan
Cinematography: Bryan Loftus
Editor: Rodney Holland
Music: George Fenton

Cast: Sarah Patterson (Rosaleen), Angela Lansbury (Granny), David Warner (Father), Tusse Silberg (Mother), Micha Bergese (Huntsman), Kathryn Pogson (Young Bride), Stephen Rea (Young Groom), Graham Crowden (Old Priest)

Mona Lisa (1986)
Production Company: Handmade Films
Producer: Patrick Cassavetti, Stephen Woolley
Executive Producer: George Harrison, Denis O'Brien
Director: Neil Jordan
Screenplay: Neil Jordan
Cinematography: Roger Pratt
Editor: Lesley Walker
Music: Michael Kamen
Cast: Bob Hoskins (George), Cathy Tyson (Simone), Michael Caine (Mortwell), Robbie Coltrane (Thomas), Clarke Peters (Anderson), Sammi Davis (May)

High Spirits (1988)
Production Company: Vision P.D.G
Producer: David Saunders, Stephen Woolley
Executive Producer: Mark Damon, Moshe Diamant, Eduard Sarlui
Director: Neil Jordan
Screenplay: Neil Jordan
Cinematography: Alex Thomson
Editor: Michael Bradshell
Music: George Fenton
Cast: Peter O'Toole (Peter Plunkett), Donal McCann (Eamon), Steve Guttenberg (Jack Crawford), Beverly D'Angelo (Sharon Brogan Crawford), Jennifer Tilly (Miranda), Liam Neeson (Martin Brogan), Daryl Hannah (Mary Plunkett Brogan)

We're No Angels (1989)
Production Company: Paramount
Producer: Art Linson
Executive Producer: Robert De Niro
Director: Neil Jordan
Screenplay: David Mamet
Cinematography: Philippe Rousselot
Editor: Mick Audsley, Joke van Wijk
Music: George Fenton
Cast: Robert De Niro (Ned), Sean Penn (Jim), Demi Moore (Molly), Hoyt Axton (Father Levesque), Bruno Kirby (Deputy), Ray McAnally (Warden), James Russo (Bobby), John C. Reilly (Young Monk)

The Miracle (1991)
Production Company: Promenade Film Productions
Producer: Redmond Morris, Stephen Woolley
Executive Producer: Nik Powell, Bob Weinstein, Harvey Weinstein
Director: Neil Jordan
Screenplay: Neil Jordan
Cinematography: Philippe Rousselot
Editor: Joke van Wijk
Music: Anne Dudley
Cast: Beverly D'Angelo (Renee Baker), Donal McCann (Sam), Niall Byrne (Jimmy), Lorraine Pilkington (Rose)

The Crying Game (1992)
Production Company: Palace Pictures/Channel 4 Films
Producer: Stephen Woolley
Executive Producer: Nik Powell
Director: Neil Jordan
Screenplay: Neil Jordan
Cinematography: Ian Wilson
Editor: Kant Pan
Music: Anne Dudley
Cast: Forest Whitaker (Jody), Miranda Richardson (Jude), Stephen Rea (Fergus), Adrian Dunbar (Maguire), Jaye Davidson (Dil), Jim Broadbent (Col)

Interview with the Vampire (1994)
Production Company: Geffen Pictures
Producer: David Geffen, Stephen Woolley
Director: Neil Jordan
Screenplay: Anne Rice
Based on the novel *Interview with the Vampire* by Anne Rice (1976)
Cinematography: Philippe Rousselot
Editor: Mick Audsley, Joke van Wijk
Music: Elliot Goldenthal
Cast: Tom Cruise (Lestat de Lioncourt), Brad Pitt (Louis de Pointe du Lac), Kirsten Dunst (Claudia), Stephen Rea (Santiago), Antonio Banderas (Armand), Christian Slater (Daniel Malloy)

Michael Collins (1996)
Production Company: Warner Bros Pictures
Producer: Stephen Woolley
Co-Producer: Redmond Morris
Director: Neil Jordan
Screenplay: Neil Jordan
Cinematography: Chris Menges
Editor: J. Patrick Duffner, Tony Lawson
Music: Elliot Goldenthal
Cast: Ian Hart (Joe O'Reilly), Julia Roberts (Kitty Kiernan), Liam Neeson (Michael Collins), Aidan Quinn (Harry Boland), Stephen Rea (Ned Broy), Alan Rickman (Eamon de Valera), Brendan Gleeson (Liam Tobin), Gerard McSorley (Cathal Brigha), Charles Dance (Soames), Jonathan Rhys Meyers (Collins' assassin)

The Butcher Boy (1997)
Production Company: Geffen Pictures, Warner Bros. Pictures, Butcher Boy Film
Producer: Redmond Morris, Stephen Woolley
Executive Producer: Neil Jordan
Director: Neil Jordan
Screenplay: Neil Jordan, Pat McCabe
Based on the novel *The Butcher Boy* by Pat McCabe (1992)
Cinematography: Adrian Biddle
Editor: Tony Lawson
Music: Elliot Goldenthal
Cast: Eamonn Owens (Francie Brady), Sean McGinley (Sergeant), Peter Gowen (Leddy), Alan Boyle (Joe Purcell), Andrew Fullerton (Phillip Nugent), Fiona Shaw (Mrs Nugent), Aisling O'Sullivan (Ma Brady), Stephen Rea (Da Brady), John Kavanagh (Dr Boyd)

In Dreams (1999)
Production Company: DreamWorks Pictures
Producer: Charles Burke, Stephen Woolley
Director: Neil Jordan
Screenplay: Neil Jordan, Bruce Robinson
Based on the novel *Doll's Eyes* by Bari Wood (1992)
Music: Elliot Goldenthal
Cinematography: Darius Khondji
Editor: Tony Lawson
Cast: Annette Bening (Claire Cooper), Katie Sagona (Rebecca Cooper), Aidan Quinn (Paul Cooper), Robert Downey Jr (Vivian Thompson), Paul Guilfoyle (Det. Jack Kay), Stephen Rea (Dr Silverman)

The End of the Affair (1999)
Production Company: Columbia Pictures
Producer: Neil Jordan, Stephen Woolley
Co-Producer: Kathy Sykes
Director: Neil Jordan
Screenplay: Neil Jordan
Based on the novel *The End of the Affair* by Graham Greene (1951)
Cinematography: Roger Pratt
Editor: Tony Lawson
Music: Michael Nyman
Cast: Ralph Fiennes (Maurice Bendrix), Stephen Rea (Henry Miles), Julianne Moore (Sarah Miles), Ian Hart (Mr Parkis), Samuel Bould (Lance Parkis)

The Good Thief (2002)
Production Company: Alliance Atlantis Communications, Double Down Films, Metropolitan Films, TNVO
Producer: Seaton McLean, John Wells, Stephen Woolley
Executive Producer: Kristin Harms, Neil Jordan, Thierry Seaward
Director: Neil Jordan
Screenplay: Neil Jordan
Cinematography: Chris Menges
Editor: Tony Lawson
Music: Elliot Goldenthal
Cast: Nutsa Kukhianidze (Anne), Ouassini Embarek (Said), Marc Lavoine (Remi), Nick Nolte (Bob Montagnet), Tchéky Karyo (Roger), Gérard Darmon (Raol), Saïd Taghmaoui (Paolo), Emir Kusturica (Vladimir)

Breakfast on Pluto (2005)
Production Company: Pathé Pictures International, Northern Ireland Film and Television Commission
Producer: Neil Jordan, Alan Moloney, Stephen Woolley
Executive Producer: François Ivernel, Brendan McCarthy, Cameron McCracken, Mark Woods
Director: Neil Jordan
Screenplay: Neil Jordan
Based on the novel *Breakfast on Pluto* by Pat McCabe (1999)
Cinematography: Declan Quinn
Editor: Tony Lawson
Music: Anna Jordan
Cast: Cillian Murphy (Patrick 'Kitten' Braden), Eva Birthistle (Eily Bergin), Liam Neeson (Father Liam), Mary Coughlan (Housekeeper), Conor McEvoy (Young Patrick Braden), Ruth McCabe (Ma Braden), Liam Cunningham (1st Biker), Gavin Friday (Billy Hatchett), Brendan Gleeson (John Joe Kenny), Ian Hart (PC Wallis), Patrick McCabe (Peepers Egan/Schoolmaster, Eamonn Owens (Jackie Timlin)

The Brave One (2007)

Production Company: Redemption Pictures, Silver Pictures, Village Roadshow Productions

Producer: Susan Downey, Joel Silver

Executive Producer: Bruce Berman, Herb Gains

Director: Neil Jordan

Screenplay: Roderick Taylor & Bruce A. Taylor. Revised by Cynthia Mort and Michael Seitzman. Current Revisions by Neil Jordan

Cinematography: Philippe Rousselot

Editor: Tony Lawson

Cast: Jodie Foster (Erica), Mary Steenburgen (Carol), Jane Adams (Nicole), Douglas J. Aguirre (CSU Detective), Naveen Andrews (David), James Biberi (Det. Pitney), Angelo Bonsignore (Cameraman)

Short film

Not I (2001)

Production Company: Blue Angel Films, Tyrone Productions, FilmFour

Producer: Stephen Woolley

Executive Producer: Michael Colgan, Alan Moloney, Joe Mulholland

Director: Neil Jordan

Based on the play by Samuel Beckett (1972)

Cinematography: Roger Pratt

Editor: Tony Lawson

Cast: Julianne Moore (Auditor/Mouth)

BIBLIOGRAPHY

Abrams, M. H. (1953) *The Mirror and the Lamp: Romantic Theory and Critical Tradition*. London: Oxford University Press.

____ (1984) 'Apocalypse: Theme and Romantic Variations', in *The Correspondent Breeze: Essays in English Romanticism*. New York: W. W. Norton, 225–7.

Anon. (1996) 'The Wombles'. Available at: http://en.wikipedia.org/wiki/The_Wombles (accessed 17 May 2006).

Bacchilega, C. (1997) *Postmodern Fairy Tales: Gender and Narrative Strategies*. Philadelphia: University of Pennsylvania Press.

Backus, M. (1999) *The Gothic Family Romance: Heterosexuality, Child Sacrifice and the Anglo-Irish Colonial Order*. Durham, NC: Duke University Press.

Bakhtin, M. (1968) *Rabelais and His World*, trans. H. Iswolsky. Boston: Massachusetts Institute of Technology Press.

____ (1981) *The Dialogic Imagination*, ed. Michael Holquist, trans. C. Emerson and M. Holquist. Austin: University of Texas Press.

Banville, J. (1994) Initial treatment of *The End of the Affair* and various correspondence in Neil Jordan's personal archives.

Baudelaire, C. (1887) *Jounaux intimes. Fusées, III*.

Beebe, J. (1997) 'He Must Have Wept When He Made You: The Homoerotic Pathos in the Movie Version of *Interview with the Vampire*', in K. Ramsland (ed.) *The Anne Rice Reader*. New York: Ballantine Books, 196–211.

Benjamin, W. (1968 [1934]) 'The Storyteller', in *Illuminations*, trans. H. B. Jovanovich. New York: Schocken, 83–110.

Bettelheim, B. (1976) *The Uses of Enchantment: The Meaning and Importance of Fairy Tales*. New York:

Alfred A. Knopf.

Bew, P. (1996) 'Collins Wrong on Essential Points', *The Sunday Independent*, 29 September, 8.

Birkhäuser-Oeri, S. (1988) *The Mother: Archetypal Image in Fairytales*, ed. M.-L. von Franz. Toronto: Inner City Books.

Blake, W. (1978) *The Complete Poems*, ed. A. Ostiker. New York: Penguin.

Booth, W. (1961) *The Rhetoric of Fiction*. Chicago: University of Chicago Press.

Boozer Jr J. (1995) 'Bending Phallic Patriarchy in *The Crying Game*', *Journal of Popular Film and Television*, 22, 4, Winter, 172–9.

Bordwell, D. (1985) *Narration in the Fiction Film*. Madison: University of Wisconsin Press.

Bottigheimer, R. B. (1987) *Grimms' Bad Girls and Bold Boys: The Moral and Social Vision of the Tales*. New Haven: Yale University Press.

Botting, F. (1996) *The Gothic*. New York: Routledge.

____ (2001) 'In Gothic Darkly: Heterotopia, History, Culture', in D. Punter (ed.) *A Companion to the Gothic*. Oxford: Blackwell Press, 3–14.

Bourke, A. (ed.) (2002) *The Field Day Anthology of Irish Literature: Irish Women's Writing and Traditions*. New York: New York University Press.

Branigan, E. (1992) *Narrative Comprehension and Film*. New York: Routledge.

Bresson, R. (1977) *Notes on Cinematography*. New York: Urizen Books.

Brooks, P. (1984) *Reading for the Plot: Design and Intention in Narrative*. Cambridge, MA: Harvard University Press.

____ (1994) *Psychoanalysis and Storytelling*. Oxford: Blackwell.

Brown, T. (1999) *The Life of W. B. Yeats*. Dublin: Gill & Macmillan.

Bruhm, S. (1994) *Gothic Bodies: The Politics of Pain in Romantic Fiction*. Philadelphia: University of Pennsylvania Press.

Bunnell, C. (1984) 'The Gothic: A Literary Genre's Transition to Film', in B. K. Grant (ed.) *Planks of Reason*. Metuchen: Scarecrow, 82–100.

Burns, E. (1972) *Theatricality*. London: Longman.

Butler, E. C. (1997) 'The Reception of *Michael Collins*', *Irish Literary Supplement*, Spring, 17–19.

Byron, G. G. (2000) *Lord Byron: The Major Works*, ed. J. J. McGann. Oxford: Oxford University Press.

Campbell, J. (1973) *The Hero With a Thousand Faces*. Princeton, NJ: Princeton University Press.

Carroll, N. (1990) *The Philosophy of Horror or Paradoxes of the Heart*. New York: Routledge.

Carter, A. (1979) *The Bloody Chamber*. London: V. Gollancz.

____ (1990) 'Introduction', in A. Carter (ed.) *The Virago Book of Fairy Tales*. London: Virago, ix–xxii.

Ciment, M. (2001) *Kubrick*, trans. G. Adair. London: Faber and Faber.

Comiskey, R. (1982) 'Interview with Neil Jordan', *The Irish Times*, 11 May, 8.

Coogan, T. P. (1991) *Michael Collins*. London: Arrow.

Creed, B. (1999) 'Horror and the Monstrous-Feminine: An Imaginary Abjection', in S. Thornham (ed.) *Feminist Film Theory: A Reader*. New York: New York University Press, 251–66.

Crowdus, G. (1997) 'The Screening of Irish History', *Cineaste*, 22, 4, 14–19.

Curtis, L. P. (1969) *Anglo Saxons and Celts: A Study of Anti-Irish Prejudice in Victorian England*. Bridgeport, CT: Conference on British Studies.

Day, A. (1996) *Romanticism*. London: Routledge.

Day, W. P. (1985) *In the Circles of Fear and Desire*. Chicago: Chicago University Press.

Delaney J., M. J. Lupton and E. Toth (eds) (1988) *The Curse: A Cultural History of Menstruation. Revised and Expanded Edition*. Urbana, IL: University of Illinois Press.

Dickinson, E. (1955) *The Complete Poems of Emily Dickinson*. London: Faber and Faber.

Donovan, K. (1995) 'Capturing the Big Fellow on Film', *The Irish Times*, 7 February, 10–12.

Dwyer, M. (1982) '10 Days that Shook the Irish Film Industry', *In Dublin*, 8 April, 24–8.

____ (1996) 'Dynamic, Thrilling, Epic Cinema', *The Irish Times*, 8 November, 12.

Eliade, M. (1960) *Myth, Dreams and Mysteries*, trans. P. Mairet. New York: HarperCollins.

____ (1963) *Myth and Reality*, trans. W. R. Trask. New York: Harper and Row.

____ (1971) *The Myth of the Eternal Return: Or, Cosmos and History*, trans. W. R. Trask. Princeton, NJ: Princeton University Press.

Falsetto, M. (2000) 'Neil Jordan', *Personal Visions: Conversations with Contemporary Film Directors*. Los Angeles: Silman-James Press, 217–54.

Fanning, R. (1997) 'The Resurrection of Michael Collins', *The Sunday Independent*, 5 January, 18–19.

Fiedler, L. A. (1966) *Love and Death in the American Novel*. New York: Dell.

FitzSimon, C. (1998) 'Patrick McCabe Interviewed', in A. Roche (ed.) *Irish University Review*, 28, 1, Spring/Summer, 174–89.

Foucault, M. (1970) *The Order of Things*. New York: Vintage Books.

____ (1980) *The History of Sexuality Volume 1: An Introduction*, trans. R. Hurley. New York: Vintage Books.

Freud, S. (1955a [1919]) 'The Uncanny', in *The Standard Edition of the Complete Psychological Works of Sigmund Freud*. Volume 18, trans. J. Strachey. London: Hogarth Press, 218–53.

____ (1955b [1920]) 'Beyond the Pleasure Principle', in *The Standard Edition of the Complete Psychological Works of Sigmund Freud*. Volume 18, trans. J. Strachey. London: Hogarth Press, 7–64.

____ (1955c [1924]) 'The Economic Problems in Masochism', in *The Standard Edition of the Complete Psychological Works of Sigmund Freud*. Volume 19, trans. J. Strachey. London: Hogarth Press, 157–80.

Frye, N. (1957) *Anatomy of Criticism*. Princeton, NJ: Princeton University Press.

Genette, G. (1980) *Narrative Discourse*, trans. J. E. Lewin. Ithaca, NY: Cornell University Press.

Gibbons, L. (1988) 'Romanticism, Realism and Irish Cinema', in K. Rockett, L. Gibbons and J. Hill (eds) *Cinema and Ireland*. Syracuse: Syracuse University Press, 194–257.

____ (1995) 'Engendering the State: Narrative, Allegory, and Michael Collins', *Éire-Ireland: An Interdisciplinary Journal of Irish Studies*, 31, 3–4, 261–9.

____ (1997a) 'Framing History: Neil Jordan's *Michael Collins*', *History Ireland*, 40, Spring, 47–51.

____ (1997b) 'Demisting the Screen: Neil Jordan's *Michael Collins*', *Irish Literary Supplement*, Spring, 16–17.

Girard, R. (1977) *Violence and the Sacred*, trans. P. Gregory. Baltimore: Johns Hopkins University Press.

Goffman, E. (1959) *The Presentation of Self in Everyday Life*. New York: Doubleday.

Gray, M. (1999) Review of *In Dreams*, *Film Ireland*, April/May, 36–7.

Greene, G. (1999) *The End of the Affair*. New York: Penguin.

Groen, R. (1998) 'Neil Jordan's writing game', *The Globe and Mail*, 3 April, C3.

Harris, E. (1996) 'The Man, the Myth, and the Mistress', *The Tribune Magazine*, 15 September, 8–10.

Hayman, D. and E. S. Rabkin (1974) *Form in Fiction: An Introduction to the Analysis of Narrative Prose*. New York: St. Martin's Press.

Herron, T. (2000) 'ContaminNation: Patrick McCabe and Colm Toibín's Pathographies of the Republic', in L. Harte and M. Parker (eds) *Contemporary Irish Fiction: Themes, Tropes, Theories*. New York: St Martin's Press, 168–91.

Hill, J. (1988) 'Images of Violence', in K. Rockett, L. Gibbons and J. Hill (eds) *Cinema and Ireland*. Syracuse: Syracuse University Press, 147–93.

Hirsch, E. (2006) 'The Immense Intimacy, the Intimate Immensity'. Available at: http://www.poetryfoundation.org/features/feature.guidebook.html?id=177209 (accessed 7 April 2005).

Hoggard, L. (2002) '*The Good Thief*', *Irish Independent*, 21 February, 1–2.

Hoskins, R. (1999) 'Portrait of the Artist', in R. Hoskins (ed.) *Graham Greene: An Approach to the Novels*. New York: Garland Publishing, 137–88.

Hughes, E. (1998) 'Tom Paulin', in J. P. Myers Jr (ed.) *Writing Irish: Selected Interviews with Irish Writers from the Irish Literary Supplement*. Syracuse: Syracuse University Press, 115–27.

Jackson, J. (1991) 'Interview with Neil Jordan', *Hot Stuff*. 5 February, 5–7.

Jaehne, K. 'Neil Jordan on The Butcher Boy', *Film Scouts*. Available at: http://www.filmscouts.com/scripts/interview.cfm?file'nea-jor (accessed 7 June 2006).

Jones, E. (1949) *On the Nightmare*. London: Hogarth Press.

Jordan, N. (1980a) *The Past*. New York: George Braziller.

____ (1980b) *Night in Tunisia*. London: Bloomsbury.

____ (1993a) 'Introduction to *The Crying Game*', in *A Neil Jordan Reader*. New York: Vintage, xi–xiii.

____ (1993b) 'Dream of the Beast', in *A Neil Jordan Reader*. New York: Vintage, 85–176.

____ (1995) *Sunrise with Sea Monster*. London: Bloomsbury.

____ (1996) *Michael Collins: Screenplay and Film Diary*. New York: Plume Books.

____ (2004) *Shade: A Novel*. London: Bloomsbury.

Jung, C. G. (1963) *The Integration of the Personality*, trans. S. Dell. London: Routledge & Kegan Paul.

Kearney, R. (1988) *Transitions: Narratives in Modern Irish Culture*. Manchester: Manchester University Press.

Kermode, F. (1973) 'Mr. Greene's Eggs and Crosses', in S. Hynes (ed.) *Graham Greene: A Collection of Critical Essays*. Englewood Cliffs, NJ: Prentice-Hall, 126–37.

Kinahan F. (1988) *Yeats, Folklore, and Occultism: Contexts of the Early Work and Thought*. Boston: Unwin Hyman.

Kristeva, J. (1982) *Powers of Horror: An Essay on Abjection*, trans. L. S. Roudiez. New York: Columbia University Press.

Lacey, C. (1998) 'Patrick McCabe', *Publishers Weekly*, 16 November, 50.

Lanser, S. (1981) *The Narrative Act*. Princeton, NJ: Princeton University Press.

Lawrence, D. H. (1994) *Kangaroo*. Cambridge: Cambridge University Press.

Lee, J. (1996) 'What the English Learn About the Irish', *Sunday Tribune*, 10 October, 16–17.

Lieberman, M. (1986) '"Some Day My Prince Will Come": Female Acculturation Through the Fairytale', in J. Zipes (ed.) *Don't Bet on the Prince: Contemporary Feminist Fairy Tales in North America and England*. New York: Methuen, 185–200.

Linehan, H. (1996) 'Always Informed More by "Now" than "Then"', *The Irish Times*, 27 November, 19–20.

Lyall, S. (1999) 'Filming the Drama Between the Novelist's Lines', *The New York Times*, 6 June, AR13.

Maconghail, M. (1996/97) 'A Triumph of the Will?', *Film Ireland*, December/January, 2–3.

Massé, M. A. (2000) 'Psychoanalysis and the Gothic', in D. Punter (ed.) *A Companion to the Gothic*. London and Malden, MA: Blackwell, 229–41.

McCabe, P. (1992) *The Butcher Boy*. London: Picador.

____ (1998) *Breakfast on Pluto*. London and New York: HarperCollins.

McCarthy, G. (2000) 'Interview with Neil Jordan', *Film West*, 39, 13–15.

McGinley, K. (1996) 'Development of the Byronic Vampire: Byron, Stoker, Rice', in G. Hoppenstand and R. Browne (eds) *The Gothic World of Anne Rice*. Ohio: Bowling Green University Press, 71–91.

McIlroy, B. (1986) 'Interview with Neil Jordan', *World Cinema 4*. Wiltshire: Flicks, 108–18.

McLachlan, S. (2003) 'Answer', on *Afterglow*. Arista Records.

Meihuizen, N. (1998) *Yeats and the Drama of Sacred Space*. Amsterdam: Rodopi.

Meisner, S. (1987) *On Acting*. New York: Vintage.

Milton, J. (2001 [1667/1671]) *Paradise Lost and Paradise Regained*, ed. C. Hicks. New York: Penguin.

Mooney, J. (1994) 'Neil Jordan Bites the Big One', *Movieline*, 6, 3, 64–9.

Moore, V. (1954) *The Unicorn: William Butler Yeats' Search for Reality*. New York: Macmillan.

Morgan, J. (2002) *The Biology of Horror: Gothic Literature and Film*. Carbondale, IL: Southern Illinois University Press.

O'Brien, G. (2000) 'The Aesthetics of Exile', in L. Harte and M. Parker (eds) *Contemporary Irish Fiction Themes, Tropes, Theories*. New York: St. Martin's Press, 35–55.

Ong, W. J. (1982) *Orality and Literacy: The Technologising of the Word*. London: Methuen.

O'Rawe, D. (2003) 'At Home With Horror', *Irish Studies Review*, 11, 2, 189–98.

Otto, R. (1958 [1923]) *The Idea of the Holy*, ed. J. W. Harvey. Oxford: Oxford University Press.

Pater, W. (1980) *The Renaissance: Studies in Art and Poetry*. Oxford: Oxford University Press.

Power, P. (1999) 'Review of *The End of the Affair*', *Film West*, 39, 61.

Pramaggiore, M. (1998) 'The Celtic Blue Note: Jazz in Neil Jordan's *Night in Tunisia*, *Angel* and *The Miracle*', *Screen*, 39, 3, 222–88.

Praz, M. (1956) *The Romantic Agony*, trans. A. Davidson. New York: Meridian Books.

Punter, D. (2002) 'Scottish and Irish Gothic', in *The Cambridge Companion to Gothic Fiction*, ed. J. F. Hogle. Cambridge: Cambridge University Press, 105–23.

Rank, O. (1914) 'The Myth of the Birth of the Hero: A Psychological Interpretation of Mythology', trans. Drs F. Robbins and E. Jelliffe Smith, *Nervous and Mental Disease Monograph Series no. 18*. New York: The Journal of Nervous and Mental Disease Publishing Company.

Rockett E. and K. Rockett (2003) *Exploring Boundaries*. Dublin: The Liffey Press.

Rose, J. (1984) *The Case of Peter Pan or the Impossibility of Children's Fiction*. Philadelphia: University of Pennsylvania Press.

Sage, L. (2001) 'The Fairy Tale', in *Moments of Truth: Twelve Twentieth-Century Women Writers*. London: Fourth Estate.

Schrader, P. (1986) 'Notes on Film Noir', in B. K. Grant (ed.) *Film Genre Reader*. Austin: University of Texas Press, 169–82.

Seiden, M. I. (1975) *William Butler Yeats: The Poet as Mythmaker, 1865–1939*. New York: Cooper Square.

Sharrett, C. (1984) 'The Idea of Apocalypse in *The Texas Chainsaw Massacre*', in B. K. Grant (ed.) *Planks of Reason*. Metuchen, NJ: Scarecrow Press, 255–76.

Sheehey, T. and D. Traynor (1996) 'Michael Collins Goes Reluctantly to the Altar', *Film Ireland*, October/November, 11–12.

____ (2000) 'A Look Over Jordan…', *Film Ireland*, 35, February/March, 16–17.

Sherry, N. (1995) *The Life of Graham Greene: Volume 2*. New York: Viking Adult.

Silverberg, L. (1994) *The Sanford Meisner Approach*. Lyme, NH: Smith and Kraus.

South Bank Show, The (1996) 'Michael Collins', LWT for ITV, tx 27 October.

Studlar, G. (1988) *In the Realm of Pleasure: Von Sternberg, Dietrich, and the Masochistic Aesthetic*. Urbana, IL: University of Illinois Press.

Swann-Jones, S. (1986) 'The Structure of Snow White' in R. B. Bottigheimer (ed.) *Fairy Tales and Society: Illusion, Allusion and Paradigm*. Philadelphia: Philadelphia University Press.

Swinburne, A. (2004 [1867]) *Chastelard: A Tragedy*. Whitefish, Montana: Kessinger Publishing.

Tatar, M. (1992) *Off With Their Head!: Fairy Tales and the Culture of Childhood*. Princeton, NJ: Princeton University Press.

Thomas, B. (1988) *An Underground Fate: The Idiom of Romance in the Later Novels of Graham Greene*. Georgia: University of Georgia Press.

Thomson, S. (1990/91) 'Interview with Neil Jordan on *The Miracle*', *Irish Stage and Screen*, 3, 7–8.

Thorslev, P. (1962) *The Byronic Hero*. Minneapolis: Minneapolis University Press.

Todorov, T. (1973) *The Fantastic: A Structural Approach to a Literary Genre*. Ithaca, NY: Cornell University Press.

Toíbín, C. (1982). 'Neil Jordan Talks to Colm Toíbín', *In Dublin*, 29 April, 152, 14–19.

Tyaransen, O. (1997) 'Jordan: The Comeback', *Hot Press*, 11–12.

Von Franz, M.-L. (1997) *Archetypal Patterns in Fairytales*. Toronto: Inner City Books.

Vonnegut, K. (1961) *Mother Light*. New York: Laurel Press.

Warner, M. (1994a) *From the Beast to the Blonde: On Fairy Tales and Their Tellers*. London: Chatto and Windus..

____ (1994b) 'Angela Carter: Bottle Blonde, Double Drag', in L. Sage (ed.) *Flesh and the Mirror: Essays on the Art of Angela Carter*. London: Virago Press, 243–56.

____ (1998) *No Go The Bogeyman: Scaring, Lulling and Making Mock*. New York: Farrar, Straus and Giroux.

Williams, A. (1995) *Art of Darkness: A Poetics of Gothic*. Chicago: University of Chicago Press.

Winarski, K. G. (1999) 'Neil Jordan's Miracle: From Fiction to Film', in J. MacKillop (ed.) *Contemporary Irish Cinema: From The Quiet Man to Dancing at Lughnasa*. Syracuse: Syracuse University Press, 98–108.

Wordsworth, W. (2000) *William Wordsworth: The Major Works*. Oxford: Oxford University Press.

Yeats, W. B. (1902 [1892]) *The Celtic Twilight*. London: A. J. Bullen.

____ (1920) *The Poetical Works of William B. Yeats*. New York: Macmillan.

____ (1966) *The Variorum Edition of the Poems of W. B. Yeats*, eds P. Allt and R. K. Alspach. New York: Macmillan.

____ (2000a [1921]) 'Easter, 1916', in M. H. Abrams (ed.) *Norton Anthology of English Literature*. Edition 6, Volume 2. New York and London: W. W. Norton, 2104–6.

____ (2000b) 'The Trembling Veil', in J. Pethica (ed.) *Yeats's Poetry, Drama and Prose*. New York and London: W. W. Norton, 240–5.

____ (2001b [1917]) 'The Rose Tree', in E. Larrissy (ed.) The Major Works. Oxford: Oxford University

Press, 88.

_____ (2002 [1892]) *Irish Fairy and Folk Tales*. New York: Metro Books.

Zipes, J. (1993) *The Trials and Tribulations of Little Red Riding Hood*. Routledge: New York.

_____ (1994) *Fairy Tale as Myth/Myth as Fairy Tale*. Lexington: University Press of Kentucky.

Zucker, C. (1993) 'The Concept of "Excess" in Film Acting: Notes Toward an Understanding of Non-naturalistic Performance', *Postscript*, 12, 2, 54–62.

_____ (1995) 'Interview with Lindsay Crouse', *Figures of Light: Actors and Directors Illuminate the Art of Film Acting*. New York: Plenum, 11–33.

_____ (1998) 'Screen Actor Pulls No Punches', *The Globe and Mail*, 3 April, C3.

_____ (1999) 'Interview with Stephen Rea', *In the Company of Actors: Reflections on the Craft of Acting*. London: A & C Black, 108–23.

_____ (2002) *Conversations with Actors on Film, Television, and Stage Performance*. Portsmouth: Heinemann.

_____ (2006) 'Love Hurts: Performance in Elia Kazan's Splendor in the Grass', *Cineaste*, Winter, 31, 4.

INDEX